George Orwell
Studies

Volume Six

No. 2

George Orwell

Publishing Office
Abramis Academic
ASK House
Northgate Avenue
Bury St. Edmunds
Suffolk
IP32 6BB
UK

Tel: +44 (0)1284 717884
Fax: +44 (0)1284 717889
Email: info@abramis.co.uk
Web: www.abramis.co.uk

Copyright
All rights reserved. No part of this publication may be reproduced in any material form (including photocopying or storing it in any medium by electronic means, and whether or not transiently or incidentally to some other use of this publication) without the written permission of the copyright owner, except in accordance with the provisions of the Copyright, Designs and Patents Act 1988, or under terms of a licence issued by the Copyright Licensing Agency Ltd, 33-34, Alfred Place, London WC1E 7DP, UK. Applications for the copyright owner's permission to reproduce part of this publication should be addressed to the Publishers.

© 2022 George Orwell Studies & Abramis Academic

ISSN 2399-1267
ISBN 978-1-84549-800-9

George Orwell

Contents

Editorial
Letters from Paris Throw New Insights on Orwell — by Richard Lance Keeble .... Page 3

Papers
Orwell and the Secret Intelligence Service – by Darcy Moore .... Page 9
The Problem with Julia – by G. Alexander Denning .... Page 17
Disassembling the Myth of the Struggling Artist in George Orwell's *Keep the Aspidistra Flying* – by Rebecca Clayton .... Page 43
A Textbook Case: Aligning Orwell and NCTJ Teaching – by Jaron Murphy .... Page 58

Articles
Joyeux Anniversaires: Peter Stansky at 90, *The Unknown Orwell* at 50 – by John Rodden .... Page 78
Retracing the Steps of Orwell and Dorothy Hare in Kent – by Neil Smith .... Page 101
Orwell's Status as a Political Prophet on the Wane – by Nicholas Harris .... Page 115
Beyond the 'Nancy Poet' Jibe: Orwell and Auden – by Richard Lance Keeble .... Page 124
Orwell, Radio and the Propaganda War – by Ron Bateman .... Page 137
In Search of Máirín Mitchell – by Martin Tyrrell .... Page 147

Book reviews
Melissa Dinsman on *Writing in the Dark: Bloomsbury, the Blitz and* Horizon *Magazine*, by Will Loxley; Martin Tyrrell on *Cold Warriors: Writers Who Waged the Literary Cold War*, by Duncan White .... Page 163

Re-Evaluation: Laurence Brander's *George Orwell* (1954)
How One of the (Now Forgotten) First Studies of Orwell Captured the Man and his Writings – by Richard Lance Keeble .... Page 175

Editors
Richard Lance Keeble — University of Lincoln
Tim Crook — Goldsmiths, University of London

Reviews Editor
Megan Faragher — Wright State University

Production Editor
Paul Anderson — University of Essex

Editorial Board
Kristin Bluemel — Monmouth University, New Jersey
Dorian Lynskey — Author, journalist
Peter Marks — University of Sydney
John Newsinger — Bath Spa University
Marina Remy — Paris Sorbonne
John Rodden — University of Texas at Austin
Jean Seaton — University of Westminster
Peter Stansky — Stanford University, US
D. J. Taylor — Author, journalist, biographer of Orwell
Martin Tyrrell — Queen's University, Belfast
Nathan Waddell — University of Birmingham
Florian Zollmann — Newcastle University

With editorial assistance from Marja Giejgo

Front cover: Cover of 1972 Constable edition of *The Unknown Orwell*

EDITORIAL

Letters from Paris Throw New Insights on Orwell

Orwell writes millions of words in his relatively short career. Most of them are collected in that towering work of scholarship, the *Complete Works of George Orwell* (1998), edited by Peter Davison, together with the additional volume, *The Lost Orwell* (2006). From time to time, previously unknown letters he composes (mainly to female friends) appear on the market throwing new insights on the man. Last November, for instance, Richard Blair, Orwell's son, handed over to the Orwell archive at University College London 50 recently discovered letters he wrote to Eleanor Jaques and Brenda Salkeld. Blair had purchased the letters from the families of the two women but wanted them to be available to the public and researchers. Orwell met both women in the early 1930s and kept in touch with them long afterwards. As biographer D. J. Taylor comments: 'The letters reveal his elegiac side. Orwell writes so much about country walks in his novels, and he was always trying to arrange walks in Suffolk with these women.'

Moreover, in the last issue of *George Orwell Studies* (Vol. 6, No. 1: 130-152), I looked at some of Orwell's fascinating writings buried in Malcolm Muggeridge's archive at Wheaton College Library, Illinois, which are missing from the *Complete Works* and largely overlooked by biographers and literary critics.

In Dorian Lynskey's wonderful, recently published *Nineteen Eighty-Four* 'biography', I noticed on page 272 a note indicating that Susie Boyt had offered to show him some unpublished letters Orwell had written to her father-in-law David Astor, the *Observer* journalist. So I contacted Dorian who, with Susie's permission, sent me photocopies of two letters Orwell sends to Astor from Paris in March and April 1945 while he is on a reporting assignment – covering the final months of World War Two for the *Observer* and *Manchester Evening News*.

The letters are short and while they contain no major revelations are still fascinating. The first he writes from Room 329 at Hotel Scribe on 10 March 1945. I have always wondered if Orwell was engaged in some sort of intelligence mission for Astor, who was

RICHARD LANCE KEEBLE

working at the time in a unit of the Special Operations Executive, the covert military unit, liaising with the Resistance movement in France. There is no indication of that in either of these letters. But here he writes: 'I have looked up a good many of the people whose names you gave me, but not all, because I have made fairly good contacts with the group surrounding the little paper, Libertes [no italics nor accent in Orwell's letter] which is more or less Tribune's [again no italics] opposite number. I have been to some quite interesting meetings of theirs and to some of their houses.' Most of the men Orwell meets in Paris – Malcolm Muggeridge, 'Freddie' Ayer, Harold Acton, Ernest Hemingway – have some connection with intelligence. Could these be the people whose names Astor gives to Orwell?

He goes on to record his intention to travel to Cologne and then to Toulouse. But while in Cologne he falls ill with a serious chest complaint and is admitted to hospital. There he learns of the death of his wife, Eileen, in an operating theatre at a Newcastle hospital and so quickly finds a military aircraft to fly him back to the UK for the funeral. He is never to travel to Toulouse.

In an essay on Orwell's war reporting in 1945 (republished in *Journalism Beyond Orwell*, Routledge, 2020 pp 49-67) I make a comment about Orwell rarely recording interviews – instead he cites conversations, discussions and overheard conversations. One of the reasons for this, I surmise, could have been because he simply did not have an efficient recording technique (shorthand or some form of rapid writing). The March letter supports this view since he complains of not being able to take down the 'military stuff' at 'the pace at which they are shot at me'.

Orwell goes on to discuss his planned move to Barnhill on the remote Scottish island of Jura where Astor owns land. 'I have heard from Eileen who has had a letter from Mrs Fletcher evidently agreeing to our taking Barnhill. She, ie Mrs Fletcher, is going over to the island in April and will see what repairs are needed. She also said apparently that after the war they are going to try and get some crofters into the other houses, which would solve the major food difficulty. So if all works out we might send the furniture up there this summer and actually go there for a week or two in the late summer. I intend sending the furniture which is in our cottage in Hertfordshire.'

His next comments are particularly intriguing: 'And meanwhile we have got to find a permanent home for ourself [a grammatical error there] somewhere in the south of England, I think in Essex. I must fix that up this year because I can't have Richard [his newly adopted son] growing up in London. The court case has been settled so he is now legally ours and can be christened.' As Richard Blair confirms in a note to me: 'In the matter of my adoption, proper legal procedures were followed, with the hearing before a judge, so I was quite correctly adopted.' But this mention of having a house (probably rented) in Essex along with Barnhill is quite a revelation.

I wrote about Orwell's addiction to cigarettes (so dodgy given his weak lungs) and the representation of smoking in his writings in the last *George Orwell Studies* issue (Vol. 6, No. 1 pp 70-84). Here, he asks Astor, if he's planning a Paris visit, to bring him 'half a pound of dark shag tobacco (dark shag not medium). Tribune have already sent me off one or two lots but nothing of that kind gets here. The cigarette situation is pretty bad. I can get four packets of English cigarettes a week from the Naafi but I can't bear English cigarettes and I swap them off for French ones when I can. Of course I brought a lot with me but I gave them all away long ago' (Orwell's generous spirit shining through at the end).

In a postscript, he mentions seeing his long essay on P. G. Wodehouse in the *Windmill* journal being reviewed in the *Observer*. He adds, somewhat intriguingly: 'But the reviewer didn't mention my contribution which I think was rather mean. I have seen the poor old man and took him out to lunch, but I won't charge the paper for that.' Orwell has been introduced to the creator of Bertie Wooster and Jeeves by Malcolm Muggeridge, who is keeping an eye on Wodehouse – suspected of being a traitor having broadcast from Germany – for MI6.

The second letter, again from Hotel Scribe, dated 10 April 1945, is much longer and mainly focuses on the current situation in Burma. Between the sending of the March 1945 letter and this one, much has happened in Orwell's life. His wife, Eileen O'Shaughnessy, dies suddenly of a heart attack during an operation at a Newcastle hospital. Orwell himself is in a hospital in Cologne at the time. He secures a military aircraft to bring him back to the UK where he attends Eileen's funeral and sorts out the arrangements for her grave in a cemetery close to the hospital. Immediately afterwards he returns to his Paris hotel and reporting assignment. Perhaps surprisingly none of these events are recorded in this new letter.

Rather, his thoughts are moving towards Burma. Having served as an Imperial Policeman in this country from 1922-1927 (and written a novel, *Burmese Days*, 1933, drawing on his experiences), Orwell continues to follow the country's politics closely. Here, he writes very forcefully in favour of giving Dominion Status to Burma. He writes that 'it would be a good solution for the country, giving them a chance of development without cutting the tie with Britain' and 'would be a much more popular solution now than it would have been 5 years ago or will be 5 years hence'. He continues:

RICHARD
LANCE KEEBLE

If we keep Burma on as a colony a fresh quisling movement will spring up and as soon as we are in difficulties again Burma will drop off into the orbit of China, the USA or whoever it may be. The various big firms, the Burma Oil Co, the Bombay Burma Trading Co etc. which more or less owned Burma and were milking it like a cow will naturally by opposed to any extension of self-government because they realise it will mean that the Burmese will be financially autonomous and will be able to levy taxes on the foreign trading concerns and no doubt set up rival organisations of their own. Of course after a decade or so of self-government Burma would be more prosperous and therefore a better market, but this makes no difference to the sectional interests who see their own profits menaced.

He says: 'The Japs are certain to be driven out this coming dry weather, ie. by May 1946 at latest, and it is after that that the future status of Burma will definitely come on the table.' But he fears 'all sorts of impressive-looking blimps will be put up to write articles, make speeches and generally deceive the public. People in general will just be bemused, and the only voice on the other side will be those American journalists with obviously doubtful motives or the sort of people like the *New Statesman* who know nothing about Burma and care less but see a chance of making mischief'.

It is in this context that Orwell makes the offer to Astor to travel to Burma, 'say from November to February to report the closing stages of the campaign and interview some of the political leaders' (that comment on interviewing to be seen alongside my earlier reference to his preference for recording overheard conversations). Afterwards, he says, he could write 'with some show of authority' further in support of Dominion Status. He continues: 'Obviously the Observer couldn't undertake it alone, but I thought it possible the Manchester E.N. and the Yorkshire Post might syndicate my articles.'

He plans to write to 'Beavan' about his ideas. This is John Beavan, editor of the *Manchester Evening News*, who arranges for Orwell to write a number of articles for his newspaper (and so earn him some money to help finance his move to Barnhill) while on the war reporting assignment. Orwell 'thanks' him by including him in his 'little list' of communist fellow-travellers he submits to the recently launched government secret propaganda unit, the Information Research Department, in 1949. Inclusion in the list hardly damages Beavan's career – he is the London editor of the *Guardian* from 1946-1955 and is made a life peer as Lord Ardwick in 1970.

In the April letter, Orwell complains of being not very well. This confirms what I reported (in the last issue of *George Orwell Studies*) from a letter, buried in Malcolm Muggeridge's archive, by Robert Verrall, a television producer who shares the room at Hotel Scribe with Orwell. Verrall writes to Muggeridge in 1957 telling of how 'very ill' Orwell had been, for instance 'lying for three days stoically in bed'. It adds to the mystery of Orwell's trip to Paris. Two previous attempts by Orwell to serve in the war effort have failed – because of his poor health. Now, when he is really very poorly, he somehow manages to evade the medical checks. How come? Interestingly, in concluding his April letter, Orwell mentions to Astor that, if he travels to Burma as a war correspondent: 'I can't pass any kind of medical if the doctor really listens to my chest.'

Is it not also intriguing to note that no letters from Orwell to Astor during 1945 are included in the *Complete Works*, edited by Peter Davison in 1998? After all, Orwell had gone to the continent on a reporting assignment specifically for his great friend. How many other letters are there still to be discovered?

As so often with Orwell, then, one is left with questions rather than answers.

- The author would like to thank Dorian Lynskey and Susie Boyt for giving me access to the letters and to Les Hurst, of The Orwell Society, for, as ever, his invaluable advice. I remain entirely responsible for all the contents.

THREE CHEERS FOR PETER STANSKY

All the editorial team at *GOS* wishes to add its thanks to Professor Peter Stansky for his outstanding contribution to the development of Orwell Studies over many years. His early biographies (in collaboration with William Abrahams) were brave and pioneering works which (given their enormous range of original insights and findings) researchers have mined ever since. Other seminal texts on Orwell have followed. Peter also played an important role in the formation of The Orwell Society and has been an enthusiastic editorial board member of *George Orwell Studies* since its launch. And in this issue, John Rodden celebrates, fittingly, both Peter's 90th birthday and the 50th anniversary of the publication of *The Unknown Orwell*.

WELCOME TO NEW EDITORIAL BOARD MEMBERS

We welcome two new members to the *GOS* editorial board. Nathan Waddell is an Associate Professor in the Department of English Literature at the University of Birmingham, UK. In addition to having written about literature and music, most recently in his book *Moonlighting: Beethoven and Literary Modernism* (2019), he has edited *The Cambridge Companion to* Nineteen Eighty-Four (2020) and the Oxford World's Classics edition of *A Clergyman's Daughter* (2021). He is currently editing *The Oxford Handbook of George Orwell*.

Dorian Lynskey is the author of *33 Revolutions Per Minute: A History of Protest Songs* and *The Ministry of Truth: A Biography of George Orwell's* 1984, which was longlisted for the Baillie Gifford and Orwell prizes. He is also a journalist for various publications and host of the podcast *Oh God What Now?*

Richard Lance Keeble,
University of Lincoln

ORWELL IN SPAIN

A paper in the last issue of *George Orwell Studies*, '"V" is for Valencia: International Brigades' Counter-Intelligence Service Reports about Eileen and Eric Blair in Spain, 1937', by Gleb Zilberstein and his colleagues, was the subject of a critical article by Masha Karp, editor of The Orwell Society's *Journal*, published on the OS website: see https://orwellsociety.com/found-and-lost/. Since the publication of that article, the editors of *George Orwell Studies* have corresponded with both Masha and Gleb. They consider the topic adequately covered in these two pieces so plan to run no further articles on it. They also decided to let Masha and Gleb know that they would not engage in any further correspondence on the matter.

The editors of GOS remain committed to high ethical standards and accuracy. Please send all comments/criticisms/corrections to the editors: Richard Lance Keeble (rkeeble@lincoln.ac.uk) and Tim Crook (t.crook@gold.ac.uk).

PAPER

Orwell and the Secret Intelligence Service

DARCY MOORE

Britain's Secret Intelligence Service (SIS) spied on Eric Blair during 1929 when he lived in Paris. Darcy Moore reveals the intelligence officer involved who had, like Blair, begun his career in the Indian Imperial Police and later approved the recruitment of the notorious double-agent, Kim Philby.

> … the Paris police are very hard on Communists, especially if they are foreigners, and I was already under suspicion. Some months before, a detective had seen me come out of the office of a Communist weekly paper, and I had had a great deal of trouble with the police (Orwell 1997 [1933]: 45).

George Orwell claimed that everything in *Down and Out in Paris and London* had really taken place at one time or another (Orwell 1998 [1903-1936]: 353). In one memorable episode, the unnamed narrator, fully aware that he risks deportation, is persuaded by his Russian friend that hundreds of francs could be earned writing articles on English politics for a Moscow newspaper (Orwell 1997 [1933]: 44). Needing money desperately and being sympathetic to the communist worldview, he reluctantly accompanies 'Boris' along a shabby street running south from the Seine bank, near the Chamber of Deputies, where a Russian secret society of communist agents recruits for the Bolsheviks (ibid).

The secret society is concealed in a laundry. Boris and the narrator are led into a small, shabby room with frosted windows and propaganda posters in Russian lettering; a huge picture of Lenin is affixed to the wall. A deal is struck. However, the offer of one hundred and fifty francs per newspaper article never eventuates and it appears they have been duped in an elaborate swindle. The narrator acknowledges that these were 'clever fellows' who played their part admirably. Their office 'looked exactly as a secret Communist office should look' (ibid: 48). The anecdote is told with so many specific details that it rings true. In 1929, there was a laundry located at 27 rue de Bourgogne which today (although residential and in the re-named rue Aristide Briand) has heavy wooden doors which open on to a courtyard and a staircase, with a landing, as described in the book (Orwell 1997 [1933]: 45; Roberts 2021: 63-64).

The narrator's aside, about being observed by a detective leaving a communist newspaper office, is particularly interesting. The most likely candidates, *Monde* or *Le Progrès Civique*, were the only two French publications that ran Blair's articles (Orwell 1998 [1903-1936]: 113). Both were printed weekly; *Le Progrès Civique*, from 1919-1939 and *Monde* (not to be confused with the highly respectable *Le Monde* founded in 1944) which began the month Eric Blair arrived in Paris, from 1928-1935. *L'Humanité* was a daily communist newspaper and it is conceivable that Blair sought work as a journalist by visiting their office or he may even have dropped in at 22 rue Delambre, where Pierre Yrondy published his four-page weekly, *le MonT-Parnasse Hebdomadaire International*, from his parental home (ibid). Yrondy, whose banned play about Sacco and Vanzetti, the Italian-American anarchists executed controversially in Charlestown State Prison in 1927, was also under surveillance (Moore 2021a).

It was not until Orwell's Security Service personnel file was released by MI5, in 2007, that incontrovertible evidence emerged confirming Eric Blair was under surveillance by a section of SIS in Paris during early 1929.

KV2/2699

The KV2 series, held at the National Archives in Kew, contains the personal files of 'suspected spies and double-agents, renegades and suspected renegades' (National Archives 2021a and 2021b). Orwell's file (KV2/2699) covers the period 1929-1952 and includes correspondence between Metropolitan Police Special Branch, Secret Intelligence Service (SIS) and the British Foreign Office who collaborated for a month to investigate E. A. Blair (National Archives, KV2/2699). The letters, written during early 1929 between Captain H. M. Miller, V. V. and Stafford include intelligence from two unknown informants in Paris, whose names were redacted before the documents were released to the public. They were reasonably well-informed about Eric Blair's activities and daily routines but almost certainly did not have a complete understanding of all his associates.

The first letter, dated 10 January from Captain Miller of Special Branch, requests passport particulars from the Foreign Office for an E. A. Blair currently residing at 6 rue du Pot de Fer. It appears Miller had received information via routine postal surveillance or an informant that Blair was offering to be the Paris correspondent for a British communist newspaper, *Workers' Life*, which later became the *Daily Worker* (Smith 2013: 114). There is no indication as to any other reason why Special Branch wished to investigate but Stafford's information, noting Blair had recently changed the profession on his passport, from 'policeman' to 'journalist', clearly aroused Miller's curiosity (ibid).

In a return letter to Stafford, he makes it clear investigations into 'the ex-Indian policeman "journalist"' will proceed and writes to V. V. seeking more information about Blair. V. V. responded to Miller three weeks later, on 8 February:

> Blair apparently states that he is the Paris correspondent for the "Daily Herald", "Daily Express", "G.K.'s Weekly", but he makes no mention of the "Workers' Weekly".
>
> Blair, [redacted] states, wrote three articles in the "Progrès Civique" of 29.12.28., 5th and 12th January, 1929, entitled "La Grande Misère de L'Ouvrier Britannique". The first article dealt with unemployment in England, which, according to Blair, is due to the war; the second with how the unemployed tramp spends his day; the third with London's beggars. He spends his time reading various newspapers, among which is "l'Humanité", but he has not so far been seen to mix with Communists in Paris and until he does [redacted] considers that the French will not interfere with him (National Archives, KV2/2699).

The analysis, that 'the French will not interfere with him' unless he mixes with communists, appears to be accurate if we take into consideration the hint that there had been 'trouble with the police' when the narrator of *Down and Out in Paris and London* was observed departing from the office of a communist weekly newspaper (Orwell 1997 [1933]: 45).

There are no other documents in the MI5 file prior to 1936, when Orwell was under surveillance while in Wigan researching a book commissioned by the Left Book Club about the plight of coal miners, the unemployed and their families in the North of England. It is unknown when the correspondence from 1929 was added to Orwell's file. However, large numbers of documents were routinely destroyed by SIS and it is conceivable these included updated information about Blair from 1929 now lost (Jeffery 2010: 338). During the 1920s, SIS received 13,000 different reports per annum plus correspondence generated by these reports so this speculation, however impossible to prove, is worth noting (ibid: 17). The regular relocation of SIS HQ also resulted in the routine destruction of documents (ibid).

The British security services are exempt from the provisions of the Freedom of Information Act 2000. Names of agents and informants, often for completely understandable reasons, are routinely redacted and are unlikely ever to be released. This makes it very challenging to undertake historical research. MI5 politely responded to a formal request made recently for more information about Orwell's personnel file, explaining that it had been released in its entirety except for minor redactions to protect the identities of two individuals. However, a little sleuthing has at least revealed the identity of 'V. V.' and why he would have been particularly interested in Miller's query about 'the ex-Indian Policeman "journalist"' (National Archives, KV2/2699).

V. V.

Valentine Patrick Terrell Vivian (1886-1969) oversaw counter-espionage for SIS from 1925 (Vivian n.d.). He was usually referred to as 'Vee-Vee', 'Val' or 'V. V.' in correspondence and was well-placed to assist Miller with information about Blair (Jeffery 2010: 195). In a strange coincidence, Vivian's early life and career mirrored Orwell's except he prospered professionally in a way that Mr and Mrs Blair would have welcomed for their only son.

Educated at St Paul's School, where he excelled in classics, Vivian decided against a curatorship at the Victoria and Albert Museum and opted for service on the sub-continent (*ODNB*). Vivian joined the Indian Imperial Police in late 1906 and began his career as a probationary assistant district superintendent (ibid). Posted to the Punjab (Orwell served in Burma, 1922-1927), he had a wide range of experiences and progressed swiftly through the ranks to senior positions in military intelligence (ibid).

Probationary assistant superintendent Valentine Vivian of the Indian Imperial Police (c. 1906), courtesy of Tony Vivian

In 1914, he was appointed as the assistant director of central intelligence, based in Simla, where he was responsible for investigating seditious activity. Vivian served in Palestine and Turkey during 1918-1919 with the Indian army, was mentioned in dispatches and awarded an OBE. By 1920, Major Vivian's career with MI1c in Constantinople, analysing military intelligence, was being recognised by influential superiors and he was recruited to SIS (also known as MI6 and made famous in the James Bond novels and films). This promotion saw Vivian transferred to London for the first six months of 1923 before serving in Germany with the British army of occupation (ibid).

Vivian formally resigned from the Indian Imperial Police in 1925 to become head of Section V, newly formed by SIS and devoted to counter-espionage (Vivian n.d.). This section particularly concentrated on countering the clandestine activities of the Comintern in proliferating Soviet communism to the rest of the world (Jeffery 2010: 195). In an unpublished manuscript, in the possession of his grandson, Vivian reflected on this period of his life:

> I had the best of two worlds at my command. If I did not like my job in the Foreign Office I could, at any time within the two years of my combined leave, withdraw my resignation and return to India, where according to Sir Edward MacLagan, a rosy future awaited me. So when I reported for duty on that New Year's Day of 1925, I had no idea that I should stay with the Intelligence Division for 28 years …
>
> Almost immediately after joining I was sent on an outside job to inspect our organisations in Holland (Rotterdam), Belgium (Brussels), France (Paris) and Germany (Berlin) … (Vivian n.d.).

Vivian was uniquely positioned as an intelligence officer to analyse the potential risk an ex-Indian Imperial Policeman such as Blair, who had resigned to become a journalist keen on publishing in radical newspapers, would pose as a communist threat.

Who spied on Blair/Orwell in the field? Possibly agents with the local Deuxième Bureau (who had a close relationship with SIS) were involved, or there may have been informants who lived in his hotel (Bowker 2004 [2003]: 110). Valentine Vivian led Section V with limited resources during the 1920s and would have had a close relationship with the station commanders operating out of the passport control department of the Foreign Office in European capitals. These officers supplied London with regular reports on communist activities despite being chronically under-staffed and poorly funded. Maurice Jeffes (1888-1954) was the head of station in Paris for most of the inter-war period (Jeffery 2010: 197). Jeffes's agents cultivated 'police officials of good standing, who have been persuaded ... to take money in exchange for information useful to SIS' (ibid). Considering that Orwell mentions, in *Down and Out in Paris and London*, 'trouble with the police', it is probable French officers supplied Jeffes or his operatives with intelligence about Blair which was passed to Vivian.

 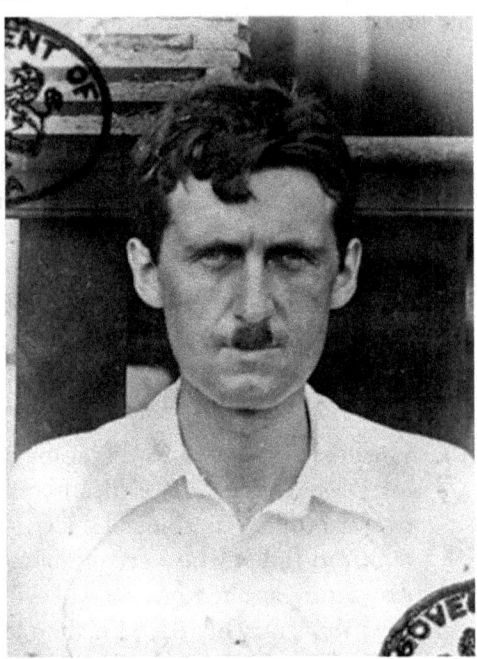

Valentine Vivian (c. 1925), courtesy of Pixie Williams, and Eric Blair (1927). Creative Commons

VALENTINE VIVIAN, KIM PHILBY AND SIS DURING WORLD WAR TWO

Valentine Vivian — described as well-groomed with crinkly hair, monocled and having an official but kindly manner — rose to the upper echelons of MI6 in a career that spanned almost three decades (Brown 1994: 19). Exploring the context in which he was responsible for recruiting one of Britain's most infamous double-agents is a lesson in class, social networks and ideology during the turbulent 1930s and 1940s. It also reveals the prevailing ethos of the Anglo-Indians that the 'unclubbable' Orwell parodied in *Burmese Days* and *Coming Up For Air* (Crick 1992 [1980]: 144; Orwell 1997 [1934]: 72; Orwell 1997 [1939]: 138-139).

In 1941, Vivian recommended the employment of Harold 'Kim' Philby (1912-1988) as an intelligence officer with SIS (Trevor-Roper 1968: 28). It was a terrible lapse in judgement as Philby was to become the most successful member of the notorious Cambridge Five spy ring. Vivian was unaware the Russians had recruited Philby in mid-1934 as the vetting of new recruits to Section V was via social networks rather than a purely professional undertaking (ibid 29-30). Vivian knew Harry St. John Bridger Philby (1885-1960) well from when they served in the Punjab and their careers had intersected many times; including socially, playing bridge at the Simla and Lahore Clubs (Brown 1994: 19). Coincidentally, the two men's wives had been childhood friends and these personal connections influenced Vivian to take an avuncular interest in the younger Philby (*ODNB*).

Vivian lunched with St John Philby, to discuss Kim Philby's suitability for SIS, at the East India and Sports Club, 'the Raj's watering hole' in London, where two king-sized elephant tusks greeted members in the lobby before they reposed on furniture covered in 'hunting pink' while dining on 'glowing curries' served by Indian waiters (Brown 1994: 257). St John Philby, described as 'an ex-Indian Civil Servant with impeccable right wing (not to say, fascist) views', was somewhat of an enigma (Trevor-Roper 1968: 30). Paradoxically (and he was always known for his lifelong and wildly fluctuating opinions) his autobiography details a personal revolt against the philosophical and political norms his class demanded; he believed himself to be 'the first Socialist to join the Indian Civil Service' (Philby 1948: 40). He was an extraordinarily talented explorer, geographer and although remaining 'quintessentially English' in his tastes converted to Islam (taking the name Sheikh Abdullah) becoming a key figure in the political development of Saudi Arabia (Macintyre 2014: 12). Vivian asked about Kim Philby's communist past at Cambridge over lunch. He later recorded that the elder Philby claimed his son was a 'reformed character' and all that was merely 'schoolboy nonsense' (ibid).

Kim Philby certainly milked this family connection explaining in his memoir (which was written under the supervision of the KGB):

> I made a point of seeing Vivian as often as possible. He was quite useless for immediate practical purposes, being mortally afraid of [Claude] Dansey and even of his own subordinate, [John Felix] Cowgill. But he probably had a better mind than either, and was of a reflective temperament which led him to discourse long and widely on SIS history, politics, and personalities, and on relations between SIS and MI5. He was a stickler for correct procedure, and his sermons on the subject told me more about the intricacies of government machinery than I could have learnt from the more slap-dash 'result-getters', such as Dansey or Cowgill. I had little idea in the early months of my cultivation of Vivian how much it would assist me in attaining the one position in SIS which I wanted above anything the service could offer (Philby 1968: 84).

DARCY MOORE   Historian Hugh Trevor-Roper was uniquely placed to observe Philby and Vivian as he worked closely with the pair as an intelligence officer in Section V during World War Two. Trevor-Roper, falsely accused of high treason by Vivian, made some useful observations regarding the rivalries and machinations in the section and how Philby capitalised on the fractious internal politics (Winter 2007: 866). Trevor-Roper claims he was 'astonished' Philby had been recruited as it was widely known he was 'a communist' (Trevor-Roper 1968: 28). He assumed Philby must have been 'an ex-communist' by 1940 as 'ex-Indian Policemen' like Vivian and other senior intelligence officers were the most virulent anti-communists of all (ibid: 29). Mostly, Colonel Vivian recruited ex-Indian policeman but 'doted' on Philby (who was also a well-educated classicist) as an 'intellectual – but not one of those unsound, irreverent intellectuals who gave so much trouble' (ibid: 38). Like Orwell perhaps?

Vivian, in his old age, was heavily criticised for his role in recruiting Philby and nurturing the traitor's career. However, his entry in the *Oxford Dictionary of National Biography* recognised that:

> … the defects of attitude and approach within SIS that failed to recognise the flaws in Philby or to detect their consequences were as much systemic as personal (*ODNB*).

Trevor-Roper made a similar assessment by suggesting other nations' secret services, which SIS penetrated and compromised, had 'exactly the same faults' (Trevor-Roper 1968: 74-75).

It was not just Trevor-Roper and Philby who were recruited to SIS during World War Two but other 'intellectuals', including men in Orwell's milieu, such as Graham Greene and Malcolm Muggeridge who were journalists and authors as well as spies (Sherry 1989: 165-175; Muggeridge 2006: 398-407). Muggeridge met Orwell in Paris when the latter was serving as a war correspondent for the *Observer*, in 1945, and possibly, it has been speculated, on an intelligence mission (Keeble 2020: 31; Muggeridge 1981: 195). Muggeridge introduced Orwell to many agents, including Trevor-Roper, who praised his writing as comparable with Samuel Johnson's work (Keeble 2020: 30-33; Muggeridge 1981: 195). The complex intersection between the press, police and intelligence-gathering in this period, and Orwell's involvement in the world of espionage, is not established (West 1992: 160-165). Speculation that Orwell had been 'caught up for a number of years with intelligence' seems completely feasible considering he authored one of 'the most chilling warnings of the threat of the emergent secret state: *Nineteen Eighty-Four*' (Keeble 2020: 36). In 1942, Orwell even acted as a referee (MI5 describing him as 'the well-known political writer') for George Kopp, his friend and former POUM commander who was being considered as an 'agent in the field' by this intelligence organisation (Orwell 2006: 86). Clues, however faint, about associations Orwell may have had during the early and later years of World War Two also warrant further investigation (Keeble op cit).

CARTER

In June 1940, Orwell reflected in his diary that 'left intellectuals' believed the Nazis would execute 'people like ourselves' and that 'C' told him there would be an effort to have 'our police records' at Scotland Yard destroyed (Orwell 1997 [1939]: 188). Orwell also mentioned the destruction of 'political dossiers' held by Scotland Yard in his 'London Letter' for *Partisan Review*, early in 1941 (ibid: 355). Inez Holden (1903-1974) thought 'C' may have been a 'mysterious man' known as 'Carter', whom Orwell's friends never met (ibid: 189). Who was Carter?

One possibility, a veteran of the Indian Imperial Police, Lieutenant-Colonel John Fillis Carré Carter (1882-1944) who oversaw all Special Branch sections from 1928, was Scotland Yard's liaison with SIS and extremely adept at cultivating relationships with the press (Bennett 2007: 128; Churton 2011: 315). Carter was referred to as 'Nick' after the fictional detective Nick Carter who had first appeared in the nineteenth century dime novel, *The Old Detective's Pupil* (Churton 2014: 43; Kaczynski 2012: 440). He worked closely, although not always harmoniously, with Valentine Vivian and Captain Miller (Bennett 2007: 132-133).

In 1930, while serving as the 'deputy assistant commissioner at New Scotland Yard', Carter wrote an article in a professional journal titled 'The Press and the Police' which revealed his expertise and interest in managing the fifth estate which he suggested 'should be treated as a close ally' (Carter 1930: 518). His article in *The Police Journal* opens:

> The problem of maintaining relations with the press has given anxious thought to most senior officers at one time or another. Misunderstandings arise sometimes, and when they do they are frequently detrimental to the police. These misunderstandings are often due to partial ignorance of the obligations of each other; and the public, who can obtain their information only from the press, consequently form wrong impressions. The press is one of the best friends the police can have: every effort should therefore be made to work in close harmony with it, keeping in view the ultimate object of giving satisfaction to the public (Carter 1930: 509).

DARCY MOORE

Carter was possibly quite sincere in upholding the even-handed ethical position that the police were the servant of the public, as in the summer of the year this article was published, Carter accused Desmond Morton, a senior SIS officer, of 'working on behalf of the Conservative Party' (Bennett and Baxter 2005: 50).

Carter, during a lengthy career, developed considerable influence and reach in London. His diary records meetings with agents and counter espionage work with G Section during World War I and he later resigned as an assistant commissioner, the third highest rank in the Metropolitan Police, on 6 September 1940 (National Army Museum 1917; *London Gazette* 1940: 5406). One of his closest friends was the former air minister in Lloyd George's wartime government, Harold Harmsworth, Viscount Rothermere (1868-1940) whose newspaper empire included the *Daily Mail, Daily Mirror, Sunday Pictorial* and *Evening News* (Orwell 1998 [1937-1939]: 184). Carter was industrious and creative in his efforts to cultivate agents and assets, as demonstrated by his recruitment of the occultist, Aleister Crowley (1875-1947). It has been suggested that Carter assisted Crowley in a reputational sense (which must have been challenging and, if true, demonstrates his influence) by arranging for positive coverage in one of Harmsworth's newspapers, the *Daily Sketch*, promoting his publications, denouncing 'exaggerated and ridiculous' gossip as well as emphasising that Crowley had 'travelled all over the world observing religious practices and philosophy' (Churton 2011: 317). After Crowley's expulsion from France in 1929 (after his name became linked to that of Prince Louis of Bourbon) there had been popular and journalistic calls for him to be charged with various crimes, including murder, and Carter funded Gerald Yorke [1] (1901-1983) to bring Crowley over from Belgium so they could meet (Baker 2022: 137-138).

Carter warmed to the notorious Crowley when they dined, in June 1929, at the stately Langham Hotel on Portland Place (Kaczynski 2012: 440). Their correspondence – with Carter often writing on official Special Branch letterhead – continued for some years, revealing a fondness for Indian restaurants and that Crowley could be indiscreet (Yorke Collection 1929-30a: OS E8; 1929-1932: OS EE2). Crowley operated in Berlin (where he was friends with novelist Christopher Isherwood and the poet Stephen Spender) during the early 1930s as a British agent, submitting regular reports to Colonel Carter (Kaczynski 2012: 448). Carter, after he had officially retired, was still meeting with Crowley as late as September 1942 (*London Gazette* 1940: 5406; Churton 2011: 398-399).

In August 1941, Orwell claimed provocatively in *Horizon* that 'the Left Book Club was at bottom a product of Scotland Yard…' (Orwell

1998 [1940-1941]: 538). What made Orwell write something so apparently dubious other than to annoy Victor Gollancz who, in 1938, had refused to publish *Homage to Catalonia* because of its criticisms of the communists? Did he have information from Carter? Maybe he was suggesting British security services enabled middle class intellectuals, socialists and others to express subversive opinions safely? During the late 1930s, the pulse of the ideological left in Britain could be taken by reading works published by the Left Book Club, founded by Gollancz, John Strachey, Harold Laski and Kingsley Martin who had been dubbed by Lord Beaverbrook's *Sunday Express*, 'the four pink horsemen of the socialist apocalypse' (Kramnick and Sheerman 1993: 364). Orwell, besides writing one of the most widely read and controversial of the Left Book Club publications, *The Road to Wigan Pier* (1937), also parodied the club in *Coming Up For Air* (Orwell 1997 [1939]: 151-158). At its peak, in April 1939, the club had 60,000 members, 1,200 affiliated study groups, close to 1.5 million books in circulation and had 'spawned a veritable mass social movement' which had become 'almost a way of life' (Kramnick and Sheerman 1993: 365).

This high-water mark receded rapidly after August 1939 when the Russian-German Non-Aggression Pact completely reversed the narrative about a 'grand struggle between Communism and Fascism' which had been unfolding since 1936 (Hewison 1988: 6-7). Many of those who had been drawn to the ideology of 'uniting the left' would continue to be cultivated as assets and come under surveillance throughout the next decade (Smith 2013: 126-127; Kramnick and Sheerman 1993: 366). It is hardly surprising that Orwell and others would have taken a keen interest in the existence of the resulting political dossiers, concerned that the Nazis would access information about left intellectuals and execute them, if the planned invasion succeeded (Orwell 1997 [1939]: 188; 355).

PHILBY AND ORWELL: THE SIMILARITIES, THE PROFOUND DIFFERENCES

In 'Why I Write' (1946), one of his most oft-quoted essays, first published in the short-lived, left-wing, pacifist periodical *Gangrel*, Orwell listed four personal motivations for putting pen to paper. He nominated 'political purpose' as particularly significant:

> Desire to push the world in a certain direction, to alter other people's idea of the kind of society that they should strive after (Orwell 1997 [1946]: 318).

Many of his contemporaries also made the effort to 'push the world' after the old imperial certainties were swept away by World War One and, regardless of how his treason is viewed, this was Kim Philby's intention too.

DARCY MOORE

Philby, like Orwell, was a King's Scholar (but at Westminster School, not Eton) and born in India. He had a gilded upbringing but an experience as a young man forever changed his outlook about privilege and disadvantage. In 1934, while in Vienna, Philby became entranced with Litzi Friedmann, an Austrian Jew and communist who taught him about what an unprivileged life was like (Macintyre 2014: 38). He witnessed the violent repression of leftists by the fascist Chancellor of Austria, Engelbert Dollfuss, married Friedmann and fled to safety in England (ibid). Shortly afterwards an agent of NKVD, the Soviet secret police, Arnold Deutsch, recruited Friedmann and Philby, along with other members of the Cambridge Five (ibid: 39). He encouraged Philby to disassociate himself from the communist movement and concentrate on infiltrating the British government. Philby never changed his allegiance from this period in his youth, until his death more than fifty years later in Moscow, aged 76, where he was commemorated as a much-decorated hero of the Soviet Union (Knightley 1989: 256).

Stamp (1990): Soviet Intelligence Agents – Kim Philby (Creative Commons)

Orwell's career trajectory was inexorably altered when he rejected serving an imperial system which was 'very largely a racket' and resigned from the Indian Imperial Police after five years of 'dirty work'. By the time he moved to Paris, Eric Blair was attracted to communism – the ideology that Orwell was to spend the rest of his life rejecting as his distrust of left-wing intellectuals whose loyalty lay with the Soviet Union deepened. His experiences during the Spanish Civil War, when, originally, he claimed to have joined a militia 'to fight against Fascism' for 'common decency' hastened his distrust of the communist movement (Orwell 1997 [1938]: 188). What Orwell witnessed in Barcelona, along with the subsequent biased coverage in the London-based press, left him with few illusions that those who spoke out against Stalinism risked their lives. Significantly, after the publication of *Animal Farm* in 1945, he purchased a German Luger for five pounds from Rodney Phillips (an Australian friend who had financed the journal *Polemic*) fearing assassination by the NKVD (Bowker 2004 [2003]: 330-331).

There is no evidence that Philby and Orwell ever met although they had much in common, were both driven to effect societal change, shared some mutual friends and were fond of the companionship the public house provided (Sherry 1989: 166-168). Both Orwell and Philby were wounded during the Spanish Civil War while ostensibly in the country to work as journalists (Macintyre 2014: 30). Muggeridge wrote in his diary that he and Philby 'engaged in much MI6 gossip' (Muggeridge 1981: 352-353). Coincidentally, the next entry records his visit to see the 'inconceivably wasted' Orwell in hospital and that, although close to death, 'his mind was still grinding over the same old political questions' (ibid). Orwell would have felt vindicated, if he had lived long enough, to learn that Peter Smollett, whom he included on a list of crypto-communists and fellow-travellers handed over – on his deathbed – to the Information Research Department, was a Soviet agent recruited by Philby (Orwell 2006: 210-211). It is unsurprising that the Austrian-born Smollett, whom Orwell was deeply suspicious of long before he was known to be a double-agent, advised Jonathan Cape not to publish Orwell's *Animal Farm* as it was an anti-Soviet allegory (ibid).

A year after Orwell's death in 1950, two of the Cambridge Five, Donald Maclean and Guy Burgess, defected and suspicion fell on Philby (as 'the Third Man') when he was the chief British intelligence representative in Washington. He was forced to resign in 1951 (Trevor-Roper 1968: 51). Unsurprisingly, after such a disastrous intelligence failure for MI6, Vivian retired in the same year (*ODNB*). Philby was publicly exonerated of treasonous activities and it was not until 1963 that he was formally unmasked as a traitor, although the general public was unaware of this development until 1967 (Page 1981: 175; Sayle 1967). He lived the rest of his life in Moscow and is widely considered the most successful double-agent of the twentieth century (Macintyre 2014: 12; Sayle 1967).

Philby, like his father (and Orwell) had quintessentially English tastes and manners and even after this defection, he obsessed over cricket scores in old copies of *The Times*, listened clandestinely to the BBC and organised for Player's cigarettes to be sent over from London (Muggeridge 2006: 398). Muggeridge described Philby as 'a boy-scout who lost his way as the cool, calculating player of a long-drawn-out traitor's role, which, I am sure, is how he would like to see himself' (ibid). Philby argued that his upper-class English manner inspired confidence and facilitated his success as a double-agent (Stasi Unterlagen Archiv 1981). In a lecture to East German agents, Philby explained that because he was a member of 'the ruling class' it was highly unlikely he would have been suspected of treason or tortured if interrogated (ibid). There is no reason to disbelieve this assertion, as unlike his memoir, no wider propaganda purpose or larger audience existed.

In 1967, an intoxicated Philby told an Australian journalist, Murray Sayle, that 'his purpose in life was to destroy imperialism' (Sayle 1967). Arguably, Orwell shared Philby's views. In December 1940, Orwell's article in *Horizon*, 'The Ruling Class', opened by saying:

> England is the most class-ridden country under the sun. It is a land of snobbery and privilege, ruled largely by the old and silly (Orwell 1998 [1940-1941]:291-292).

He goes on to posit that 'at any normal time the ruling class will rob, mismanage, sabotage, lead us into the muck…' but the nation is, despite it all, 'a family' (ibid). Orwell, although always a contrarian, was ultimately a patriot and would have despised Philby's paradoxical, obsessive, traitorous and unreflective commitment to communism. The scene in *Nineteen Eighty-Four*, Orwell's last personal attempt to 'push the world in a certain direction', where Winston Smith expresses his commitment to O'Brien, the master puppeteer and double-agent, reveals Orwell's deep unease at the immorality of what revolutionaries would undertake to further their cause:

> 'You are prepared to commit murder?'
>
> 'Yes.'
>
> 'To commit acts of sabotage which may cause the death of hundreds of innocent people?'
>
> 'Yes.'
>
> 'To betray your country to foreign powers?'
>
> 'Yes.'
>
> 'You are prepared to cheat, to forge, to blackmail, to corrupt the minds of children, to distribute habit-forming drugs, to encourage prostitution, to disseminate venereal diseases – to do anything which is likely to cause demoralisation and weaken the power of the Party?'
>
> 'Yes.'
>
> 'If, for example, it would somehow serve our interests to throw sulphuric acid in a child's face – are you prepared to do that?'
>
> 'Yes' (Orwell 1987 [1949]: 179-180).

Orwell could never have supported a regime, as Philby did, that needed 'a pyramid of corpses every few years' in the misguided belief that the ends justified the means (Orwell 1998 [1940-1941]: 141).

Philby and Orwell – and indeed, Vivian – shared similar backgrounds and experiences. They were Anglo-Indians moulded by their schooling, war, choice of career, the primacy of loyalty, friendship and the cold reality of secrecy and betrayal. There is more than a little irony – which Orwell would have savoured – that Valentine Vivian, a fellow ex-Indian Policeman organised the surveillance of Blair, the potential agent provocateur, considering they both ultimately shared the same concerns about communist ideology. The fact that Vivian erred by recruiting a Russian agent, named after the eponymous character in Rudyard Kipling's great imperial spy novel *Kim*, may have also provided Orwell with more than a little mirth.

- The author would like to express his warm thanks and appreciation to Tony Vivian, who kindly provided newspaper clippings and photographs. Also, to Valentine Vivian's grandchildren, Kim and Pixie, who generously assisted by providing previously unpublished material and photos. An earlier version of this article was published at his blog: https://www.darcymoore.net/2021/07/04/orwell-in-paris-under-surveillance/.

NOTE

[1] While at Eton, Orwell and his friend, Steven Runciman, infamously fashioned candle wax into the image of another student they did not like — and snapped off the leg. Disturbingly soon afterwards, the boy, Phillip Yorke, broke his leg and died of leukemia. His brother, Gerald Yorke, subsequently became keenly interested in the occult and mysticism and contacted Aleister Crowley to learn about magic (Yorke Collection 1929-1932). Even though his family thought it disgraceful, Yorke became a close associate of Crowley's until the occultist's death in 1947 (Bowker 2004 [2003]: 56-57). Jacintha Buddicom, Orwell's childhood companion, was also a friend of Crowley's towards the end of his life (Moore 2021b).

REFERENCES

Baker, Phil (2022) *City of the Beast: The London of Aleister Crowley*, London: Strange Attractor Press

Bennett, Gill (2007) *Churchill's Man of Mystery*, London and New York: Routledge

Bennett, Gill and Baxter, Christopher (2005) *The Records of the Permanent Under-Secretary's Department, 1873-1939*, Foreign, Commonwealth and Development Office, FCDO

National Archives (2021a) The Security Service: Personal (PF Series) Files, KV2. Available online at https://discovery.nationalarchives.gov.uk/details/r/C14997, accessed on 8 August 2021

National Archives (2021b) MI5 file on George ORWELL alias Eric Arthur BLAIR, KV2/2699. Available online at https://discovery.nationalarchives.gov.uk/details/r/C11377649, accessed on 8 August 2021

National Army Museum (1917) Diary of Major John Fillis Carré Carter, 19 September 1917-12 November 1917, Available online at https://collection.nam.ac.uk/detail.php?acc=2004-06-94-1, accessed on 10 March 2022

Bowker, Gordon (2004 [2003]) *George Orwell*, London: Abacus

Brown, Anthony Cave (1994) *Treason in the Blood: H. St John Philby, Kim Philby and the Spy Case of the Century*, Boston: Houghton Mifflin Company

Carter, J. (1930) 'The Press and the Police', *The Police Journal: Theory, Practice and Principles*, Vol. 3, No. 4, October pp 509-518

Churton, Tobias (2011) *Aleister Crowley: The Biography*, London: Watkins Media, Kindle edition

Churton, Tobias (2014) *Aleister Crowley: The Beast in Berlin*, Rochester: Inner Traditions, Kindle edition

Crick, Bernard (1992 [1980]) *George Orwell: A Life*, Harmondsworth, Middlesex: Penguin, second edition

Greene, Graham (2007) *A Life in Letters*, Toronto: A. A. Knopf

Hewison, Robert (1988) *Under Siege: Literary Life in London 1939-1945*, London: Methuen

Jeffery, Keith (2010) *MI6: The History of the Secret Intelligence Service 1909-1949*, New York: The Penguin Press

Kaczynski, Richard (2012) *Perdurabo: The Life of Aleister Crowley*, North Atlantic Books, Kindle Edition.

Keeble, Richard Lance (2020) *George Orwell, the Secret State and the Making of Nineteen Eighty-Four*, Bury St Edmunds: Abramis

Knightley, Phillip (1989) *The Master Spy: The Story of Kim Philby*, New York: Alfred A. Knopf

Kramnick, Isaac and Sheerman, Barry (1993) *Harold Laski: A Life on the Left*, New York: Allen Lane, Penguin Press

London Gazette (1940) No. 34940, 6 September p. 5406

Macintyre, Ben (2014) *A Spy Among Friends: Kim Philby and the Great Betrayal*, London: Bloomsbury

Moore, Darcy (2021a) Orwell in Paris: *le MonT-Parnasse*. Blog post available online at https://www.darcymoore.net/2021/07/18/orwell-in-paris-le-mont-parnasse/

Moore, Darcy (2021b) Cini & The Beast. Blog post available online at https://www.darcymoore.net/2021/12/04/cini-the-beast/

Moore, Darcy (2021c) Orwell in Paris: Under Surveillance. Blog post available online at https://www.darcymoore.net/2021/07/04/orwell-in-paris-under-surveillance/

Muggeridge, Malcolm (1981) *Like It Was: The Diaries of Malcom Muggeridge*, London: Collins

Muggeridge, Malcolm (2006) *Chronicles of Wasted Time: An Autobiography*, Vancouver: Regent College Publishing. Originally published in two volumes, *The Green Stick*, 1972, and *The Infernal Grove*, 1973

Orwell, George (1997 [1933]) *Down and Out in Paris and London, The Complete Works of George Orwell, Vol. I*, London: Secker & Warburg

Orwell, George (1997 [1934]) *Burmese Days, The Complete Works of George Orwell, Vol. II*, London: Secker & Warburg

Orwell, George (1997 [1937]) *The Road to Wigan Pier, The Complete Works of George Orwell, Vol. V*, London: Secker & Warburg

Orwell, George (1997 [1938]) *Homage to Catalonia, The Complete Works of George Orwell, Vol. VII*, London: Secker & Warburg

Orwell, George (1997 [1945]) *Animal Farm, The Complete Works of George Orwell, Vol. VIII*, London: Secker & Warburg

Orwell, George (1997 [1949]) *Nineteen Eighty-Four, The Complete Works of George Orwell, Vol. IX*, London: Secker & Warburg

Orwell, George (1998) *A Patriot After All: 1940-1941, The Complete Works of George Orwell, Vol. XII*, London: Secker & Warburg

Orwell, George (1998) *Smothered Under Journalism: 1946, The Complete Works of George Orwell, Vol. XVIII*, London: Secker & Warburg

Orwell, George (1998) *Our Job Is to Make Life Worth Living: 1949-1950, The Complete Works of George Orwell, Vol. XX*, London: Secker & Warburg

Orwell, George (2006) *The Lost Orwell: Being a Supplement to the Complete Works of George Orwell*, Davison, Peter (ed.) London: Timewell Press

ODNB: *Oxford Dictionary of National Biography* – Blishen, A., Vivian, Valentine Patrick Terrell (1886-1969)

Page, Bruce, Leitch, David and Knightley, Phillip (1981) *The Philby Conspiracy*, New York: Ballantine Books

Philby, Harry St John Bridger (1948) *Arabian Days: An Autobiography*, London: Robert Hale Ltd

Philby, Kim (1968) *My Silent War*, London: MacGibbon & Kee

Roberts, Duncan (2021) *Orwell and the Russian Captain*, Unpublished Manuscript

Sayle, Murray (1968) London-Moscow: The spies are jousting, *Sunday Times*, 6 January

Shelden, Michael (1994) *Graham Greene: The Man Within*, London: Heinemann

Sherry, Norman (1989) *The Life of Graham Greene, Vol. Two: 1939-1955*, New York: Viking

Smith, James (2013) *British Writers and MI5 Surveillance, 1930-1960*, Cambridge: Cambridge University Press

Stasi Unterlagen Archiv (1981) Podiumsveranstaltung mit Kim Philby in 'Haus 22' der Stasi-Zentrale [Panel discussion with Kim Philby in 'House 22' of the Stasi headquarters]. Available online at https://www.stasi-mediathek.de/medien/podiumsveranstaltung-mit-kim-philby-in-haus-22-der-stasi-zentrale-2/ accessed on 20 January 2022

Trevor-Roper, Hugh (1968) *The Philby Affair*, London: Kimber

Vivian, Valentine (n.d.) *Cobwebs of the Past*, Unpublished manuscript

West, Nigel (2019 [1983]) *MI6: British Secret Intelligence Service Operations, 1909-45*, South Yorkshire: Frontline Books

West, W. J. (1992) *The Larger Evils: Nineteen Eighty-Four: The Truth Behind the Satire*, Edinburgh: Canongate Press

Wilson, Ray (2005) *Special Branch: A History, 1883-2006*, London: Biteback Publishing, Kindle edition

Winter, P. R. J. (2007) A higher form of intelligence: Hugh Trevor-Roper and wartime British Secret Service, *Intelligence and National Security*, Vol. 22, No. 6 pp 847-880. DOI: 10.1080/02684520701770642

Yorke Collection (1929-1930a) *Letters from Colonel Carter to Aleister Crowley*, 27 October 1929-6 February 1930, Yorke Collection OS E8: Warburg Institute Library

Yorke Collection (1929-1932) *Letters between Colonel Carter and Gerald Yorke*, 13 May 1929-25 March 1932, Yorke Collection, OS EE2: Warburg Institute Library

DARCY MOORE NOTE ON THE CONTRIBUTOR

Darcy Moore is a deputy principal at a secondary school in New South Wales. He teaches English and History and has worked as an academic in post-graduate teacher education at the University of Wollongong. His interest in Orwell began at school, thirty-eight years ago, when he was enthralled by *Animal Farm* and *Nineteen Eighty-Four*. He is currently writing *Orwell in Paris: The Making of a Writer* which appears to be morphing into a longer book about Eric Blair in the 1920s. He blogs at *darcymoore.net* and his Twitter handle is @Darcy1968. His Orwell Studies Library can be accessed at darcymoore.net/orwell-collection/.

PAPER

The Problem With Julia

G. ALEXANDER DENNING

The problem in understanding the character of Julia in George Orwell's Nineteen Eighty-Four *is that her role is determined by whether or not she is a spy. The fact that she is mentioned at least forty times before we are given her name, only adds to this uncertainty. Through a careful analysis of the text, this paper will argue that she is not a spy, and that her interest in Winston is honourable. It will then examine the nature of her political resistance, showing that unlike Winston, she is more concerned with personal survival than political change. The paper will broaden its investigation of her role to show how her use of the sexual relationship provides Orwell with a unique paradigm with which to develop his political agenda. It will show how Julia's relationship with Winston strikes at the heart of the weakest point in the totalitarian state. Far from being what Matthew Hodgart calls 'an uninteresting character' (1971: 141), it will be shown that she is both complex and misunderstood.*

Keywords: Julia, *Nineteen Eighty-Four*, Party spy, sexual politics

JULIA'S APPEARANCE

She is bold looking, about twenty-seven, with thick dark hair, a freckled face and swift, athletic movements and shapely hips (Orwell 1949 [1989]: 11). Later we are told she is twenty-six (ibid: 136). She has light brown eyes, with dark lashes (ibid: 126) and swears, which is not allowed among Party members (ibid: 128). She has short hair, and she tells Winston in their secret room above Mr Charrington's shop that she is going to be 'a woman, not a Party comrade' (ibid: 149) and will replace her 'bloody trousers' for lipstick, rouge, powder, eye liner, scent, frock, silk stockings and high-heels (ibid). She is sexy rather than attractive, strong minded rather than submissive; what would pass today for 'a modern woman' – albeit, one living in an authoritarian state.

HER JOB

She works in the Fiction Department, where she has a mechanical job on one of the novel-writing machines, as evidenced by her oily hands and the fact that she often carries a spanner (ibid: 11). She has long fingers with shapely nails and a work-hardened palm with a row of callouses (ibid: 122), no doubt caused by her running and servicing a powerful but tricky electric motor – a job she enjoys (ibid: 136) – which requires her to swing round a big kaleidoscope on which the plots of novels are 'roughed in' (ibid: 111). She likes using her hands and feels at home with machinery (ibid: 136). While she knows how to compose a novel mechanically, she does not see herself as a writer, nor does she care for reading. She sees books as 'a commodity that had to be produced, like jam or bootlaces' (ibid). In her younger days she worked in a sub-section of the Fiction Department known as Pornosec (nicknamed 'Muck House'), which produced pornography for the proles (ibid: 137). Again, she insists she is not literary and was never in the 'Rewrite squad' (ibid). When she visits Winston in the room above the shop, she is carrying 'a tool-bag of coarse brown canvas, such as he had sometimes seen her carrying to and fro at the Ministry' (ibid: 147). In other words, she is more the 'grease monkey' than the writer, and practical in manual tasks. With her short hair and boyish overalls (ibid: 149), she would probably pass for a regular 'tomboy'.

HER INTERESTS

She is a model Party member. She had been the hockey captain at school, had won the gymnastics trophy two years running, had been a troop leader in the Spies and a branch secretary in the Youth League before joining the Junior Anti-Sex League. She is considered an excellent character, proof being that she is chosen to work in Pornosec. Her free time is filled with lectures, demonstrations, distributing literature, preparing banners and fundraising which she sees as camouflage in order to deceive the Party (ibid: 135-137).

HER FAMILY

We know nothing of her family, except that her grandfather, who disappeared before the Revolution when she was eight (ibid: 136), had taught her the nursery rhyme, 'Oranges and Lemons', before he was vaporised (ibid: 153). She lives in a hostel with thirty other girls, which has made her hate women because of their smell (ibid: 136). She had her first sexual experience when she was sixteen with a sixty-year-old Party member who later committed suicide to avoid arrest (ibid: 137). When Winston tells her about his mother, she drifts off to sleep (ibid: 171). This may hide a deeper problem she has with her own mother (parents) and may account for her early promiscuity.

SOURCES FOR HER CHARACTER

Much has been made about the women on whom Orwell may have based the character of Julia.[1] Hilary Spurling argues she is based on Sonia Brownell, Orwell's second wife (2002: 93); Dorian Lynskey opts for Celia Paget or Inez Holden and says that Sonia and Julia didn't look or think alike (2019: 174); D. J. Taylor, likewise, is not persuaded by the Sonia theory (2019: 41), preferring Eleanor Jaques and Brenda Salkeld, both of whom emanated from Orwell's Suffolk days, and the theory put forward by W. J. West, that she is based on the female character in Inez Holden's novel *Night Shift* (1941). Not much is gained in pursuing such an enterprise; she is probably a composite of several women anyway.

HER PRAGMATISM

Unlike Winston, who dreams of a future (beyond his lifetime) when life will be better without Big Brother, Julia lives for the moment. When he says: 'We are the dead,' Julia responds: 'We're not dead yet' (Orwell 1989 [1949]: 142). The narrator describes her inner thoughts:

> She would not accept it as a law of nature that the individual is always defeated … it was possible to construct a secret world in which you could live as you chose. All you needed was luck and cunning and boldness. She did not understand that there was no such thing as happiness, that the only victory lay in the far future, long after you were dead, that from the moment of declaring war on the Party it was better to think of yourself as a corpse (ibid).

To make her frugal life under Big Brother more bearable, she steals from Party members the niceties she brings to their rented room (ibid: 147). But the most important thing she steals from the Party is her privacy. More than Winston, who can only find refuge in the room above the shop, Julia has found many secret places to escape surveillance, some of which they share together.

She participates with enthusiasm in the activities of the Party. She tells Winston: 'Always yell with the crowd. It's the only way to be safe' (ibid: 128). Her theory of survival is: 'If you kept the small rules you could break the big ones' (ibid: 135). While her pragmatism may be seen as selfish, in light of the authoritarian regime under which she lives, it is more an issue of self-preservation.

HER POLITICS OF EXPEDIENCY

Julia's pragmatism explains her mistrust of politics and her disinterest in the machinations of the Party. The narrator explains:

> You wanted a good time; 'they', meaning the Party, wanted to stop you having it; you broke the rules as best you could … it was just as natural that 'they' should want to rob you of your pleasures as that you should want to avoid being caught. … She hated the Party . . . but she made no general criticism of it. Except where it touched upon her own life she had no

G. ALEXANDER DENNING

interest in Party doctrine … she never used Newspeak words, except the ones that had passed into everyday use. She had never heard of the Brotherhood, and refused to believe in its existence. Any kind of organized revolt against the Party, which was bound to be a failure, struck her as stupid. The clever thing was to break the rules and stay alive all the same … not rebelling against its authority but simply evading it, as a rabbit dodges a dog (ibid: 137-138).

She is far less susceptible to Party propaganda than Winston and only questions its teachings when they impact on her own life. The difference between truth and falsehood is not important to her (ibid: 160). The war against Eurasia was not happening. The rockets which fell daily on London were probably fired by the government of Oceania itself (ibid). During the Two Minutes Hate she has difficulty in not laughing (ibid). She sees the issue of whether or not the Party had invented aeroplanes as 'totally uninteresting' (ibid: 161), just as she is not interested in who is fighting with whom in the war against Oceania. 'Who cares?' she says, '… It's always one bloody war after another, and one knows the news is all lies anyway' (ibid). She is not worried by Winston's job of changing the facts in the Records Department (ibid), neither is she interested in the story of Jones, Aaronson and Rutherford and the alteration of the facts surrounding their disappearance (ibid: 161). She is not interested in the ramifications of Party doctrine, the principles of Ingsoc, doublethink, the mutability of the past, the denial of objective reality and the use of Newspeak words. '[It] was all rubbish,' the narrator tells us. '… She knew when to cheer and when to boo, and that was all one needed. If [Winston] persisted in talking of such subjects, she had a disconcerting habit of falling asleep' (ibid: 163), which she does when he later reads to her from the book by Emmanuel Goldstein, leader of the dissident Brotherhood (ibid: 226). When Winston tells her he is interested in 'leaving a few records behind, so that the next generation can carry on where we leave off' (ibid: 163), she responds: 'I'm not interested in the next generation, dear. I'm interested in *us*' (ibid, italics in the original).

Julia's political ambivalence toward Big Brother anticipates the question as to whether or not she is a spy.

IS JULIA A SPY?

The narrator tells us that Winston hates nearly all women: 'It was always the women … who were the most bigoted adherents of the Party, the swallowers of slogans, the amateur spies and nosers-out-of-unorthodoxy' (ibid: 12). But when Julia walks into the Two Minutes Hate session, she fills him with 'black terror' when he fears she may be an agent of the Thought Police (ibid: 12). Later, in the canteen, he thinks she is an amateur spy and probably not a member of the Thought Police (ibid: 65). Whatever she is, the text is clear that Winston doesn't trust her.

If she is a spy, it is improbable to imagine her acting alone, or acting without O'Brien's knowledge, when he is the most senior member of the Party. This is why the spy theory (also called the 'honeytrap' or 'sexpionage' theory) is often associated with the role of O'Brien (the 'Collusion' theory).

D. J. Taylor suggests that 'there is at least a suspicion that Julia is O'Brien's willing accomplice, the honeytrap expressly set in place with the aim of luring Winston into danger and throwing him into the hands of the Thought Police' (2019b: 82). He concludes that Julia 'is very probably an agent provocateur' (ibid: 144). Gordon Bowker agrees that 'in the world of the book she could, like O'Brien and Charrington, also be a dissembler leading Winston straight into the arms of the Thought Police' (2004 [2003]: 388). Dorian Lynskey asks: 'Is Julia a member of the Thought Police after all?' (2019: 177). And Nathan Waddell says: 'For much of the novel, Winston's paranoia means he can never quite shake the suspicion that Julia is spying on him ... that she is a member of the Thought Police' (2020: 7). While according to Richard Lance Keeble, she may be 'a highly politicised agent of the state, influencing events in major ways' (2020: 20).

A crucial scene is when O'Brien and Julia walk into the Two Minutes Hate session (Orwell 1989 [1949]: 11). Keeble wonders whether they are 'friends' (2020: 19). But the text does not say they came in 'together'; rather, that they came into the room 'unexpectedly' (Orwell 1989 [1949]: 11), and that they did not sit together but in separate rows (ibid: 13). There is no evidence they are there for the same reason, other than to be present at the session, or that they are meant to be there together, least of all on a joint mission to trap Winston. There is nothing to indicate they even know each other. We simply don't know why they are there at the same time.

Another argument against the 'collusion theory' is the scene in O'Brien's apartment (see ibid: 179-184) when he is annoyed that they have arrived together, and cautions them to leave separately. He describes how they both may be given new identities involving the modification of face, movement, hands, hair, voice – even the amputation of a limb. This is not what you would tell a fellow conspirator. There is also the extraordinary moment when Julia is about to leave. O'Brien hands her a tablet to place on her tongue so the lift attendant will not smell the wine on her breath. These actions are unlikely if O'Brien and Julia are colluding against Winston, but more believable if Winston and Julia have come to him because they trust him. After all, before this meeting, we were told that 'it seemed natural to [Julia] that Winston should believe O'Brien to be trustworthy' (ibid: 159).

The 'collusion theory' assumes that O'Brien only feigns loyalty to the Secret Brotherhood in order to trap Winston. But a careful analysis of the text may suggest otherwise. There is no evidence that Winston doubts his belief that O'Brien is someone he can trust. Not even under torture does his allegiance to him waver. The Appendix, with its reference to 'Winston Smith' (Orwell 1989 [1949]: 320), assumes that his diary was preserved. O'Brien is the only person who knew of its existence. Therefore, it could be argued that O'Brien is a genuine member of the secret Brotherhood, responsible for preserving the name of Winston Smith for future generations.[2]

OTHER ARGUMENTS AGAINST THE SPY THEORY

When the girl with dark hair follows Winston through the prole district, we are told: 'There was no doubting any longer that the girl was spying on him' (ibid: 104). Keeble suggests it is 'the strongest hint Orwell offers that Julia is actually a spy' (2020: 19). But if you examine the following scene – the passing of the love note (Orwell 1989 [1949]: 113) – the impression is that her intentions have been honest from the beginning. In fact, that same night, when Winston had time to reflect, we are told that he 'did not consider any longer the possibility that she might be laying some kind of trap for him' (ibid: 115).

Keeble refers to the fact that she already knows Winston's name, and that she tells him she is better than him at finding things out, as signs that she has 'all the attributes of a conscientious spy (who knows) the name of her target' (2020: 20). But this is what any woman would seek to find out about a love interest, especially one capable of deception and stealing from the Party.

The fact that she already knows the essential parts to the story of Winston's marriage is further evidence that she could be a 'well-briefed spy', according to Keeble (ibid). But it may simply be that she understands, only too well, 'the frigid little ceremony' (Orwell 1989 [1949]: 139) that women like Katharine, Winston's estranged wife, are forced to go through on the same night every week by a regime that had outlawed sexual intimacy. As if to reinforce this point, when Winston asks her to guess what his wife calls it, Julia already knows: 'Our duty to the Party' (ibid).

Keeble sees the issue of her falling asleep during the reading of Goldstein's book as further evidence that she could be a spy. He comments: '… as a spy, she is completely uninterested in it' (2020:

20). However (as mentioned above), it may be that she is simply not interested in politics.

As for the argument that we never know if she (like Winston) is tortured (see ibid: 20), it may not be stated, but the text says: 'One of the men had smashed his fist into Julia's solar plexus, doubling her up like a pocket ruler. She was thrashing about on the floor, fighting for breath. … Then two of the men hoisted her up by the knees and shoulders and carried her out of the room like a sack' (Orwell 1989 [1949]: 232) – not a good way to treat a spy who has led them to their target. There is also the scene in the Chestnut Tree café, where Winston reminisces about his last meeting with Julia: 'Her face was sallower, and there was a long scar … across her forehead and temple' (ibid: 304). She also exhibits the same zombie-like responses as himself – surely hallmarks that she too has suffered electric shock treatment.

There is the issue about the room above the shop. Julia agrees to rent it with 'unexpected readiness', even though she knows it is 'lunacy' and they are 'intentionally stepping nearer to their graves' (ibid: 146). She would only agree to do this, knowing the diabolical consequences, if she is on Winston's side. Besides, if she is a spy, one would imagine she would have nothing to fear after he was caught. Presumably, she would be released to continue with other clandestine assignments for the Party.

Waddell questions whether she tells Winston about the rats 'because she actually saw it happen? Or does she tell him this because she's a goading agent of the Thought Police?' (2020: 13). But before her seeing the rat, she does not know that Winston fears them. It seems to be a natural observation on her part (Orwell 1989 [1949]: 150). Besides, the room is under surveillance (c.f. the iron voice behind the picture at their arrest, ibid: 130). The Party doesn't need a goading agent when they already know of his fear of rats.

There are further elements of the story that can help in refuting the spy theory: firstly, the secrecy surrounding their meetings. There are many references to Julia's diligent planning of their meetings. The following are but a few examples: 'Don't come up to me until you see me among a lot of people' (ibid: 19); 'don't look at me' (ibid: 119); she pretends to read a poster (ibid: 120); there is no conversation until a dense mass of people forms to drown out their voices (ibid: 120); she speaks 'with lips barely moving' (ibid: 121); her plans have a 'military precision that astonished him' (ibid); she is careful to avoid hidden mikes (ibid: 125); they leave by different routes and at different times which she has worked out (ibid: 133); if she judged that the coast was clear 'she would blow her nose … otherwise he was to walk past her' (ibid: 134); she had developed a system she called 'talking by instalments' so they could speak to each other while not quite abreast (ibid: 135); she doesn't go by the same way twice (ibid: 143); she draws a map in the dust with a twig from a pigeon's nest (ibid). Her attention to detail, combined with her attempts to avoid detection by the Party, renders the spy theory implausible. It is the Party she wants to deceive and not Winston.

Secondly, the genuine nature of their romance: perhaps the strongest argument against the 'spy theory' is the evidence of their love. However, Bernard Crick argues that Winston is mistaken to think that Julia really loves him and that, at most, it is 'mutual trust' (2007: 151) rather than a genuine love affair. He writes: 'Indeed, that Julia really loves him is shown in the story to have been a mistake on Winston's part. She falls asleep when he reads Goldstein's testimony and she is bored by his tale of the photograph; and for her part promiscuity is a gesture of contempt for the regime …' (ibid). His first two objections can be explained by the fact that, unlike Winston, she is not interested in political argument. As for the matter of promiscuity, it is true that in Part 1, their relationship (at least on Winston's side) is nothing more than 'erotic fantasy' (see Orwell 1949 [1989]: 17), but in Part 11 we see the flowering of their love. It starts with Julia's orchestrated fall wherein she passes Winston the love note. From this point on, we are told, he is convinced she is not a spy because of her 'unmistakable agitation' (ibid: 115), presumably because she actually suffered pain in her attempt to make contact with him.

Their first attempt at sex has all the hallmarks of a genuine relationship, if only for the fact that she understands his failure to gain an erection. She puts her arm around his waist and says tenderly: 'Never mind dear. There's no hurry. We've got the whole afternoon' (ibid: 126). Later, he tries again. The narrator says: 'Their mouths clung together; it was quite different from the hard kisses they had exchanged earlier. When they moved their faces apart again both of them sighed deeply' (ibid: 130). This is not a woman feigning intimacy with a hidden agenda.

There is the highly personal moment when Julia calls off their meeting because of her menstrual cycle. When he asks her why, she replies: 'Oh, the usual reason. It's started early this time' (ibid: 145). The text makes it clear that his anger quickly dissipates when she gives the tips of his fingers a quick squeeze 'that seemed to invite not desire but affection' (ibid: 146). When the rat appears in their room above the shop, she affectionately calls him 'dearest' (ibid: 151). But the text goes further: 'She pressed herself against him and wound her limbs round him, as though to reassure him with the warmth of her body' (ibid). Clearly, Julia shows a genuine concern to comfort him. And meeting in the room above the shop, Julia pledges her allegiance: 'What you do, I'm going to do' (ibid: 173). In O'Brien's apartment, when he asks them if they are prepared to separate and never see each other again, Julia is the first to object. She places love ahead of political expediency – even to the secret Brotherhood (ibid: 180).

During their last meeting above the shop, they are deeply secure in each other's presence: 'The sun on his face and the girl's smooth body touching his own gave him a strong, sleepy, confident feeling. He was safe, everything was alright' (ibid: 226). But they are not safe; everything is not alright; they are about to be arrested; they know this is their ultimate fate (see ibid: 173). The point of the scene is to show a love which knows no bounds.

Once their relationship is established, there is never a question as to where Julia's loyalty lies. This is why terms like 'sexpionage' and 'honeytrap' are misnomers when applied to her use of sex. They imply a loyalty to the Party when the text is clear that her loyalty stands with Winston.

HER POLITICISATION OF SEX

Julia tells Winston she has had sex with Party members on scores of occasions, but not with Inner Party members – 'those swine' (ibid: 131), she calls them – and presumably, not with proles. From this we can infer that she obtains the niceties she shares with Winston in their room above the shop by using sex to bribe those Outer Party members who steal from their Inner Party bosses. For Julia, sex on this level is simply a means of retaliation: firstly, to steal from the Party for her own gratuitous pleasure and, secondly, to engage in an intimate act that is forbidden. But she does not use sex as a weapon of espionage to advantage the Party. This is why it is better to talk about her 'politicisation' of sex and not its 'weaponisation'. The latter term hides her subtle use of sex to undermine the Party. Even though she says she is not political, her use of sex in this way is still a political act. It may be gratuitous, but it is not motivated by self-indulgence alone. It is also a deliberate act of defiance.

Her distinctive use of sex to undermine the Party can be seen if we compare her attitude to sex with that of Winston. With him it is the physicality of the act which he uses against the Party. This is evidenced at their first intimate encounter, when they meet in the countryside (the Golden Country of his dreams). The narrator tells us that what motivates him about the sexual act is 'the animal instinct, the simple undifferentiated desire: that was the force that would tear the Party to pieces' (ibid: 132); and later, the words used are descriptive of warfare: 'Their embrace had been a battle, the climax a victory. It was a blow struck against the Party' (ibid: 133). But for Julia, it is the emotional energy released in the sexual act that has political importance. At a rendezvous in the church belfry tower, she explains:

> When you make love you're using up energy; and afterwards you feel happy and don't give a damn for anything. They can't bear you to feel like that. They want you to be bursting with energy all the time. All this marching up and down and cheering and waving flags is simply sex gone sour. If you're happy inside yourself, why should you get excited about Big Brother ... and the rest of their bloody rot? (ibid: 139).

According to the narrator, Winston acknowledges the connection between 'chastity and political orthodoxy'; that the sex impulse was 'dangerous to the Party' (ibid: 140)].[3] But he fails to see the power behind Julia's belief that the emotional release of sex (happiness, in particular) is just as potent in undermining the Party. This is why he is 'abruptly' sidetracked into thinking about his wife Katharine and betrayal within the family unit (ibid). His failure becomes obvious later when, in their room above the shop, he says: 'You're only a rebel from the waist downwards' (ibid: 163). This is the 'Achilles' heel' in his attitude towards women, Julia in particular.

Many feminists argue[4] that Orwell demeans the role of women by not attributing to them a serious political interest. Daphne Patai says that Julia is motivated by sexual pleasure and is totally uninterested in the politics of the society that oppresses her (1984: 243). The fact that she is only given a first name simply reflects that she is 'an insignificant female' (ibid: 244). Beatrix Campbell writes that Julia's rebellion is 'essentially sexual' and lacking in 'political consciousness' (1984: 129). Likewise, Deirdre Beddoe says that Julia, unlike Winston who is inspired by intellectual concepts, only objects to the regime 'because it stops her having a good time' (1984: 147). But these criticisms underestimate the political power Orwell gives to her character. With her subtle use of sex, she challenges the Party as effectively as Winston does with his use of rational argument. Far from Orwell demeaning the role of women in the political process, he shows in the case of Julia how sex can play a pivotal role in counteracting the forces of totalitarianism.

Even scholars who acknowledge Julia's sexual politics appear to miss the importance she places on emotion, settling on a more 'idealised'[5] version of her politics. Michael Shelden sees her use of sex as a liberating force for freedom in the release of passion (1991: 472), while Robert Colls sees her as the conveyor of hope in Winston's dismal life (2013: 215-216), and Jeffrey Meyers, a symbol of Winston's lost mother's love (2000: 284). These explanations, however, are not enough to explain her true political influence on the plot.

THE ROLE OF JULIA

So, what is ultimately the role of Julia? D. J. Taylor suggests her role is 'figurative rather than decisive ... we learn very little about Julia, and what goes on in her mind ... her importance rests on what she symbolizes – youth, impulse, free-spiritedness – rather than what she actually is' (2019a: 41). But Taylor underestimates her role. We know a lot about what she thinks: she opposes the Party's propaganda (Orwell 1989 [1949]: 160f); she manipulates the Party for her own limited happiness (ibid: 142); she learns to share Winston's trust for O'Brien (ibid: 159); she is willing to join the secret Brotherhood (ibid: 177); she is prepared to commit various atrocities for the sake of the cause (179); she vows to stay loyal to Winston at any cost (ibid: 180). She is not just a seductive female but is prepared to risk everything (except her love for Winston) for the sake of the cause.

Richard Lance Keeble argues (see 2020: 20-22) that her role serves the broader context of Orwell's reflections on truth and objectivity as reflected in the epistemological debate between Winston and O'Brien. Winston asserts his belief in objective truth in contrast to O'Brien's attack on the idea of mind-independent reality. The fact that we don't know whether Julia is a spy 'highlights the essential unknowingness of reality ... whether Julia is actually a spy or not will remain forever an "unsolved riddle"' (2020: 22). Similarly, by assuming that Julia is (or may be) a spy, Gordon Bowker argues (2004 [2003]: 388) that the uncertainty over whether Julia is a spy supports the novel's idea of the deceptive nature of truth, making it a novel about 'the slippery, unstable nature of meaning' (ibid: 389). But if she is not a spy (which this essay suggests), these arguments are less convincing.

Dorian Lynskey has a slightly different view of her role. He says that while O'Brien claims there is no such thing as objective truth, and Winston says that there is, Julia maintains that *'it doesn't matter'* (2019: 174, italics in the original). He argues that she lives entirely in the present and is not interested in the society she inhabits or in its politics. She has a 'cynical, even nihilistic, intelligence' (ibid), which is what totalitarian states depend upon from their citizens.[6] But this is to trivialise her role, and has led feminist scholars, like Deirdre Beddoe, to criticise Orwell's treatment of women. She says: 'Whereas Winston is inspired by intellectual concepts like integrity of history and the notion of freedom, Julia is only "a rebel from the waist downwards"' who 'objects to the regime because it stops her having a good time' (1984: 147). Again, these views disregard Julia's distinctive use of sex to undermine the state. It is the element of emotional intimacy which Orwell brings to her relationship with Winston that is the game changer.

G. ALEXANDER DENNING

HER EMOTIONAL VIEW OF REALITY

A number of scholars assert that Winston – like his creator, Orwell – is a believer in objective truth as opposed to the relativism of totalitarianism. David Dwan calls Winston 'a convinced empiricist – a firm believer in the "evidence of your senses", or the "evidence of your eyes and ears" as the foundation for knowledge' (2019: 153).[7] They are less inclined to see the importance that Julia gives to emotions.

For Julia, truth is based on a person's emotional response to reality. She asks Winston: 'Which would you sooner sleep with, me or a skeleton? Don't you enjoy being alive? Don't you like feeling: This is me, this is my hand, this is my leg, I'm real, I'm solid, I'm alive! Don't you like *this?*' (1989 [1949]: 142, italics in the original). Later, she applies her 'no nonsense' view of reality to the way a person thinks. She tells Winston: 'They can make you say anything – *anything* – but they can't make you believe it. They can't get inside you' (ibid: 174, italics in the original). According to the narrator, Winston agrees: 'With all their cleverness, they had never mastered the secret of finding out what another human being was thinking' (ibid). Or what we might assume Julia would say: what another person was 'feeling'.

Interestingly, when Winston is tortured, O'Brien accuses him of not giving up his feelings: 'The Party is not interested in the overt act: the thought is all we care about. ... We convert him (the heretic), we capture his inner mind, we reshape him' (ibid: 265-267). It is Julia's insistence on feelings that provides the emotional underpinning to Winston's rational view of reality. This is what the text refers to when it says: 'she had got into the texture of his skin' (ibid: 293). It is this which makes him cry out in a moment of reckless honesty: 'Julia! Julia! Julia, my love! Julia!' (ibid). The last bastion of resistance is his emotions. This is what sends him to Room 101 when O'Brien admonishes him: 'You are improving. Intellectually there is very little wrong with you. It is only emotionally that you have failed to make progress' (ibid: 295). Ironically, it is because of Julia that he is holding on to his emotions.

HER REDEFINITION OF THE NATURE OF LOVE

With the sexual relationship between Winston and Julia, it is important to recognise the importance Orwell gives to intimacy and not merely the physical act in itself. Yes, she is promiscuous, but not with Winston. She seeks him out in a loving relationship, and in this context, sex represents:

- intimacy in a world where feelings are despised;
- commitment in a world where the individual is left to their own devices;

- family in a world where children inform on their parents;
- sacrifice in a world where progress is measured by the increase in pain.

Pivotal to Julia's influence on their relationship is the way she changes Winston's view of sex. Before their first meeting, he is aware of its political power, seeing it (according to the narrator) as a form of 'rebellion' and 'thoughtcrime' (ibid: 71). But at this early stage in the plot, his attitude to sex is also driven by his mental psychosis. Two examples will suffice. Firstly, when he transfers his hatred from the image on the telescreen to his imaginings of what he would do to Julia: 'He would flog her to death with a rubber truncheon. He would tie her naked to a stake and shoot her full of arrows like Saint Sebastian. He would ravish her and cut her throat at the moment of climax' (ibid: 17). Secondly, when he writes in his diary about his encounter with the harlot: *'She threw herself down on the bed, and at once, without any kind of preliminary, in the most coarse, horrible way you can imagine, pulled up her skirt'* (ibid: 70, italics in the original).

These examples of sexual eroticism may be the product of Winston's failed sexual relationship with his wife, Katharine (see ibid: 138), combined with his longing for his mother and his jealousy of his younger sister's demand on her time (see ibid: 168-171).[8] Winston's distorted view of sex is a far cry from the intimacy he later shares with Julia. Their sexual relationship is a metaphor for how love can overcome the tyranny of hatred. The Party may want to 'abolish the orgasm' (ibid: 280) as O'Brien proudly boasts, but the love which Julia and Winston share is emotional as much as it is physical, and consequently far more difficult to abolish. They both vow not to betray the other and, though they eventually do, it is the highest form of love which they aspire to.[9] And when torture by electric shock destroys their love (which it does), it doesn't mean that it wasn't genuine.

AFTERWORD

This paper has sought to show the importance of Julia's character in Orwell's last and greatest work. Rather than dismissing her as a youthful and promiscuous spy of the Thought Police who uses her sex appeal to trap the unsuspecting Winston, the essay has shown that she shares his opposition to the Party and has her own unique strategy of resistance. The paper has also examined her relationship with Winston, arguing that her emphasis on emotional intimacy in their love-making elevates the sexual act into a more sophisticated political 'tactic' than what is implied by the cold-hearted use of the word 'weapon', which is often attributed to the stereotypical female spy. While they both agree that the Party cannot get inside their heads, according to Julia, neither can it get inside their hearts. Of course, the fact that it does get inside both their heads and their hearts – they betray themselves and each other – does not negate the fact that love like theirs will inevitably defeat the Party. They know it will not be in their lifetime (ibid: 163) – O'Brien tells them as much (ibid: 183). They know they are doomed from the start (ibid: 146; 159). Their love is a tragedy of Shakespearean proportions; it is also a blow which will strike against the Party and ultimately bring about its destruction.

The paper has also highlighted the tricky pathway by which Orwell navigates the reader through the concepts of truth and meaning in a world where fact and memory are whatever the Party says they are. Scholars have argued that the uncertainty over Julia's motives is yet another example of Orwell playing with the idea of what is truth. But her character may also be an Orwellian decoy designed to show us that truth is not only an intellectual exercise, an epistemological game 'fought' between opposing sides over what is actually real and what can be said to be real for the purposes of propaganda, it also has an emotional component: it is real because it feels real, like it is the good and right thing to do. The emotional and intellectual are like twin towers which must be preserved if society is not to collapse under the pressure of totalitarianism.

Julia's role is that of a 'modern woman'. Orwell may well have pre-empted the sexual revolution of the sixties and the modern feminist movement which followed, in seeing the importance of the sexual relationship in bringing about social and political change. Through their sexual union, Orwell shows how the breaking of the puritanical hold of the Party on its members is a form of revolt. The giving of oneself to the other is a life-changing union which the Party cannot take back. It is what the Party truly fears; what will bring about the 'annihilation of a whole culture' (ibid: 33), of 'a whole civilization' (ibid: 131). This is the emotional legacy which the character of Julia leaves to future generations.

NOTES

[1] Richard Lance Keeble summarises these theories in his essay (2020: 15)

[2] For a detailed analysis of this view see essay by G. Alexander Denning (2020)

[3] Cass Sunstein has an alternative view on Orwell's position that there is a connection between chastity and political orthodoxy, arguing that there is no link between sexual repression and political repression. Sunstein says the text actually argues against Orwell's thesis, because after Winston and Julia become sexual partners, they enlist in a political conspiracy against the Party by joining the secret Brotherhood

[4] For a summary of these views see Richard Lance Keeble's essay (2020: 16)

[5] The term is Richard Lance Keeble's. The scholars referenced are cited in his essay (ibid: 17)

[6] Lynskey refers to a line from an earlier draft: 'It was characteristic of the two of them that whereas it was Winston who dreamed of overthrowing the Party by violent insurrection, it was Julia who knew how to buy coffee on the Black Market' (2019: 174). But the very fact that this was discarded by Orwell may actually show that he wasn't happy with this portrayal of Julia as someone with little political insight of her own

[7] For an extended discussion on Orwell's ideas on truth see Dwan, David (2019): 139-168)

[8] Sigmund Freud called this the 'Oedipus complex' in his groundbreaking book: *The Interpretation of Dreams* (1899), whereby a child displays an unconscious and unhealthy sexual desire for the opposite-sex parent and a hatred for the same-sex parent. However, Bowker reminds us that Orwell would have been well aware of Freud's theory of infantile sexuality and theories of probing into the human mind aimed at changing human behaviour and human thought (see 2004 [2003]: 9). He cautions that Orwell himself was not so much negatively affected by his own mother who generally supported him, but by the effect that his time at St Cyprian's prep school had on his self-worth and self-respect, leaving him with 'an intense sense of guilt and self-hatred' (ibid: 49)

[9] Homer and the Ancient Greeks referred to this highest form of love as 'agape', meaning 'unconditional love' as distinct to 'eros', meaning sexual/erotic love

REFERENCES

Beddoe, Deirdre (1984) Hindrances and help-meets: Women in the writings of George Orwell, Norris, Christopher (ed.) *Inside the Myth: Orwell: Views from the Left*, London: Lawrence and Wishart pp 139-154

Bowker, Gordon (2004) [2003] *George Orwell*, London: Abacus

Campbell, Beatrix (1984) Orwell: Paterfamilias or Big Brother?, Norris, Christopher (ed.) *Inside the Myth: Orwell: Views from the Left*, London: Lawrence and Wishart pp 128-136

Colls, Robert (2013) *George Orwell: English Rebel*, Oxford: Oxford University Press

Crick, Bernard (2007) *Nineteen Eighty-Four*: Context and controversy, Rodden, John (ed.) *The Cambridge Companion to George Orwell*, Cambridge: Cambridge University Press pp 146-159

Denning, G. Alexander (2020) O'Brien in *Nineteen Eighty-Four*: A new interpretation, *George Orwell Studies*, Vol. 5, No 2 pp 62-75

Dwan, David (2018) *Liberty, Equality and Humbug: Orwell's Political Ideals*, Oxford: Oxford University Press

Gottlieb, Erika (1992) *The Orwell Conundrum: A Cry of Despair or Faith in the Spirit of Man?*, Ottawa, Canada: Carleton University Press

Hodgart, Matthew (1971) From *Animal Farm* to *Nineteen Eighty-Four*, Gross, Miriam (ed.) *The World of George Orwell*, New York: Simon and Schuster pp 135-142

Keeble, Richard Lance (2020) *George Orwell, The Secret State and the Making of Nineteen Eighty-Four*, Bury St Edmunds: Abramis Academic Publishing

Lynskey, Dorian (2019) *The Ministry of Truth: A Biography of George Orwell's 1984*, London: Picador

Meyers, Jeffrey (2000) *Orwell: Wintry Conscience of a Generation*, New York and London: W. W. Norton and Company

Orwell, George (1989 [1949]) *Nineteen Eighty-Four*, London: Penguin

Patai, Daphne (1984) *The Orwell Mystique: A Study in Male Ideology*, Amherst: University of Massachusetts Press

G. ALEXANDER DENNING

Shelden, Michael (1991) *Orwell: The Authorised Biography*, London: William Heinemann

Spurling, Hilary (2003*) The Girl from the Fiction Department: A Portrait of Sonia Brownell*, London: Penguin

Sunstein, Cass R. (2005) Sexual freedom and political freedom, Gleason, Abbott, Goldsmith, Jack and Nussbaum, Martha C. (eds) *On* Nineteen Eighty-Fou*r: Orwell and Our Future,* Princeton and Oxford: Princeton University Press pp 233-241

Taylor, D. J. (2019a) Who was Julia? *Nineteen Eighty-Four's* many heroines, *George Orwell Studies*, Vol. 3, No 2. pp 39-43

Taylor, D. J. (2019b) *On* Nineteen Eighty-Four, New York: Abrams Press

Waddell, Nathan (2020) Introduction: Orwell's book, Waddell, Nathan (ed.) *The Cambridge Companion to* Nineteen Eighty-Four, Cambridge: Cambridge University Press pp 1-20

NOTE ON THE CONTRIBUTOR

G. Alexander Denning trained as an ordained Baptist minister, having attained a degree in theological studies at Whitley College, Melbourne. Since leaving the ministry, he has been involved in a number of entrepreneurial businesses before his retirement. For many years he has been interested in writing poetry and novels, all of which are unpublished. His interest in George Orwell was aroused in the late 1990s when a friend gave him a copy of *Nineteen Eighty-Four*. Being fascinated with the character of O'Brien, he wrote a paper which lay dormant in his bottom drawer for twenty years until its recent publication, with some revision. This has aroused his interest in other aspects of the novel.

PAPER

Disassembling the Myth of the Struggling Artist in George Orwell's *Keep the Aspidistra Flying*

REBECCA CLAYTON

The myth of the struggling artist is an enduring one; it appears in literature in many forms. It can be characterised by self-exile, inertia and refusing materiality in favour of pure aestheticism. George Orwell's 1936 novel Keep the Aspidistra Flying *builds upon this myth, repositioning the archetype in relation to the contemporary moment. Orwell employs the character of Gordon Comstock as a device through which he constructs and dismantles the myth of the struggling artist; he does so to interrogate the extent to which the artist has a responsibility to their present historical moment. In this paper, I first examine how Orwell's style of narration and presentation of Comstock helps to construct this persisting myth. I then explore how Comstock's conversations with Rosemary and Ravelston, and his obsession with the unassuming aspidistra plant, show the myth of the struggling artist to be deeply flawed.*

Keywords: *Keep the Aspidistra Flying*. 'Inside the Whale', struggling artist, artistic responsibility, self-exile

In James Joyce's 1916 novel *A Portrait of the Artist as a Young Man*, the protagonist, Stephen Dedalus, asserts that 'when a man is born ... there are nets flung at it to hold it back from flight. You talk to me of nationality, language, religion. I shall try to fly by those nets' (Joyce 1992 [1916]: 157). Here, Dedalus articulates an intention to separate himself from the reality he inhabits. The word 'nets' suggests that Dedalus found these social and cultural forces to be constricting; he felt that to be absolutely free he must exile himself, live beyond these nets.

In Orwell's 1940 extended essay 'Inside the Whale', he remarks that the group of writers to which Joyce broadly belonged all shared one defining characteristic: namely, 'pessimism of outlook' (Orwell 2002 [1940]: 228). Orwell asserts that:

> What is noticeable about all these writers is that what purpose they have is very much up in the air. There is no attention to the urgent problems of the moment, above all no politics in the narrower sense. Our eyes are directed to Rome, to

REBECCA CLAYTON

Byzantium, to Montparnasse, to Mexico, to the Etruscans, to the Subconscious, to the solar plexus – to everywhere except where things are actually happening (Orwell 2002 [1940]: 228).

Orwell describes the way these writers, who included Joyce, D. H. Lawrence, T. S. Eliot, and Aldous Huxley amongst others, tended to ignore current affairs in Europe. Instead of looking outward, this group, broadly termed 'modernists', focused their attention almost exclusively inward. When Dedalus laments the ties of 'nationality, language and religion' he saw as so incongruous to his artistic ambitions (Joyce 1992 [1922]: 157), he was giving a voice to an impulse that was gaining traction amongst the literary intelligentsia during a period ravaged by a global war. Philip Bounds notes Orwell's 'jaundiced tone' (Bounds 2009: 105) towards the Joyce-Eliot group in 'Inside the Whale'. Orwell purports to admire such authors, in particular Joyce, whom he declares a 'pure artist' (Orwell 2002 [1940]: 228). However, he simultaneously goes out of his way to declare the group's political irresponsibility. As much as Joyce is to Orwell, a 'pure artist' (ibid), he takes umbrage with his view that 'literature was somehow hermetically sealed from the world around them' (Bounds 2009: 106). As Bounds states, Orwell thought that their belief in 'aesthetic autonomy condemned them to a species of political obscurantism' (ibid).

This idea, that the artist should not be bound by the material conditions of their being but to the immaterial facets of their art, lies at the heart of the myth of the struggling artist. The perceived separation between the artist and the reality they inhabit is key to understanding the myth. Their collective renunciation of the material in their work led many to forgo material comforts in their lives. Thus, the notion that the artist must be seen to live without affluence and outside the bounds of polite society, was borne. Orwell argues, in 'Inside the Whale', that that sense of disillusionment amongst the writers of the 1920s was actually a luxury afforded to them by the relative prosperity and peace felt throughout Europe after the First World War. One might argue against this, that the tendency towards apathy was partly a symptom of the trauma felt amongst the public after the horrors of a global war. The reasons behind these feelings are complex; nevertheless, although Dedalus framed it as a sort of flight, the reality was that writers retreated inward and backward over the course of the decade, taking more abstract historical, spiritual, and psychological themes as their muse.

This attitude of withdrawal from society, both physically and artistically, became an object of fierce contention amongst Orwell's contemporaries. In the wake of the rise of fascism in Europe, artistic inertia seemed ludicrous to the young writers of the 1930s. The poets and novelists of this decade largely diverged from the path trodden by their predecessors. They had no intention of, to paraphrase Orwell, directing their eyes elsewhere. As Orwell surmised: 'If the keynote of the writers of the 'twenties is "tragic sense of life" the keynote of the new writers is "serious purpose"' (Orwell 2002 [1940]: 230). Their attitude was one of staunch commitment rather than disavowal. In 'Inside the Whale', Orwell grapples with himself over the extent to which the artist should stay on the periphery of the community they comment upon. He wonders whether art's role truly is, as Dedalus believes, to break from the constraints of the present to create art; or whether it is, conversely, only active participation in the present that can lead us to portray the truth.

'Inside the Whale' is Orwell's exposition of his literary tussle with Henry Miller. Miller happened to be one of the few artists of the thirties who remained a proponent of this 'pessimism of outlook' (ibid: 228) made fashionable by the Joyce-Eliot group. Orwell stopped at Miller's Parisian apartment in late 1936 as he made his way to northern Spain to report on the Spanish Civil War; 'Inside the Whale' to a large extent, follows on from that meeting. Far from being Miller's adversary, Orwell is fascinated by Miller's politics of refusal. He praises Miller's command of language, but resists his attitude of apathy. Orwell argues that the 'monstrous trivialities' of Miller's prose are 'engrossing' (ibid: 216). However, he also argues later in the essay that Miller's unambiguous espousal of political apathy was 'a declaration of irresponsibility' (ibid: 216, 241). He uses the metaphor of the whale, a not-so-oblique reference to the Biblical story of Jonah and the whale and Herman Melville's *Moby Dick* (1851), to explain this conundrum. He argues that Miller is a 'willing Jonah' (ibid: 243). He is trapping himself within the system that confines him in his absolute refusal to participate in society.

Another 'willing Jonah' who rears their head in Orwell's oeuvre is Gordon Comstock. In his 1936 novel *Keep the Aspidistra Flying*, Comstock deliberately suffers as a form of protest to what he sees as the tenets of amoral bourgeois living. Comstock isolates himself from his friends, quits his decent job and deliberately descends into poverty. He removes himself from the strictures of decency, just as Dedalus sought to do. As Comstock himself relates: 'he had a feeling that if you genuinely despise money you can keep going somehow, like the birds of the air' (Orwell, 1980 [1936]: 55). He, like Dedalus, takes the flight of a bird as the model by which he lives. In his desire to break free of society's rules, he aligns himself with the generation of writers who subscribe to this 'twilight of the gods' mentality (Orwell 2002 [1940]: 230). In Comstock, we can identify the archetype of the struggling artist.

REBECCA CLAYTON

Keep the Aspidistra Flying examines the role self-exile plays in the creative output of the poet and the usefulness of political ideology, or lack of it, within literature. Considering the integrity of the poet who lives outside the society but refuses to confront the reality of that decision, Orwell explores the opposition between a literary philosophy that shuns artistic responsibility and an emerging school of thought that favoured active participation. Comstock constructs for himself this mantle of the struggling artist, reproducing, in a way, the tussle between Orwell and Miller in 'Inside the Whale'. As the novel progresses, the archetype unravels and we are made to see that it is but a veil, thinly held up to cast a shadow over the parochial nature of Comstock's self-image.

ASSEMBLING THE STRUGGLING ARTIST

In his study of Orwell, Raymond Williams says this of the writers, at the turn of the twentieth century:

> If the only orthodox test of achievement was 'social' recognition and success, then this could be opposed by a simple negation. The 'writer', the true writer, had no commercial aims, but also, at root, no social function and, by derivation, no social content (Williams 1975: 31).

If the artist had lost their audience, then there was no longer any need for them to appease that audience or relate their work to current popular opinion. The decline of the social function of the artist led to art works themselves becoming less contingent upon social issues and more reliant on the subjective experience of the artist (ibid: 32). Williams identifies, in Orwell, this struggle with the social obligation of the writer to their present moment. Williams writes that Orwell 'became the socially conscious writer of the thirties rather than the aesthetic writer of the twenties' (ibid).

Keep the Aspidistra Flying explores the nuances of this evolution.

At the beginning of the second chapter, Comstock returns to his hovel. The narrator explains that: 'When he had chucked up everything and descended into the slime of poverty, the conception of this poem had been at least a part of his motive' (Orwell 1980 [1936]: 36). In the 1984 study, *George Orwell: The Search for a Voice*, Lynette Hunter says that 'the close relationship between narrator and character points to a difference in perspective rather than a difference in intelligence' (Hunter 1984: 38). By this, Hunter means that there is a symbiotic relationship between the mind of the narrator and of Comstock that leads the reader to develop a far more comprehensive idea of Comstock than if the gap between narrator and protagonist were more distinct. In the text, Comstock's own thoughts and feelings invade those of the omniscient narrator, plunging the narrative into moments of profound subjectivity. It is this intermeshing of the objective and subjective that allows the reader to understand Comstock's 'motive' (Orwell 1980 [1936]: 36) for taking this slow descent into penury.

This amalgamation of the interior and exterior within the narrative style is present from the beginning, when the narrator describes Comstock's dishevelled figure: 'even from above you could see that his shoes needed resoling' (ibid: 7). This observation is a consummate metaphor for the relationship between the narrator and Comstock; even from the narrator's external viewpoint, you can perceive the inner turmoil lurking beneath Comstock's surface. The narrator not only describes Comstock as one might come across him in the street, but also gives voice to Comstock's subjective interior monologue. Not only are we made aware of Comstock's bedraggled appearance, but also of the façade Comstock enlists to mask it. He does everything he can to dispel others' suspicions of his precarious financial situation, both in the way he interacts with others and the way he holds himself. For example, the narrator relates that Comstock carries himself 'very upright, throwing a chest, with a you-be-damned air which occasionally deceived simple people' (ibid: 9). Here, the reader is shown that Comstock is a man who thinks deeply about the way others regard him. The soles of his shoes are synecdochic of this; they embody both the conflict between Comstock's external and internal self, and the battle for narratorial dominance within the text.

This opposition between the internal and external bleeds into other aspects of the novel. When Comstock returns to his lodgings, he laments: '… night after night, always the same, the lonely room, the womanless bed; dust, cigarette ash, the aspidistra leaves' (ibid: 40). It is clear from this remark that Comstock places great importance on his physical surroundings, and in doing so, allows his poverty to define him. This betrays the character of Comstock as a caricature of a writer rather than an authentic artist. He panders to the spectacle of the writer rather than the reality of writing. He is both a person and a type. His conception of himself is immediately familiar to us as the archetype of the struggling artist.

Hunter also acknowledges that the narrator injects a 'humorous voice' (Hunter 1984: 36) into the novel. In paying such close attention to the physicality of Comstock, the narrator is partaking in a joke. The joke is on Comstock and, by extension, all those budding writers who suffer poverty in the name of art. Bernard Crick says, of Orwell's humour, that it 'lies in literal truth-telling, removing all euphemisms, a way of wrapping unpalatable deep truths in sardonic homely observations' (Crick 2011 [2008]). Here, the humour present in Orwell's characterisation of Comstock lies in his ability to lay the character bare, without judgement and without embellishment. It is the quotidian nature of Comstock's existence that is so amusing because he is unable to perceive the ordinariness of his circumstance. Comstock imbues himself with a certain romantic grandeur; it is a grandeur that the narratorial style shows to be a figment of his poetic imagination. The humour present in *Keep the Aspidistra Flying* relies on the presence of a voice other than Comstock's. The narrator casts a wry eye over Comstock, and it is the discordance between the narrator's reality and Comstock's self-image that makes us smile.

It becomes increasingly obvious that Comstock's poverty is a deliberate act rather than a result of accidental misfortune. Comstock continually alludes to his desire to be 'under ground, under ground! Down in the safe soft womb of earth...' (Orwell 1980 [1936]: 217). It is the deliberate nature of Comstock's descent into poverty that marks him as a struggling artist more than any suffering he undertakes. He explains to himself:

> There are two ways to live, he decided. You can be rich, or you can deliberately refuse to be rich. You can possess money, or you can despise money; the one fatal thing is to worship money and fail to get it (ibid: 50).

This viewpoint becomes a common mantra for Comstock. He sees society as a system that one either believes in or is cast out from – there is no middle ground. For Comstock, there is no way to be a part of society whilst also remaining critical of it. It is this that places him in the direct lineage of the struggling artist. As Elizabeth Wilson argues in her seminal *Bohemians: The Glamorous Outcasts*, artists 'pictured themselves as embattled geniuses defending Art against a vulgar bourgeoise' (Wilson 2000: 6). Here, Comstock takes on the mantle of the embattled genius, recognising that modern society is fuelled by the desire for money and status. For him, it is this greed that dominates our relationship with the world around us. According to Wilson, bohemians specifically sought 'to reconcile the economic uncertainty of the artistic calling with ideas of the artist's genius and superiority' (ibid: 3). This is at the root of the struggling artist's self-exile: in the absence of economic security and class identity, the artist must create their own creed.

The irony of this is that artists felt no affiliation towards those on the lower end of the class spectrum. Indeed, they felt quite the opposite, as John Carey argues in *The Intellectuals and the Masses*. Carey says that artists in the early twentieth century saw themselves as a sort of 'natural aristocracy' (Carey 1992: 71) that had no need of wealth or social position to flourish quite independently of society. Carey notes that there was a common feeling that intellectuals should occupy a more rarefied place in the common order. He uses the example of Clive Bell who argued that artists, since they possessed the ability to detect 'pure form' in works of art (ibid: 80), should be treated differently from others. Whilst the power of English and continental aristocracies was on the wane, artists saw themselves as their natural successors. This led many writers to separate themselves both physically and mentally from society: they were neither low class nor high class; they stood, or tried to, outside of the economic system.

Orwell's characterisation of Comstock illustrates Carey's point. In the second chapter of *Keep the Aspidistra Flying*, Comstock indulges in a remarkable appraisal of an old couple who visit the bookshop. He says of them: 'A couple of old creatures, a tramp or beggar and his wife, in long greasy overcoats that reached almost to the ground, were shuffling towards the shop. Book-pinchers, by the look of them' (Orwell 1980 [1936]: 19). The irony of his discernment is unmistakable – although he romanticises poverty, he also treats the lower classes with disgust and disdain. The language he uses to describe their physical appearance is loaded with the revulsion he feels towards them. He describes them as the 'throw-outs of the money-god. All over London, by tens and thousands, draggled old beasts of that description; creeping like unclean beetles of the grave' (ibid: 21). The language he uses here is dehumanising, and it has the effect of separating Gordon from those he is observing. It shows that, although he has socialist pretensions, Comstock is predominantly concerned with himself. Like other writers, he saw his art as a means of excommunication from the criterion of ordinary success. He is not like others, he is saying. He subscribes to no ideology other than that of the struggling artist.

DISASSEMBLING THE STRUGGLING ARTIST

Raymond Williams argues that, in *Keep the Aspidistra Flying*, 'what begins as a protest becomes a whine' (Williams 1975: 36). He says that the 'remaking of an active self, is steadily cut out' (ibid: 36). The error Williams makes is mistaking Comstock's final resolution as a surrender to submission. When viewed in relation to 'Inside the Whale,' it becomes clear that his declaration is precisely the opposite. Rather than cutting the active self out, Comstock is resolving to actively participate in life. As Gordon Bowker notes in his biography of Orwell, *Keep the Aspidistra Flying* signals 'the abandonment of an old unfulfilled poetic part of himself' (Bowker 2003: 169). David Kubal goes one step further in his 1973 study *Outside the Whale*, to say that the novel 'clearly marks Orwell's transition from protest to commitment' (Kubal 1972: 89). It is fair to say that *Keep the Aspidistra Flying* marks a transformation in Orwell's view on artistic responsibility in relation to politics, enacted through Comstock. Rather than submitting himself to the trapping of the 'money-god' (Orwell 1980 [1936]: 21), Comstock realises that his commitment to the creed of the struggling artist is ill-founded and unhelpful. More than a celebration of the archetype, Orwell's characterisation of Comstock is intended to highlight the shortcomings of the myth.

Gordon Comstock's conversations with his love interest Rosemary work to dismantle the archetype of the struggling artist because they foreground the precariousness of Comstock's aesthetic and social views. Before Rosemary appears in person, Comstock laments her lack of correspondence with him, writing a petulant note: 'You have broken my heart' (Orwell 1980 [1936]: 85). After he writes this sullen note, he muses: 'Rather neat it looked, all by itself, there in the middle of the sheet, in his small "scholarly" handwriting. Almost like a little poem in itself' (ibid). This encapsulates the way Comstock's attitude toward literary endeavour influences his relationships. In this passage, Comstock makes a link between romantic hardship and poetic inspiration. He views his interactions with Rosemary as fuel for his literary output, but also as a catalyst for his self-professed 'war on money' (ibid: 225). His attitude towards Rosemary, as with all his close relations, becomes an extension of his poetic verbiage and is inevitably tainted by aesthetic exaggeration.

After he sends this note she visits him, and they argue about money. Rosemary points out the lack of care he takes over his appearance, and Comstock replies: 'Everything costs money. Cleanness, decency, energy, self-respect – everything. It's all money. Haven't I told you that a million times?' (ibid: 117). Comstock is consumed by what he sees as society's unjustness, and this impacts his relationship with Rosemary. His obsession with his own self-image leads him to interpret Rosemary's statements as something starkly different from their reality. Comstock accuses her of wanting him to go back to his 'proper' job at the New Albion. He says: '… you think I ought to have stayed on at the New Albion, don't you? You'd like me to go back there now and write slogans for Q. T. sauce and Truweet Breakfast Crisps. Wouldn't you?' (ibid: 121). She replies: 'No I wouldn't. I never said that' (ibid). Gordon bites back: 'You thought it, though. It's what any woman would think' (ibid). This shows how he persistently projects on to her to justify his opinions. He views Rosemary as his adversary because he sees her as an extension of society's expectations of him. However, his tendency to exaggerate Rosemary's criticism of him shows us his opinions are fallible and at times, bordering on fantasy.

Martha C. Carpentier argues that Rosemary may be seen as 'responsible for the perpetuation of restrictive social systems' (Carpentier 2019: 115). Comstock's petulant remark that: 'It's what any woman would think' (Orwell 1980 [1936]: 121) confirms Carpentier's analysis. Here, Rosemary becomes an emblem of his difficult relationship with society. He immediately associates Rosemary with a path that epitomises the middle-class aspirations of marriage, mortgages and procreation. However, his love for Rosemary is indicative of his own repressed desire to participate in society. As Carpentier argues, Rosemary 'gives Gordon what he secretly pined for' (Carpentier 2019: 115); to exist and be accepted within society. In the face of Rosemary's steadfast affection for him, even amidst his fulminations of the role of women in his poetic self-destruction, his perspective falters and is eventually dismantled.

Comstock has a similarly discordant relationship with his friend and occasional publisher Ravelston.[1] It is through their conversations that the discrepancies in Comstock's worldview become apparent. Their conversations, which work to undermine Comstock's position, making it plain that his ideas are by no means indisputable, invariably revert to talk of one fateful thing – money. Comstock lives on the poverty line. Ravelston, in comparison, lives a life of comfort and luxury. As Orwell writes: 'Gordon on the pavement, Ravelston leaning out of the window above' (Orwell 1980 [1936]: 86). The physical distance between them gestures toward the tension that money, or lack of money, imbues upon their friendship. Ravelston occupies the lofty heights afforded to him by his opulently furnished flat; Comstock inhabits the streets of London. This polarity lies at the heart of their friendship and makes it difficult for them to relate to one another, despite their shared political and artistic interests.

Ravelston is a self-professed socialist, but he is a socialist in an 'ill-defined way' (ibid: 87). He is described as a man who is constantly trying to prove his bohemian credentials, without giving up his comfortable existence. It is said that Ravelston:

> … wore the uniform of the moneyed intelligentsia; an old tweed coat… He made a point of going everywhere, even to fashionable houses and expensive restaurants, in these clothes, just to show his contempt for upper-class conventions (ibid: 87).

This quotation illustrates Ravelston's superficial attitude towards socialism. Ravelston wants others to perceive him as being less wealthy than he is. His penchant for wearing the same clothes, even to exclusive establishments, defies the etiquette of the upper classes. However, this is a pretence; he has merely acquired the affectations of the artist. In doing so, Ravelston buys into the façade of the struggling artist. On one point, Comstock observes that 'he seemed always in the act of stepping out of somebody else's way' (ibid: 88).

This gives the impression of a deferential man who is vehemently self-aware, almost apologetically so. Ravelston has as much inner conflict about his own status as Comstock does. Ravelston is often found to be very embarrassed by his affluence, and at every instance tries to deflect attention away from it.

However, it is not entirely true that Gordon is made completely awkward by Ravelston's wealth. Comstock is aware of the imbalance, and he is embarrassed by it, but he also does everything in his power to perpetuate it. After they leave one another Comstock muses: 'It was queer how talking with Ravelston always bucked him up. The mere contact with Ravelston seemed to reassure him somehow' (ibid: 107). One could interpret this as being evidence of the quality of friendship that exists between the two men. Yet, whilst they sit at opposite ends of the spectrum, both Ravelston and Comstock encourage each other's aspirations of literary prowess by buying into the idea of the struggling artist. Their meetings have the effect of encouraging each other's literary endeavours whilst reassuring themselves of the integrity of their own divergent opinions. Comstock is energised by Ravelston's presence because, by comparison, he sees himself as a true artist. In a contrary way, it is through Ravelston's attempts to render himself fiscally emaciated that Comstock reassures himself of the authenticity of his position.

During one of their debates, Ravelston and Comstock have the following exchange:

> 'And you think principles are all right so long as one doesn't go and put them into practice?'
>
> 'No. But the question always is, when is one putting them into practice?'
>
> 'It's quite simple. I've made war on money. This is where it's led me….
>
> 'The mistake you make, don't you see, is in thinking one can live in a corrupt society without being corrupt oneself. After all, what do you achieve by refusing to make money? You're trying to behave as though you could stand right outside our economic system. But one can't. One's got to change the system, or one changes nothing' (Orwell 1980 [1936]: 225)

This exchange lies at the core of *Keep the Aspidistra Flying*. Ravelston is disparaging of Comstock's philosophy of inaction and maligns his attitude of acceptance. He tries to convince Comstock that, far from exiling himself from the trappings of the 'money-god' (ibid: 21), his privations merely have the effect of making him and everyone around him miserable. He points out that Comstock's principles are admirable, but he misplaces them by using them as an excuse not to engage in real life. Comstock's attempt to 'stand right outside our economic system' (ibid: 225) is futile because, in refusing to make money, one is still beleaguered by the issues that money brings. As Kubal says: 'It is the little poet-rebel who is more beset with money than the businessman … it is the thought of money, rather than the lack of it, that enervates Gordon spiritually and creatively' (Kubal 1973: 93).

Gordon Comstock's conversations with Ravelston ventriloquise a larger debate that was raging during Orwell's time of writing. Comstock's enactment of the myth of the struggling artist embodies a worldview that favoured political disengagement. This was unfashionable at the time, as poets such as W. H. Auden, Louis MacNeice and Christopher Isherwood were attempting to respond to both political and humanitarian crises in their poetry. As Samuel Hynes says in *The Auden Generation*, 'a whole generation of writers had a war ahead of them and a war behind them'. As a result, 'the middle classes began to speak for and to the poor' (Hynes 1992 [1976]: 9). It was the working poor whom these poets attempted to speak on behalf of, those who had no alternative other than to continue their fruitless employment. However, many of the poets who aimed to speak for the poor had never experienced real poverty. It is this 'hypocrisy' to which Orwell objected, and it is his acknowledgement of the hypocrisies of the left that seeps into his depiction of Ravelston[2] who articulates the views of the rich socialist who 'mouths Marx whilst living in guilty ease' (Kubal 1973: 101). Ravelston is a wealthy man who talks at length on the advantages of socialism without even attempting to live according to the tenets of socialism himself.

Two sides of the same coin: Ravelston and Comstock each belong to the same school of thought. Nevertheless, they go about their principles in starkly different ways: Comstock promotes the philosophy of passive acceptance espoused by the 1920s generation while Ravelston proffers the double standards of the Auden Generation who are full of ideas regarding social justice without any real knowledge of the poor and oppressed. In creating these two characters, Orwell offers his critique of both ideologies. As ever in Orwell, we find a writer unafraid to highlight the hypocrisies of the left.

Hence the significance of the symbol of the aspidistra. It is from the aspidistra that the novel takes its name, and in a sense, it is from the aspidistra that Comstock takes his principles. The aspidistra is ever-present within the novel, providing Comstock with comfort when he is miserable and something to protest against when he is embittered.

REBECCA CLAYTON

In the Edwardian era, amongst the bourgeoisie, the aspidistra became popular because of its ability to withstand the often-unaccommodating environment of the English Victorian terrace. With its robust nature it became a prominent symbol of suburban life. For this reason, Gordon despises the aspidistra more than any other plant – when he is alone in his lodgings he laments: 'That was what it meant to worship the money-god! To settle down, to Make Good, to sell your soul for a villa and an aspidistra!' (Orwell 1980 [1936]: 53). The aspidistra represents the quaintness of middle-class existence, the middle-class desire for wealth and sophistication – but also the failure to achieve it. As Comstock says: 'The one fatal thing is to worship money and fail to get it' (ibid: 50). The aspidistra symbolises the system that we are all, either wittingly or unwittingly, embroiled in. It is this system that the upper classes benefit from, the middle classes attempt to exploit, and the working classes are the victims of.

It is important that, despite Gordon's grievances towards the aspidistra, it never leaves his side. He even takes it with him when he moves into his poet's garret at his lowest point in the novel. He complains:

> It was an aspidistra. It gave him a bit of a twinge to see it. Even here, in this final refuge! Hast thou found me, O mine enemy? But it was a poor weedy specimen – indeed, it was obviously dying (Orwell 1980 [1936]: 222)

Gordon admits that the aspidistra, and all that it symbolises, is his 'enemy' (ibid). The aspidistra epitomises everything that the artist should be against – the steadfastness of ordinary life. The private torments of the artist and the physical hardships imposed on the artist by the bourgeoisie are synthesised through the image of the aspidistra. The aspidistra is an emblem of everything the artist felt they must struggle against in the twentieth century; the aspidistra is almost indestructible, yet provides little beauty. In the same way, bourgeois living endures yet provides little glamour.

Conversely, it is for this reason that Comstock is never quite able to give up the aspidistra. Although 'he had furtively attempted to kill it – starving it of water, grinding hot cigarette-ends against its stem, even mixing salt in with its earth' (Ibid: 33), it never dies. The aspidistra survives the privations it endures. This can be construed as Orwell's commentary on the pitfalls of the image of the artist as suggested by his predecessors, the 'modernists'. Despite the mythologisation of the struggling artist, it is much preferable for the artist to encounter society on practical terms. Although the writers of the 1920s would never advocate the qualities of the aspidistra, it becomes apparent that the writers of the 1930s must do so if they are to survive. The aspidistra becomes a metaphor for Comstock's realisation that the romantic notion of the struggling artist is precisely that: a romantic notion that does not correlate to the reality of experience.

CONCLUSION: THE ANTI-FLIGHT OF THE ARTIST

We have seen how Orwell undermined the myth of the struggling artist in *Keep the Aspidistra Flying*. Gordon Comstock personifies the evolution of the literary scene in the early twentieth century, as passivity in the face of adversity was no longer deemed an option. This begs the question, namely, of why Orwell felt the need to write such a novel. Orwell completed the manuscript between 1935 and 1936; this was less than a year before he took up arms alongside Republican revolutionaries in the Spanish Civil War. That Orwell should still be struggling with questions of literary pacifism seems to fly directly in the face of his convictions at that time.

The answer is twofold. Firstly, it stems from Orwell's self-professed adolescent predilection for 'purple passages' (Orwell 2002 [1946]: 1081). In 'Why I Write', Orwell recounts that he was about sixteen when he 'suddenly discovered the joy of mere words, i.e., the sounds and associations of words' (ibid: 1081). He goes on to say that his initial aim when setting out to be a writer was to 'write enormous naturalistic novels with unhappy endings, full of detailed descriptions and arresting similes, and also full of purple passages in which words were used partly for the sake of their sound' (ibid: 1081). He was enticed by the generation of writers which preceded him; those whose creative freedom was unfettered by political ideology. Comstock, in the initial stages of the novel, follows on from that tradition. He is staunchly committed to pure aestheticism within art, and he wants his life to be a symbol of that: the writer who privileges mere words above societal practicalities.

These adolescent fantasies are modulated by an early adulthood spent protesting at the hypocrisies of the middle-class left. This leads to the second reason as to why Orwell chose to write *Keep the Aspidistra Flying*. The hypocrisies of the political left are laid bare in the characters of Comstock and Ravelston. Bernard Crick, in his introduction to his biography of Orwell, argues that 'what was remarkable about Orwell was not his political position but that he demanded publicly that his own side should live up to their principles' (Crick 1992 [1980]: xv). It is Orwell's willingness to criticise the left's methods of engagement that sets him apart from other political writers of the period. Crick says that 'he made his name as a journalist by his skill in rubbing the fur of his own cat backwards' (ibid). This tendency of Orwell comes to fruition within *Keep the Aspidistra Flying*. In this way, the novel is primarily a rendering of Orwell's own literary evolution. It is his own pretences and prejudices that he enacts through Comstock; he lands upon, finally, this philosophy of commitment to reality. There is nothing inherently either right-wing or left-wing within this philosophy. He simply argues for action over inaction, enthusiasm over apathy.

Unlike Joyce's *Portrait,* in which it is only by escaping society that the artist can be satisfied, *Keep the Aspidistra Flying* shows that it is by encountering society that one produces something worth reading. We began with Stephen Dedalus's famous quote; 'When a man is born … there are nets flung at it to hold it back from flight' (Joyce 1992 [1922]: 157). As if in dialogue with Joyce's protagonist, Comstock attests: 'he forgot that birds of the air don't pay room-rent' (Orwell 1980 [1936]: 55). In this way, the novel is an example of anti-flight; it challenges the idea that artists must detach themselves from the day-to-day to create great art. When Comstock resolves to keep the aspidistra 'flying', he accepts that the artist must remain grounded in the present moment and to their fellow man. As Comstock realises: 'Life on two quid ceases to be a heroic gesture and becomes a dingy habit. Failure is as great a swindle as success' (ibid: 63). Comstock eventually arrives at the same conclusion as Orwell: that self-imposed exile is a dangerous affront to both political and social progress.

NOTES

[1] It is widely accepted that the character of Ravelston is a friendly caricature of Orwell's real-life friend and publisher Sir Richard Rees, the editor of *The Adelphi* (Bowker 2003: 169). His gentle mocking of Rees in the character of Ravelston is another hint to the sardonic comic tendencies of Orwell as noted by Crick

[2] Orwell caused controversy amongst his own side upon the publication of *The Road to Wigan Pier*, which he was commissioned to write by Victor Gollancz, director and publisher of the Left Book Club. *The Road to Wigan Pier* was a surprise and an embarrassment to Victor Gollancz, so much so that Gollancz felt the need to write an apologetic Foreword to the club's first edition in 1937 (Hynes 1992 [1976]: 273)

REFERENCES

Bounds, Philip (2009) *Orwell & Marxism: The Political and Cultural Thinking of George Orwell,* London: I. B. Tauris & Co.

Bowker, Gordon (2003) *George Orwell,* London: Little, Brown

Carey, John (1992) *The Intellectuals and the Masses: Pride and Prejudice among the Literary Intelligentsia, 1880-1939,* London: Faber and Faber

Carpentier, Martha C. (2019) Poem, creed, letter, foetus: George Orwell's *Keep the Aspidistra Flying, Mosaic: An Interdisciplinary Critical Journal,* Vol. 52, No. 3 pp 101-117. Available online at https://www.jstor.org/stable/26781581, accessed on 11 March 2022

Crick, Bernard (2011) Orwell as a comic writer, The Orwell Foundation. Available online at https://www.orwellfoundation.com/the-orwell-foundation/orwell/articles/bernard-crick-orwell-as-a-comic-writer/, accessed on 7 February 2022

Crick, Bernard (1992 [1980]) *George Orwell: A Life,* London: Penguin Books

Hunter, Lynette (1984) *George Orwell: The Search for a Voice*, Milton Keynes: Open University Press

Hynes, Samuel (1992 [1976]) *The Auden Generation: Literature and Politics in England in the 1930s,* London: Vintage

Joyce, James (1992 [1922]) *A Portrait of the Artist as a Young Man*, Hertfordshire: Wordsworth Classics

Kubal, David (1972) *Outside the Whale: George Orwell's Art and Politics,* Indiana: University of Notre Dame Press

Orwell, George (1980 [1936]) *Keep the Aspidistra Flying,* Middlesex: Penguin

Orwell, George (2002 [1940]) Inside the Whale, Carey, John (ed.) *Essays,* London: Everyman's Library pp 211-248

Orwell, George (2002 [1946]) Why I Write, Carey, John (ed.) *Essays*, London: Everyman's Library pp 1079-1085

Williams, Raymond (1975) *Orwell,* Glasgow: Fontana Books

Wilson, Elizabeth (2000) *Bohemians: The Glamorous Outcasts,* London: I. B. Tauris & Co.

NOTE ON THE CONTRIBUTOR

Rebecca Clayton is a freelance writer. She gained a First-Class Honours in BA English Literature and Language from King's College London in 2018. She completed her Master's in English: Issues in Modern Culture at UCL (University College London) in 2020. Her work has been published *in The New Voice* and *Rock & Art* magazine. Her research interests include the role of the artist in both historical and contemporary contexts, poststructuralist ideas surrounding neoliberalism in the present day and the works of Bob Dylan.

PAPER

A Textbook Case: Aligning Orwell and NCTJ Teaching

JARON MURPHY

This paper reflects on the appearance of two extracts from Orwell's essay 'Politics and the English Language' (1946), which are framed as excellent advice on developing a writing style in the latest National Council for the Training of Journalists' (NCTJ) guide for trainee journalists. Noting that attention to these extracts arises briefly towards the back of the expanded new guide, this paper nevertheless highlights three positives for both Orwell scholarship and journalism education. Firstly, Orwell's inclusion is a noteworthy difference from the previous, longstanding guide which did not mention him at all. Secondly, Orwell's inclusion provides licence for his incorporation into NCTJ teaching practice, opening up creative possibilities for tutors to enhance learning for their UK and international students. Lastly, Orwell's inclusion is, in fact, a significant development in the context of NCTJ publications historically. Through archival research, this paper finds a general absence of reference to Orwell (who died in 1950) in NCTJ literature since the organisation's inception in 1951.

Keywords: Orwell, National Council for the Training of Journalists (NCTJ), journalism, education

Jonathan Baker's *Essential Journalism* (2021), the updated and official 'NCTJ Guide for Trainee Journalists', was released a couple of months before the start of the 2021-2022 academic year with a brief but encouraging foreword from Alex Crawford, Sky News special correspondent and NCTJ patron. 'Strap yourself in,' she advises. 'You are about to have the ride of your life' in 'one of the toughest and most gratifying professions there is' (Baker 2021a: ix).

Excluding a series of 'further reading' lists at the end and the index, the book consists of 437 pages – quite hefty but certainly value for money as 'a core resource' for its target market, according to the back-cover blurb, of 'journalism trainees and undergraduates' as well as 'seasoned practitioners and lecturers'. In particular, the book is pitched as 'a practical guide to all aspects of modern journalism' for those who wish to undertake the NCTJ Diploma 'and become a qualified journalist in the UK'. As Baker explains in the preface, the NCTJ is 'the UK's principal training body' and 'the book is aligned to the Programmes of Study, or syllabus, laid out in the Diploma' (2021a: x). Although the Diploma is not the only NCTJ qualification available, it is the primary route for many students to employment. The NCTJ website states there are more than 80 NCTJ-accredited courses 'at some 40 universities, further education colleges and independent training centres across the UK', with the NCTJ's stamp of approval 'the hallmark of excellence in journalism training, providing a world-class industry standard that is recognised throughout the media' (NCTJ 2022a).

This paper concerns, primarily, a brief but significant passage among the wide-ranging contents of Baker's new NCTJ manual on the fundamentals of journalism. It singles out for scrutiny what might readily seem, from an Orwell studies perspective, the pertinent and to-be-expected invoking by Baker, for the purpose of instruction on the development of a writing style, of what he calls Orwell's 'celebrated essay' (2021a: 401) entitled 'Politics and the English Language' (1946) – albeit on page 401 and thus notably close to the end. After all, the essay showcases magnificently Orwell's obsession with English language usage and writing style, bound up with his acute awareness of verbal gymnastics in politics. The essay has been a revered text for generations of journalists – not least subeditors tasked with checking and improving copy – in the UK and internationally.

Industry veneration of the essay was inaugurated by proprietor-editor David Astor who, as Jonathan Heawood writes in his introduction to *Orwell: The Observer Years* (2003), had a copy 'distributed to every new *Observer* writer' following its publication in the April 1946 issue of *Horizon*. 'Even now,' Heawood adds, 'it is quoted in the house style guide' (ibid: xii); and this tradition continues online (for instance, see *Guardian* 2020). Yet, as this paper will show by way of archival research, Baker's reference to Orwell and inclusion of two extracts from his much-admired essay is, in fact, a new development in NCTJ publications. With Baker's book coinciding with the NCTJ's 70th anniversary celebrations, the paucity of evidence of the impact of Orwell's legacy on NCTJ literature historically, given that he died in 1950 shortly before the NCTJ was founded in its initial form in 1951, is intriguing.

ORWELL'S WRITING ADVICE ACKNOWLEDGED – AT LAST

Baker briefly turns the spotlight on Orwell and the essay in the final part of the book which focuses on specialist journalism practice and where he encourages developing a writing style as a feature writer. Although this attention to Orwell occurs at a late stage and requires readers' stamina and interest in becoming a feature writer to arrive at, it fits well in the context of feature writing given not only the applicability of the two extracts to practice but also considering, from an Orwell studies perspective, that Orwell's journalism encompasses a number of the 'sorts of features' (2021a: 384) outlined by Baker, including reportage, profiles, analysis or 'think pieces' and reviews. Describing Orwell as 'both a novelist and a journalist', and among 'the most famous proponents of the plain and simple approach', Baker explains that Orwell 'summarised his thoughts' in a celebrated essay entitled 'Politics and the English Language' (ibid: 401). Baker then reproduces what Orwell described as writing 'rules' to support decision-making 'when instinct fails' (Orwell 2000: 359). In doing so, Baker turns the Roman numerals into numbers:

> 1. Never use a metaphor, simile or other figure of speech that you are used to seeing in print.
>
> 2. Never use a long word when a short one will do.
>
> 3. If it is possible to cut out a word, always cut it out.
>
> 4. Never use the passive when you can use the active.
>
> 5. Never use a foreign phrase, a scientific word or a jargon word if you can think of an everyday English equivalent.
>
> 6. Break any of these rules sooner than say anything outright barbarous (ibid: 401).

Baker immediately reproduces another portion of Orwell's essay, adding numbers for each question:

> A scrupulous writer, in every sentence that he writes, will ask himself at least four questions, thus: 1. What am I trying to say? 2. What words will express it? 3. What image or idiom will make it clearer? 4. Is this image fresh enough to have an effect? And he will probably ask himself two more: 1. Could I put it more shortly? 2. Have I said anything that is avoidably ugly? (ibid).

These two short extracts lead to Baker's encouragement to experiment and discover one's own writing style:

> This excellent advice holds good for everything that you write, of whatever sort and for whatever medium. It is a very good place to start, as you begin to experiment with your writing. As with all your other journalistic output, keep it clear, keep it simple. But as you grow in confidence, feel emboldened to add a little colour to the plainness. Try your hand at various techniques: a short sentence, or several short sentences, followed by a longer one; or vice versa. A paragraph that builds tension, which is then resolved with a smart conclusion. Extended metaphors (Orwell only advised us not to use hackneyed and overused metaphors and similes; there is nothing wrong with coming

up [sic] something fresh of your own) or a bit of word play perhaps. Try things out and see whether or not they come off. But, to repeat: in the end you are looking for a style that suits you and with which you feel at ease, not one you have copied from somewhere else and which feels laboured and not natural to you (ibid).

Baker's harnessing of Orwell's essay as a quick 'writing by numbers' tutorial to spur trainee journalists' development of a writing style is an astute educational strategy and to be applauded. However, an obvious downside is that, by dealing with Orwell's essay at a basic level for beginner journalists, Baker confines his approach to only one aspect of Orwell's overall argument – the English language – and completely neglects the other, ultimately inseparable component – politics. It is easy to appreciate why Baker sidesteps the complication of the link to politics, within a chapter on feature writing in general and in keeping with the apolitical ethos of NCTJ practical training, but context matters – especially in journalism teaching and practice, at any level – and the political dimension could helpfully have been signposted beyond the essay title. As Baker wrote in a blog on the NCTJ website, in advance of the book's release:

> … in some respects at least – the more things have changed, the more they have stayed the same. Even in a much-changed world, reporting at its most fundamental level is still about finding things out and telling people about them; journalism is still about building on that by adding context, explanation, background and anything else the audience might need in order to understand what is going on in the world, and to have the means to become informed and engaged citizens (Baker 2021b).

ORWELL'S CRUCIAL LINKING OF POLITICS AND LANGUAGE

So too in journalism teaching. Within Orwell's essay, the second extract precedes, of course, the first and leads to the key sentence: 'It is at this point that the special connexion between politics and the debasement of language becomes clear' (2000: 355). Perceiving that language stems from and, in turn, shapes thought and there is, thus, a potential for mutual corruption, Orwell is championing here the value of mental effort: a firm pushback against the intellectual laziness of using 'ready-made phrases' that 'will construct your sentences for you – even think your thoughts for you, to a certain extent' and readily 'perform the important service of partially concealing your meaning even from yourself' (ibid: 355).

JARON MURPHY

The first extract, in context, is squarely in line with the second. Leading to it, Orwell upholds again the value of 'conscious effort' (2000: 358) and advocates a process by which 'one can choose – not simply accept – the phrases that will best cover the meaning, and then switch round and decide what impression one's words are likely to make on another person' (ibid: 358-359). Before listing his six rules, he writes that this 'last effort of the mind cuts out all stale or mixed images, all prefabricated phrases, needless repetitions, and humbug and vagueness generally'; and following his list of rules, he expressly clarifies that he has 'not here been considering the literary use of language, but merely language as an instrument for expressing and not for concealing or preventing thought' (ibid: 359). Proceeding to close his essay, the political component of Orwell's overall argument remains crystal-clear: 'One ought to recognize that the present political chaos is connected with the decay of language, and that one can probably bring about some improvement by starting at the verbal end' (ibid). Significantly, Orwell is not concerned solely with improvement of language usage by writers, to achieve clarity and directness. He is also warning that political obfuscation and deception can occur *through* language usage which, by its contortions, typically signals their occurrence. He writes: 'Political language – and with variations this is true of all political parties, from Conservatives to Anarchists – is designed to make lies sound truthful and murder respectable, and to give an appearance of solidity to pure wind' (ibid). Orwell, therefore, elevates improved language usage to a form of duty and resistance, in the interests of better standards of public discourse: 'One cannot change this all in a moment, but one can at least change one's own habits, and from time to time one can even, if one jeers loudly enough, send some worn-out and useless phrase – some *jackboot, Achilles' heel, hotbed, melting pot, acid test, veritable inferno* or other lump of verbal refuse – into the dustbin where it belongs' (ibid: 359-360, italics in the original).

This denouement chimes with what are perhaps the essay's most well-known sentences (which appear in the online '*Guardian* and *Observer* style guide: O'), featuring one of Orwell's most striking images, in which he perceives that 'inflated style is itself a kind of euphemism' and argues powerfully: 'The great enemy of clear language is insincerity. When there is a gap between one's real and one's declared aims, one turns as it were instinctively to long words and exhausted idioms, like a cuttlefish squirting out ink' (ibid: 357). It also chimes with his claim that silly words and expressions 'have often disappeared … owing to the conscious action of a minority': 'Two recent examples were *explore every avenue* and *leave no stone unturned*, which were killed by the jeers of a few journalists' (ibid: 358, italics in the original). Detecting and calling out agendas, insincerity and falsehoods in politics is, of course, central to the traditional functions of journalists (or the Fourth Estate) in democratic societies. As Baker writes in Chapter 2, 'The nature of journalism: the nature of news': 'One of the jobs of a free media is to make sure that politicians and people in public office, or people who manage public money, behave as they promised they would or as they are supposed to. This idea is often referred to as "holding power to account"' (2021a: 26).

Moreover, the importance of questioning and, if need be, challenging those in authority, for the public's benefit, extends to many areas of society involving power dynamics: journalists are routinely required to examine and interpret language usage and motives in the form of press releases, speeches, interviewees' responses, reports, documentation, etc, in researching and constructing what should be accurate, fair and balanced stories. This is allied to another traditional function of journalism: to foster and inform discussion and debate among a diversity of voices in the public sphere (or as Baker described it in his NCTJ blog, to provide the 'means to become informed and engaged citizens'). Therefore, from a pedagogical perspective, Orwell's essay could be drawn upon to a much greater degree in training journalists to fulfil their roles in society than the confines of the brief tutorial provided by Baker – and this paper urges an enlarged and integrated approach. Journalists' intellectual effort and competence in writing and editing should be united with the ability to recognise and appropriately deal with, to be blunt, 'BS' dressed up in language that is, for instance, convoluted, opaque, evasive and/or dishonest – wherever a journalist may encounter it.

That said, Baker's reference to Orwell and inclusion of extracts from 'Politics and the English Language' is a welcome development as a visible NCTJ Diploma-aligned teaching approach, introducing these engaging elements into students' learning experience within the scope of exploring and discovering their own feature writing style. Yet, at a basic level, Orwell's advice can be applied to journalistic writing and editing more generally, without necessarily abandoning the pro-democratic rationale of a free press which traditionally underpins the roles of journalists in society. By utilising Orwell to spur students to become adept feature writers, Baker provides not only a licence for NCTJ tutors to follow suit but effectively opens up creative possibilities for tutors to incorporate Orwell into wider teaching of the NCTJ Diploma syllabus.

JARON MURPHY

ORWELL'S ADVICE APPLICABLE TO STORYTELLING

As we have seen, Baker suggests that Orwell's plain and simple approach 'holds good', as a starting point, for all journalistic writing. As Baker also wrote in his NCTJ blog: 'The central elements of my new guide for young journalists … are all about story-finding and storytelling. All storytelling requires good, clear, simple and unambiguous writing' (Baker 2021b). Orwell could just as easily have been invoked, then, much earlier in the book in relation to writing, not least Chapter 11 on 'Storytelling: language and style' (2021a: 192) where, for instance, it is stated that the aim is 'for an easy and accessible style, uncomplicated, unambiguous and capable of immediate comprehension' (ibid: 193) while 'Acid test' (ibid: 212) is top of a list of common clichés. Orwell's essay could also have been included among the subsequent recommended 'further reading' where it does not even appear correspondingly on the 'Feature writing' (2021a: 440) list.

This is not to suggest, absurdly, that Orwell has never formed part of journalism teaching in a broad sense – far from it. As one of the foremost Orwell experts, Richard Lance Keeble, writes in *Journalism Beyond Orwell* (2020): 'I have certainly used Orwell extensively in my teaching: on media ethics, literary journalism, investigative reporting, war correspondence, on the links between Fleet Street and the secret state and so on' (2020: 2). Teachers of journalism, including NCTJ tutors, have been free to draw upon Orwell (and myriad other journalists in UK and international contexts) as they please. The author of this paper has taken the liberty of doing so, too, in both industry and academia. However, as we shall see in more detail, attention to Orwell and, therefore, visible sanction for tutors to utilise Orwell for the purposes of teaching aligned to the NCTJ Diploma (and for that matter, other NCTJ qualifications), has tended not to arise explicitly in the NCTJ literature until Baker's book. This development may encourage NCTJ tutors who have never included Orwell in their teaching to consider the benefits of doing so. However, a note of caution is warranted if referring to Orwell via Baker's book.

Unfortunately, the only other explicit reference to Orwell in the book is dubious. In Chapter 2, crediting Lord Northcliffe with the assertion that 'News is what people do not want you to print. All the rest is advertising', Baker adds: 'This thought is also attributed to George Orwell, substituting "public relations" for "advertising"' (2021a: 29). However, an entry on the Quote Investigator website, with input from researcher Barry Popik and updated in 2015, concludes that attributions to 'Alfred Harmsworth (Lord Northcliffe) and several other individuals' appeared later than

1953 and the 'popular variant using "public relations" instead of "advertising" was in circulation by 1979'. It adds: 'The linkage to George Orwell is very weak. Based on current data QI would label the adage anonymous' (Quote Investigator 2015). Mentioning attribution to Orwell here without reservation is not, then, the best example for trainee journalists who must quickly appreciate the importance of fact-checking and accuracy as part and parcel of writing and editing.

Nevertheless, the point made by Baker is an important one, that 'news will often mean publishing things that the people involved would like to keep out of the public domain' (2021a: 29); and, all in all, Baker's references to Orwell and extracts from 'Politics and the English Language' in the new NCTJ guide constitute a positive and noteworthy change from Orwell's absence in the immediately preceding NCTJ guide entitled *Essential Reporting* which was written by Jon Smith and released in September 2007. Interestingly, although Orwell was a print and broadcast journalist who died in 1950, his appearance in the new NCTJ guide forms part of the revised and expanded content in response to the evolving demands on journalists of working in the digital age. In the preface, duly acknowledging Smith's book as 'the forerunner', Baker explains that when it was published in 2007 the 'digital revolution, then only in its infancy, was soon to make its presence felt'. In 2021, 'the scope of this book, its successor, has had to be much wider and multi faceted [sic]'.

Nevertheless, Baker reflects that 'so much of Smith's wisdom, common sense and explanations of the basics of good, accurate, ethical journalism remain highly relevant and applicable today' and he expresses his gratitude to both Smith and the NCTJ for permitting transferral of 'so much of that wisdom' (2021a: xiii) to the new book. In this vein, Baker wrote in his NCTJ blog that journalism 'needs to cling to the principles and values of good journalistic practice that long predate the digital age, but whose relevance and worth remain undiminished' (2021b). Notably, in the expansion of content to 451 pages, compared to Smith's 264 pages (both including the index and 'further reading' recommendations), Baker reworks and adds substantially to Smith's 'Features' chapter (17). Baker's Chapter 21, 'The feature writer', encompasses the print, broadcast and online environments with an emphasis on developing initial 'core skills that are regarded as essential to good journalism in whatever form' (2021a: 383) – hence its abiding concern with good writing practice.

The inclusion of, and numbering within, the two extracts from Orwell's essay certainly brings a sharper focus on language usage and writing style than before; and the extracts also complement

Baker's prior examples of aspects of feature writing and his account of narrative structure. Orwell also informs the summaries which close the chapter. For instance, Baker asserts that the completed feature will have 'an accurate, grammatically sound and authentic narrative, using simple and direct language, and avoiding over-complexity in its sentence structure' (ibid: 402). Among his 'Top tips for feature writing', Orwell's relevance is recognisable in the advice, for instance, to strive 'to pinpoint the exact word(s) to convey your meaning'; to use 'simple, familiar words'; to ensure that for any long sentences 'the writing is clear, the meaning is quickly absorbed and the reader will not be held up trying to work out what you are trying to say'; to avoid 'clichés and over-worn phrases, especially in descriptive passages'; and to use 'active language not passive' (ibid).

ORWELL'S ADVICE APPLICABLE TO NEWS REPORTING

Here again, NCTJ tutors could gain impetus from Baker to incorporate Orwell into their teaching – not just in relation to feature writing but also other areas of the Diploma syllabus. As Baker points out, many of his tips 'would apply equally to news reporting'; and he argues that features 'are not a separate and discrete branch of journalism' but 'simply offer a different, and richly rewarding, medium for storytelling' (2021a: 402). Although Orwell's journalism outputs included much that could be categorised as feature writing, such as his 'hundreds of reviews', and he produced only 'a clutch of news reports, most of them for the *Observer*' (Anderson 2008: 38), his example as a journalist and aspects of his writing advice are eminently suited, this paper expressly foregrounds, to the teaching and learning of basic news reporting and editing skills, too, in delivering the Diploma syllabus for UK and international students.

By bridging these forms of journalism, Baker makes more explicit and detailed what had been touched upon in Smith's book. Comparing and contrasting the nature and functions of features with those of basic news reports, Baker draws attention to how there is more that 'unites than divides them' (2021a: 386). Shaping Baker's approach, Smith had highlighted that features 'like news, require keen observation, careful research, a focus on people, meticulous accuracy, and disciplined construction' (2007: 229) although for features one could 'use metaphors, similes and other literary devices inappropriate in news stories' (ibid: 232). More's the pity, then, that Orwell was not explicitly utilised by Smith whose book served as the NCTJ guide on journalism fundamentals for around 14 years. By the light of Baker's book, students could retrospectively recognise Orwell's relevance in the 'forerunner' by Smith. For instance, among the advice on writing features dispensed by Smith is that they 'are not an excuse for long rambling essays in flamboyant language'; 'there is no place for waffle' (ibid: 229); they are not an opportunity 'to over-indulge in extravagant language or intricate sentences' (ibid: 232); and 'time-battered clichés' (ibid: 238) should be avoided.

Notably, while Smith's features section is near the end of the book and this shapes its similar placement in Baker's book, it is in relation to news reporting rather than feature writing that Smith's book is most reminiscent of Orwell's writing advice. For instance, in Chapter 10, 'Writing the Words', his immediate advice is to 'keep it short, keep it simple, tell it straight': 'The secret of news-writing is as short, simple and straightforward as that' (ibid: 119). Smith proceeds to elaborate: 'Use short words'; 'Cut out unnecessary words' (ibid: 120); 'Be active, not passive'; 'Be wary of clichés' (2007: 121). This is augmented in the next chapter, 'English Matters', with advice on good grammar and punctuation, lists of sloppy 'language errors' (ibid: 139) and redundant as well as problematic words, and encouragement to master house style.

HOW ORWELL GOES MISSING IN NCTJ PUBLICATIONS

Given that Orwell was not referred to in Smith's book, it might be asked: what about in NCTJ publications between 1951 and 2007? Library searches and, in particular, kind permission to access Bournemouth University's Segrue Collection were helpful in identifying and consulting clearly NCTJ-issued or NCTJ-aligned texts historically. The earliest publication located, in the Segrue Collection, was the second edition (revised) of the *Handbook of Training* (1953) of what was then the National Advisory Council for the Training and Education of Junior Journalists. It states: 'As the central advisory body, the Council will administer the Training and Education Scheme, and will be responsible for the examinations for the General Proficiency Test and the National Diploma' (NACTEJJ 1954: 1). The book provides detailed context on the origins and nature of the journalism training scheme at that time and can be squared with the NCTJ's account on its website of its emergence in the 1950s (see NCTJ 2022b for 'Our History'). Both sources quote the same passage from the report of the Royal Commission on the Press in 1949 concerning the 'problem of recruiting the right people into journalism, whether from school or from university, and of ensuring that they achieve and maintain the necessary level of education and technical efficiency…' (NACTEJJ 1953: v; NCTJ 2022b).

Although the writing approach that Orwell espoused is in evidence, there is no mention of Orwell in the book – and it is not difficult to appreciate why, for the same reason that Smith can hardly be criticised for leaving Orwell out of his book decades later. The plain and simple approach to writing was not the sole preserve of Orwell, of course, but widely accepted 'best practice' ratified by style guides in the journalism industry long before he put his own stamp on it in 'Politics and the English Language'. In covering the 'Three-Year Basic Course: Vocational Training', for instance, the *Handbook of Training* states: 'Writing of simple, direct, grammatical English is essential. ... An office "style book" should always be at hand in a junior's training' (1954: 17). This is mirrored, as might be expected, in a National Advisory Council pamphlet, also in the Segrue Collection and entitled *Summary of Training and Education Scheme* (1954). It stipulates that juniors must become 'able to write reports in clear, concise and grammatical English' (NACTEJJ 1954: 4); and it is recommended that vocational training should include, among other experiences, 'the preparation of practice reports which will be corrected by a senior' and 'instruction in the mechanics of sub-editing' (ibid: 5). Also notable is the stipulation that juniors should 'pursue systematic courses of study' throughout, with 'English Language and Literature' (ibid) a constant each year.

Orwell is absent, too, from the 1960s texts consulted. Unsurprisingly, in the *Training in Journalism: Handbook of the National Council for the Training of Journalists* (1964), also in the Segrue Collection, the line is repeated verbatim: 'Writing of simple, direct, grammatical English is essential'; and it is advised again that a style book 'should be available to every junior, who should refer to it regularly' (NCTJ 1964: 25). However, this time it is highlighted that juniors 'sometimes become confused' about style and, with there being 'various styles which journalism is likely to demand', the NCTJ's new book *Daily English* 'and the English syllabus to be launched at the Colleges in September 1964, should help considerably in clearing up this confusion' (ibid).

The need for English proficiency is repeatedly accentuated. For instance, it is also reported that the NCTJ's intention is to raise, in 1965, 'its recommended educational qualifications for new entrants ... to *at least five* Ordinary level subjects (including English Language and Literature)... ' (ibid: 13, italics in the original). Later, it is argued (with the male bias of that time which would be called out, as we shall see, in an NCTJ manual in 1997): 'In subjects such as English language, government and current affairs, the journalist must be better informed than the average reader of the newspaper for which he writes, if he is to write to any real purpose at all' (ibid: 31); and it is revealed that among the 'educational targets which a junior must achieve to be eligible to sit for the Proficiency Test' is 'English Language and/or Literature: from September 1964, the National Council's own course...' (ibid: 33). In *Daily English: A*

Course in Practical English for Young Journalists (1964), also in the Segrue Collection, the stated purpose is to help young journalists present news 'clearly, accurately and cogently' (Liddle and Pardoe 1964: 5). Orwell is not among its 'representative selection of modern newspaper writing' (ibid: 7) nor on its list of Recommended Books which includes by then already decades-old texts like *Modern English Usage* (1926) and *The King's English* (1930) by H. W. and F. G. Fowler and *An A. B. C. of English Usage* (1936) by H. A. Treble and G. H. Vallins. These texts are repeated, as might be expected, in the English Language section of a 16-page NCTJ pamphlet entitled *Reading List* (1967), also in the Segrue Collection. Again, Orwell is missing but, notably, the 1943 Penguin edition of *Scoop*, by Evelyn Waugh, first published by Chapman & Hall in 1938, appears in the Fiction section (NCTJ 1967: 7).

In *The Practice of Journalism* (1963), by John Dodge and George Viner, produced under the auspices of the NCTJ and National Union of Journalists (NUJ), similar 'best practice' advice compatible with Orwell's approach to writing is offered. For instance, in the chapter 'Good English' by the pseudonymous contributor 'Dr Syntax', it is argued that the 'shorter and simpler the words and phrases we use, the better, as a general rule; but a good writing style grows only out of careful thought, constant vigilance, good sense, knowledge, and experience' (Dodge and Viner 1963: 121). Dr Syntax adds: 'The prime necessity for every writer is to have something to say; but it is also necessary to take care about *how* we say it. Plain, short words in crisp, short sentences are always better than long, pretentious words which mean the same thing as the short words, and long sentences which use many words to say little' (ibid). Dr Syntax is alluding in the first portion of the sentence to the Victorian poet-critic Matthew Arnold. As Baker highlights shortly before turning his attention to Orwell: 'One of the best-known comments about style was made by the Victorian poet Matthew Arnold: Have something to say and say it as clearly as you can. That is the only secret of style' (2021a: 401).

Baker does not provide a text source but this dictum is attributed to Arnold in G. W. E. Russell's *Collections and Recollections* (1898). Amusingly, in a full-page article by Preston Benson in the *Journalist* in November 1963 promoting *The Practice of Journalism*, with the headlines 'TRAINING MAKES NEWS: THE TEXTBOOK'S OUT – COURSES GROW' and 'First comprehensive guide to the skills of British journalism', Orwell's close friend Malcolm Muggeridge and the television personality, Nancy Spain, are criticised for their response on TV to a question from 'a youth' aspiring to become a journalist on 'what the functions of journalism were: "To sell newspapers, I suppose," murmured Malcolm uneasily. Nancy lamely concurred'. Benson adds scathingly: 'When journalists of

JARON MURPHY

distinction are as witless as this about their craft surely they need a refresher course and luckily for them it is to hand' (Benson 1963: 7).

Orwell is also neglected in *The Practice of Journalism*'s companion volumes published under the auspices of the NCTJ: *Practical Newspaper Reporting* (1966) by Geoffrey Harris and David Spark; and John F. Goulden's *Newspaper Management* (1967), also in the Segrue Collection. With four editions, *Practical Newspaper Reporting* has enjoyed remarkable longevity: the first edition appeared in 1966, the second in 1993, the third in 1997, and the substantially updated fourth version in 2011. The latter can, therefore, be considered contemporary with Smith's NCTJ *Essential Reporting* guide and another NCTJ resource (also sans Orwell), Andy Bull's *The NCTJ Essential Guide to Careers in Journalism* (2007). Predictably, the *Practical Newspaper Reporting* first edition contains the familiar industry 'best practice' advice which Orwell had, in his own way, advocated: 'Newspaper English needs to be simple and straightforward. Use active verbs, not passives… ' (Harris and Spark 1966: 107). The reader is urged: 'Do not be content with abstract phrases. … Obviously your sentences must be simple and clear…'; 'Use simple and direct words. … Try to use the exact word for the meaning you want to convey' (ibid: 108); opt for readily understandable words 'in common use' (ibid: 113); beware difficulties presented by 'Technical and foreign words' and ambiguities even in 'simple English' (ibid: 116); avoid 'lazy thinking' (ibid: 119).

In a section under the subheading 'Worn phrases', advice to attempt 'to devise and use new similes and images of your own which exactly convey the meaning you want' is followed by a list including 'acid test' with the comment: '"Acid" has gone with test so often that it has ceased to add any meaning to it' (ibid: 122). With slight revisions and some new subheadings, the wording of the advice is largely the same (including 'acid test') in the second edition as well as the third edition, although the latter incorporates several new elements.

For instance, there is a list of pointers drawn from Keith Waterhouse's celebrated text *On Newspaper Style* (1989), such as using 'specific', 'concrete' and 'plain' (Harris, Spark and Hodgson 1997: 77) words; a section on 'codes' (distinguished from the attention again to 'Technical language') which reiterates that journalism is about 'communicating with readers in clear, simple and vivid language' (ibid: 79); a section on 'Political correctness' which warns 'it produces clumsy phrases, seeks to hide realities behind euphemisms … and it sometimes seems more interested in evading criticism than in expressing meaning' (ibid: 88) but also, positively, highlights that a 'marked success of the feminists has been to persuade writers that they can no longer use "his" or "him" to include "her" when making a generalization' (ibid: 89); and a section on 'Loaded words' which points out the '*Times Style Guide* bans all euphemisms for murder' (ibid).

In the 'completely rewritten' (Spark and Harris 2011: xii) fourth edition, which is responsive to the demands of contemporary online journalism as well as key issues within the journalism industry such as diversity and ethics, there is still close attention to English language usage, writing style, and forms of journalism like news reports and features: ample topics, then, for which Orwell could have been explicitly drawn upon but, once again, is not. However, here too, it remains possible to recognise Orwell's approach to writing in the 'best practice' advice. For instance, in Chapter 5, 'Newswriting: choose the words', it is stated that readers 'like journalists to use clear, fresh words' (2011: 63). A range of problems like repetition, jargon, clichés, mixed metaphors and 'tired words' are highlighted. Although the 'acid test' example is gone, a sincerity-clarity link reminiscent of Orwell's essay underpins an argument that reference to '*loved ones*' rather than specific family members like father, mother, etc, 'radiates insincere compassion' (ibid). Imaginative originality is encouraged: 'Why copy the overused imagery and vocabulary of other journalists, when you could use fresh images of your own?' (ibid: 68). The wide-ranging advice is augmented by Chapter 6, 'Newswriting: getting the words in order', which urges, for instance, writing succinctly and avoiding 'muddled thinking' (ibid: 79) as well as long sentences.

Overall, the only explicit reference to Orwell in the NCTJ literature historically, besides Baker's book, occurs fleetingly in the distinctly male-orientated *Newsman's English* (1972), the first of a five-volume series by Harold Evans under the auspices of the NCTJ but also geared towards journalists internationally (and covering, in order, *Handling Newspaper Text*, *News Headlines*, *Picture Editing*, and *Newspaper Design*). According to Hugh Cudlipp, Evans believed 'we cannot have healthy democracy without efficient and honest newspapers' (1972: vii) – a position firmly in the tradition of journalists as the Fourth Estate, shared by Orwell. Commencing Chapter 2, 'Good English', Evans reproduces a longer quotation attributed to Matthew Arnold containing the same portion alluded to by Dr Syntax and later quoted by Baker: 'People think I can teach them style. What stuff it is [!]' leads into: 'Have something to say and say it as clearly as you can. That is the only secret of style.' Evans proceeds to argue that the 'penny-a-liner, who is disappearing anyway, is a petty corrupter of the language by comparison with Her Majesty's Government and the Pentagon'. In lines in accord with Orwell's approach, Evans holds that 'English has no greater enemy than officialese' and observes: 'Daily the stream of language is polluted by viscous verbiage. Meaning is clouded by vague abstraction, euphemism conceals identity, and words, words, words weigh the mind down.' Meaning, he insists, 'must be unmistakable, and it must also be succinct' (Evans 1986 [1972]: 16).

Elaborating on the role of 'the deskman' 'in 'protecting the reader from incomprehension and boredom', Evans explains the necessity of language usage 'which is specific, emphatic and concise'. Each sentence 'must be clear at one glance' and there 'must be no abstractions'. This, he declares, 'places newspaper English firmly in the prose camp of Dryden, Bunyan, Butler, Shaw, Somerset Maugham, Orwell, Thurber. The style to reject is the mandarin style … which is characterised by long sentences with many dependent clauses, by the use of the subjunctive and conditional, by exclamations and interjections, quotations, allusions, metaphors, long images, Latin terminology, subtlety and conceits' (ibid: 17). In this vein, Evans subsequently advises to 'Be Active': 'Vigorous, economical writing requires a preference for sentences in the active voice' (ibid: 23); to 'Avoid Needless Repetition' (ibid: 45); to 'Care for Meanings' (ibid: 53); and to 'Avoid Clichés' (ibid: 58). Topping the list of 'Stale Expressions' is the familiar 'acid test' (ibid: 80).

CONCLUSION: A CALL TO THE NCTJ TO UTILISE ORWELL STILL MORE IN THE FUTURE

As Evans's book indicates, Orwell can be counted within a rich tradition of critics and writers of prose in English which deeply informs journalism 'best practice'. That Orwell has been subsumed into a vast corpus of acclaimed prose works by renowned writers, and thus a cultural swirl of anecdotes and writings about writing which are pertinent to journalism, helps to explain the paucity of references to him in NCTJ publications historically even as these publications appear to be awash with writing principles he espoused. Besides obvious irrelevance to some topics (for instance, Orwell was for a time Literary Editor at the *Tribune* but never worked in newspaper management), another factor could be Orwell's complex relation to the standard 'objective' journalism of the mainstream or corporate press which, in Orwell's view, often served the interests of its wealthy proprietors. Although he supported 'a readiness to present news objectively', Orwell also believed prominence should be given 'to the things that really matter' (Orwell 2008 [1946]: 330). In similar vein, Orwell also took issue with schools of journalism and formulaic writing courses which prioritised money-making at the expense of 'telling unpleasant truths about present-day society' (ibid: 191).

As Keeble conveys, Orwell was 'a progressive journalist committed to the alternative media' on the left of the political spectrum, with his journalism reflecting 'an overall political activist approach' (Keeble 2020: 2). Such an approach differs markedly from the injunction to be impartial or unbiased which is usually enshrined in style guides in the newspaper industry and, accordingly, drummed into trainee journalists as essential to accurate, fair and balanced coverage deriving from apolitical professional practice.

Even Orwell's 19 articles as a war correspondent for the *Observer* and *Manchester Evening News* in 1945, 'the only time Orwell worked to strict deadlines as a reporter for mainstream newspapers' (Keeble 2007: 101), are highly subjective. Moreover, Orwell has been better known as the author of *Animal Farm* (1945) and *Nineteen Eighty-Four* (1949) than as a journalist and essayist. Historically, Orwell does not seem to have readily stood out, then, as a go-to exemplar or suitable case study for NCTJ textbooks for beginner journalists. Yet, as Baker's updated NCTJ guide shows, Orwell could not be more relevant to the need for beginners to understand industry expectations and develop best practice in terms of English language usage and writing style. This paper not only endorses Baker's harnessing of Orwell for educational purposes aligned to the Diploma but calls for further visible and wide-ranging utilisation of Orwell in future NCTJ textbooks and teaching. Orwell could potentially be applied in a range of areas: for example, the mandatory Essential Journalism, e-portfolios and ethics modules; and the optional magazine, editing skills and sports journalism modules.

Although Orwell's radio work as a talks producer for the BBC Eastern Service has not been examined here, reference to it could enrich teaching of the broadcast/radio journalism modules. Baker's professional background in BBC radio, television and multimedia newsgathering, as well as his leadership of training of BBC journalists globally as head of the College of Journalism (2010-2013), would have made him acutely cognisant of the value of Orwell's writing advice – which helps to explain its inclusion in Baker's new NCTJ guide. 'Politics and the English Language' appears, for instance, on the further reading list on page 85 of the *The BBC News Styleguide* (2003) written by John Allen, when Baker was World News Editor at the BBC Television Centre in London. A quotation from the essay opens the section on 'Clichés and Journalese': 'By using stale metaphors, similes and idioms, you save much mental effort, at the cost of leaving your meaning vague, not only for your reader but for yourself' (Allen 2003: 23; Orwell 2000 [1946]: 354-345).

As Tim Crook argues in 'Orwell and the radio imagination' (2015), Orwell's six rules can be extrapolated at various points in

Allen's guide. Crook speculates that it 'is perhaps no coincidence that Orwell's two years of toil, industry and creativity at the BBC were followed by the writing of two seminal essays' – 'Politics and the English Language' and 'Poetry and the Microphone' (1945) – 'that have had such a powerful influence on radio journalistic writing and the presentation and communication of poetry on the radio'. 'Politics and the English Language,' he argues, 'underpins the professional ethic of impartial, clear, and unpretentious writing in radio news.' He adds: 'I believe the stripped down, cautious and spoken word style of broadcasting English reverberated with Orwell's desire to resist the propagandizing and politicization of English communication. His enduring struggle against academic gobbledygook and determination to fight staleness of imagery and lack of precision is the stalwart aim of anybody writing scripts in spoken English style for the radio' (Crook 2015: 11).

Moreover, there is wider evidence of inclusion of Orwell in textbooks for the purposes of journalism training which predate Baker's NCTJ guide: for example, both editions of *Writing for Broadcast Journalists* (2005, 2010) by Rick Thompson. Although not explicitly branded as such, these editions appear to be compatible with teaching aligned to the Broadcast Journalism Training Council (BJTC) which, like the NCTJ and Professional Publishers Association (PPA), accredits journalism courses in the UK. In Chapter 3, 'The language of broadcast news', the identical quotation from 'Politics and the English Language' which appears in Allen's 2003 BBC guide opens the section 'Clichés' on page 29 of the first edition and on page 31 of the second edition. 'Orwell's summary' can be found near the end of both editions: 'Every journalist should develop his or her own style, avoiding clichés and stale formulae. In broadcasting, never forget that the words will be heard, not read.' Before quoting Orwell's six rules which, as we have seen, are later reproduced by Baker, Thompson argues there 'is no better summary of the way the spoken word should be written than the advice given by George Orwell in his 1946 essay *Politics and the English Language*' (2005: 151, 2010: 163). The essay appears on the further reading list for 'The Development and Use of the English Language' in both editions (2005: 176, 2010: 188).

Notably, in the revised section on 'Officialese from politicians' in Chapter 3 of the second edition, Thompson's argument is in accord with this paper's foregrounding of the value, in the 'apolitical' training of journalists, of expressly recognising Orwell's political awareness; and therefore in accord with this paper's call for change from Baker's exclusive attention to the English language aspects at the expense of the ultimately inseparable political dimension of Orwell's writing approach. Thompson highlights that, in 2008, the

Centre for Policy Studies published a 'Lexicon of Contemporary Newspeak' pointing out that 'what George Orwell described as *euphemism, question-begging* and *sheer cloudy vagueness* now dominates political discourse' (2010: 25, italics in the original). He adds that the director of the think-tank, Jill Kirby, was scathing about this 'often impenetrable vocabulary' and believed 'the corruption of language has infected all political parties, is endemic in public service, and is rapidly spreading in the media' (ibid: 25-26). Thompson stresses this 'serious point' and rightly argues: 'All good broadcast journalists not only must avoid this kind of political jargon and stick to everyday spoken English, they should also point out to their audiences, through direct quotes or attribution, that their elected leaders are deploying this kind of obfuscation' (ibid: 26).

Yet this should apply, of course, to *all* journalists fulfilling their function to hold power to account; and it illustrates, again, how relevant Orwell remains and how useful he could be if incorporated into teaching aligned to the NCTJ Diploma in a wide-ranging but integrated manner. Students could benefit not just from improved language skills across media platforms but enhanced appreciation of why they, as journalists, matter to society. Given recent calls in the US for the media to improve its approach to 'democratic backsliding' (Maruf 2021) and 'to start championing an unapologetic pro-democracy bias, before it's too late' (Klaas 2021), Orwell could serve to stimulate discussion that helps UK and international students to develop, fundamentally, a strong sense of professional identity and purpose that will shape – and sharpen – their practice as journalists.

Above all, Orwell's insistence on plain truth-telling stands as a perennial beacon for trainee and working journalists. The Ipsos Veracity Index 2021 showed that British adults' level of trust in journalists to tell the truth was only 28 per cent – a slight improvement on 2020 and 'back to their previous highest scores' since 1983. The only professions less trusted were government ministers and politicians generally at 19 per cent each, and advertising executives at 16 per cent (Clemence 2021). To borrow from the quotation alongside Orwell's statue at BBC headquarters in London, these are facts that journalists would not necessarily 'want to hear' but must if the profession is to rise to new heights.

ACKNOWLEDGEMENT

The author extends special thanks to the Archives and Special Collections Team at the Sir Michael Cobham Library, Bournemouth University, for facilitating access to the Segrue Collection while he was researching this paper.

REFERENCES

Allen, John (2003). *The BBC News Style Guide*, London: BBC Training and Development

Anderson, Paul (ed.) (2008 [2006]) Introduction, *Orwell in* Tribune – *'As I Please' and Other Writings 1943-7*, London: Methuen Publishing Ltd pp 1-39

Baker, Jonathan (2021a) *Essential Journalism – The NCTJ Guide for Trainee Journalists*, Abingdon: Routledge

Baker, Jonathan (2021b) The future of journalism: Old skills, new values. Available online at https://www.nctj.com/latestnews/jonathan-baker-blog, accessed on 26 February 2022

Benson, Preston (1963) First comprehensive guide to the skills of British journalism, *Journalist*, November p. 7

Clemence, Michael (2021) Ipsos Veracity Index: Trust in the police drops for the second year in a row. Available online at https://www.ipsos.com/en-uk/ipsos-mori-veracity-index-trust-police-drops-second-year-row, accessed on 17 March 2022

Crook, Tim (2015) Orwell and the radio imagination, Keeble, Richard Lance (ed.) *George Orwell Now!*, New York: Peter Lang pp 193-208. Accepted version available online at https://research.gold.ac.uk/id/eprint/11328/, accessed on 17 March 2022

Dodge, John and Viner, George (1963) *The Practice of Journalism*, London: Heinemann

Evans, Harold (1986 [1972]) *Editing and Design, Book One: Newsman's English*, London: Heinemann

Guardian (2020) The Guardian and Observer *Style Guide: O*. Available online at https://www.theguardian.com/guardian-observer-style-guide-o, accessed on 26 February 2022

Harris, Geoffrey and Spark, David (1966) *Practical Newspaper Reporting*, London: William Heinemann Ltd, first edition

Harris, Geoffrey, Spark, David and Hodgson, F. W. (eds) (1997) *Practical Newspaper Reporting*, Oxford: Focal Press, third edition

Heawood, Jonathan (2003) Introduction, *Orwell: The* Observer *Years*, London: Atlantic Books pp x-xiii

Keeble, Richard (2007) *The Journalistic Imagination: Literary Journalists from Defoe to Capote and Carter*, Abingdon: Routledge

Keeble, Richard Lance (2020) *Journalism Beyond Orwell: A Collection of Essays*, Abingdon: Routledge

Klaas, Brian (2021) Why the media should have a pro-democracy bias, *Washington Post*, 16 December. Available online at https://www.washingtonpost.com/opinions/2021/12/16/why-media-should-have-pro-democracy-bias/, accessed on 27 February 2022

Liddle, George and Pardoe, F. E. (1964) *Daily English: A Course in Practical English for Young Journalists*, London: NCTJ

Maruf, Ramishah (2021) 'News outlets should be openly pro-democracy', journalism professor says, *CNN Business*, 12 December. Available online at https://edition.cnn.com/2021/12/12/media/jay-rosen-reliable-sources-political-coverage-democracy/index.html, accessed on 27 February 2022

NACTEJJ (1953) *Handbook of Training*, London: NCTJ

NACTEJJ (1954) *Summary of Training and Education Scheme*, London: NCTJ

NCTJ (1964) *Training in Journalism: Handbook of the National Council for the Training of Journalists*, London: NCTJ

NCTJ (1967) *Reading List*, London: NCTJ

NCTJ (2022a) Become an accredited course. Available online at https://www.nctj.com/employers-and-trainers/Becomeanaccreditedcourse, accessed on 26 February 2022

NCTJ (2022b) Our History. Available online at https://www.nctj.com/about-us/history, accessed on 26 February 2022

Orwell, George (2000 [1946]) Politics and the English Language, *George Orwell: Essays*, London: Penguin Classics pp 348-360

Orwell, George (2008 [1946]) 'As I Please' 62, 22 November; in Anderson, Paul (ed.) *Orwell in Tribune – 'As I Please' and Other Writings 1943-7*, London: Methuen Publishing Ltd pp 328-331

Quote Investigator (2015) News is what somebody does not want you to print. All the rest is advertising. Available online at https://quoteinvestigator.com/2013/01/20/news-suppress/, accessed on 27 February 2022

Smith, Jon (2007) *Essential Reporting*, London: SAGE Publications Ltd

Spark, David and Harris, Geoffrey (2011) *Practical Newspaper Reporting*, London: SAGE Publications, fourth edition

Thompson, Rick (2005) *Writing for Broadcast Journalists*, Abingdon: Routledge, first edition

Thompson, Rick (2010) *Writing for Broadcast Journalists*, Abingdon: Routledge, second edition

NOTE ON THE CONTRIBUTOR

Jaron Murphy is a Senior Lecturer in Communication, Journalism and Literature at Bournemouth University. In 2018, he appeared on a list of 238 most respected journalists following research commissioned by the NCTJ which asked journalists working in the UK and Ireland 'which living journalist they felt most embodies the values of journalism that they respect and adhere to'. He holds a DPhil in Literature from the University of Oxford.

JOYEUX ANNIVERSAIRES: PETER STANSKY AT 90, *THE UNKNOWN ORWELL* AT 50

Much of Peter Stansky's work – arguably 'the precious stone set in the silver sea' of his numerous and diverse contributions to British Studies – has been devoted to the life and career of George Orwell. The following 'homage to Peter' honours his immense contribution as a biographer of Orwell on the occasion, in 2022, of his recent ninetieth birthday – which coincides with the fiftieth anniversary of *The Unknown Orwell*. It is the first of an outstanding two-volume Orwell biography in the 1970s that Stansky co-authored with William Abrahams. This essay/memoir tells 'the biography of the biography': the fascinating, dramatic story of how the biography came to be. In doing so, John Rodden unveils the surprising and largely 'unknown' history of its conception and composition – and of the 'prehistory' of failed efforts throughout the 1950s and 1960s by Orwell's publishers, friends and colleagues to persuade his widow Sonia to approve a biographer.

The year 2022 represents a double landmark in the history of Orwell biography. This winter has already witnessed, on 18 January, the ninetieth birthday of Peter Stansky, the Stanford University historian of Victorian and modern Britain, whose indispensable and pioneering contributions to scholarship on Orwell range from co-authoring a two-volume biography of Orwell in the 1970s to publishing numerous other articles and essays (including an edited collection, in 1983, *On Nineteen Eighty-Four*) devoted to Orwell's life and works. Moreover, the first volume of the Orwell biography, *The Unknown Orwell* – co-authored with his close colleague, the late book editor and poet-novelist William Abrahams – has its own anniversary worthy of recognition in 2022: it entered the world fifty years ago this September. Its publication was followed seven years later by a second volume, *Orwell: The Transformation* (1979), also co-authored with Abrahams, which took the story of Orwell's life up to 1937, covering the circumstances that gave rise to Orwell's first great book, *Homage to Catalonia* (1938), along with the personal and political 'transformation' entailed by his Spanish Civil War experience.

To those who know Peter personally – not just the scholar-teacher but also the man – it was no surprise that almost 700 people registered to attend a 'Zoom *festschrift*' that his colleagues sponsored during the week of his January birthday to celebrate his lifetime of contributions to Victorian and Modern British Studies. That wonderful event blossomed into a 'Homage to Peter' and it represented a wholehearted outpouring of love and respect for the man and his work.

My aim in this *hommage* to Peter Stansky, as he enters his tenth decade – and joins three eminent British figures (Peter Davison, Ian Angus and Ian Willison) as the American representative of this august nonagenarian quartet of elders in Orwell Studies – is twofold: to sketch a portion of the life story of the life storyteller and to address the background, composition and achievement of the dual biography, particularly *The Unknown Orwell*.

THE BOY IS FATHER TO THE BIOGRAPHER?

Let me begin with a mini-biography of the biographer. Born in 1932 in Manhattan, Peter and the rest of the Stansky family soon moved to Brooklyn and then returned to Manhattan later in the decade. Although his father was a lawyer in New York City, Stansky *père* possessed both artistic taste and a sophisticated interest in the art world. His legal clients included the owners of New York art galleries as well as regional antique dealers. Peter attended high school in New York City. Robert Gottlieb, the well-known editor and critic, was a schoolmate in the class ahead of him in high school. Later Gottlieb became a family friend – and edited both volumes of the Orwell biography.

In the spring of 1954, Stansky entered Yale University where he discovered his life-long passion for history, specialising in modern British history. His work as a history major culminated in an outstanding senior thesis (which he modestly dismisses as 'jejune' in a privately published memoir-cum-essay collection, *Twenty Years On: Views and Reviews of Modern Britain,* 2020), devoted to the participation of British writers in the Spanish Civil War. The writers? The poets Julian Bell (son of Clive and Vanessa), John Cornford (great-grandson of Charles Darwin), Stephen Spender – and the man of letters George Orwell. He later recalled: 'I put my work as a senior at Yale aside, never thinking I might return to it' (Stansky 2020: 111; unless otherwise noted, all further Stansky quotations are from this source).

As it would turn out, Peter would return within a decade to the topic of that work again and again. Beginning in the mid-1960s, assisted by William Abrahams, he would publish books and articles galore throughout the next six decades, all the way up to *Twenty*

JOHN RODDEN

Years On, in 2020. The 'jejune' Yale College thesis would serve as the point of departure for several landmark studies forming the core of Stansky's *oeuvre*.

After graduation Stansky matriculated at Cambridge University in order to pursue a second BA degree. 'I was not at all sure what I would do next: law or academics.' He soon chose 'academics'. He proceeded to gain his BA degree at King's College, Cambridge, and then decided against pursuing further studies in England. Instead, he would return to the US and attend Harvard for a PhD.

The rest is, shall we say, 'history'. Over the course of the next five decades, Peter Stansky joined the history department at Stanford University, where he taught for forty years and became the Frances and Charles Field Professor of History, also serving a stint as Dean of the Faculty of Arts and Sciences.

Stansky became one of the world's leading scholars of British Studies too, specialising in Victorian and Modern Britain. Quite apart from his dual biography of George Orwell, Stansky authored or edited more than twenty books devoted to Victorian and twentieth-century Britain. His most cherished Victorian figure has been William Morris (*Redesigning the World: William Morris, the 1880s, and the Arts and Crafts*, 1985). Among his best-known works dealing with modern Britain are multiple studies discussing Virginia and Leonard Woolf and the Bloomsbury circle (*On or About December 1910: Early Bloomsbury and its Intimate World*, 1996), British writers in the Spanish Civil War (*Journey to the Frontier*, 1966; *Julian Bell: From Bloomsbury to the Spanish Civil War*, 2012), and Britain's experience of World War Two (*The First Day of the Blitz*, 2007), respectively. Stansky's distinguished career has been duly crowned by numerous honours. For instance, he has been a fellow of the American Academy of Arts and Sciences as well as of the Royal Historical Society.

Having introduced – albeit all too briefly – the 'man within the biographies', this commemorative essay will now showcase those aspects of Peter Stansky's life and work most relevant to Orwell Studies, focusing above all on *The Unknown Orwell* across three distinct topic areas: its prehistory, its conception and composition, and its contribution to Orwell Studies. I am concerned throughout to convey 'Stansky's Orwell', that is, the image of George Orwell that emerges from the first volume of the Orwell biography as well as the texture of experience that the reader undergoes when perusing it. My twin focus spotlights the approach to Orwell adopted by Stansky and Abrahams, as well as the struggles they endured to write this trailblazing two-volume work, whose excellence is attested by the honours that each volume garnered on publication: the American editions of both *The Unknown Orwell* and *Orwell:*

The Transformation were nominated (1973, 1981) for the National Book Award in biography.[1]

THE UNKNOWN PREHISTORY: BACKGROUND OF A BIOGRAPHY

When the historiography of Orwell biography one day comes to be written, *The Unknown Orwell* will warrant an important chapter. But the preface to that chapter will be the story of what preceded this formal biography and decisively conditioned both its style and content.

So let me first address a 'struggle' little known except to Orwell scholars: the difficulty of getting *any* biography of George Orwell into print. Let us examine in some detail this obscure, fascinating and well-nigh unprecedented aspect of Orwell historiography, which is not only significant in its own right but also germane to the Stansky-Abrahams dual biography. What may be termed the 'unknown prehistory' of *The Unknown Orwell* exerted a direct impact both on that volume and its successor. What is 'unknown' to most readers of the volumes is the endless saga of arduous attempts – and, ultimately, misfires – to secure a biographer under contract to write Orwell's biography. Researching and writing Orwell's life became a protracted process for complicated reasons, chiefly having to do with Orwell's widow, Sonia.

As we shall see, this prehistory was also unknown to Stansky and Abrahams when they began to conduct research and contact potential interviewees. Little did they realise that they were fated to endure treatment equally difficult and capricious from Sonia, though – in the end – they did prevail.

On 18 January 1950 – fatefully, the day that young Peter celebrated his eighteenth birthday – George Orwell signed his last will and testament. He died three days later. In that document he asked that 'no biography be written'. He also made it clear – in the same paragraph of his will – that he wished for no funeral service, burial or memorial of any sort.

Those last two requests were immediately violated; his widow Sonia (Brownell) authorised Malcolm Muggeridge and Anthony Powell, good friends and close literary colleagues of Orwell, to arrange a funeral and a subsequent burial, both of which occurred on 28 January 1950, exactly a week after his death. He is buried in Sutton Courtenay, his tombstone reading simply: 'Here Lies Eric Blair.'

The biographical saga, with its plethora of paradoxes and puzzles, begins here. Let us examine this 'prehistory' of Orwell biography at some length, for it exerted a shaping influence on the Stansky-Abrahams dual biography.

ARTICLE

JOHN RODDEN

Having already ignored Orwell's express wishes by holding an Anglican church funeral and formal burial in a churchyard, why did Sonia insist on maintaining the other clause, namely that 'no biography be written'?

Concurring with the judgement expressed by Orwell's good friend and (one-time) co-executor Richard Rees – who held a casual attitude toward the 'no biography' clause and advised Stansky and Abrahams 'not to take this stipulation too seriously' – scholars generally have concluded that Orwell himself was not particularly opposed to a biography. He was, indeed, sceptical toward the perils of so-called Stracheyism, that is, the tendency in the wake of Lytton Strachey's sensational *Eminent Victorians* (1918) for biographers to wield iconoclastic, revisionist cudgels and seek to cut 'eminent' figures down to size. Nonetheless, he was keenly interested in biography and reviewed biographies throughout his life. (Already in 1930, the 26-year-old 'E. A. Blair' was expressing strong admiration in John Middleton Murry's *New Adelphi* for Lewis Mumford's Melville biography.) Regarding Orwell's request in his will to have no biography, one of Orwell's best biographers, Gordon Bowker, held that it was actually Sonia, not George, who was severely antipathetic to the genre of biography and was the motive force behind that request. According to Bowker, the request that 'no biography be written' reflected not 'Orwell's expressed intentions' – but rather Sonia's own.[2]

My own research involving Orwell's 'afterlife' in the George Orwell Archive at University College London supports this view. For various reasons having to do with both her perceived role as his literary executrix and her desire to maintain her own privacy, Sonia strongly opposed the idea of a biography. She did not want to license the possibility of Orwell being cut down to size, and she also did not relish her own background being looked at too closely – and probably subjected to critique. If anything, her fears had deepened by the early 1960s, when Stansky and Abrahams came calling with their book proposal. She had just gone through a very painful four-year marriage to Michael Pitt-Rivers that ended in divorce.

In any case, during the early 1950s there were numerous old friends and colleagues of George Orwell who approached Sonia and requested her approval to write a biography. Moreover, both his British and American publishers (Fredric Warburg at Secker & Warburg, William Jovanovich at Harcourt, Brace) were avid to have a biography reach print – for obvious financial as well as scholarly reasons.

The first serious biographical 'suitor', as it were, was T. R. 'Tosco' Fyvel, who had published an admiring personal appreciation of Orwell just months after his death in June 1950. He was also at work on a longer sketch of Orwell, which might be expanded into a full-fledged biographical portrait (if not biography). Fyvel had befriended Orwell as early as 1938 when they co-edited the Searchlight Book series, and had stayed in close contact, succeeding Orwell as literary editor of *Tribune*. Both Fyvel and his wife Mary were good friends of both George and Eileen O'Shaughnessy, his first wife. None of this counted for much with Sonia, however, who turned him down flatly in the spring of 1954. Fyvel, nevertheless, went on to publish his biographical sketch – which featured his interpretation of the Blair/Orwell distinction – in 1959. However, he did not publish his book of recollections until after Sonia's death: *George Orwell: A Personal Memoir,* 1983.

Next in line was Julian Symons who approached Sonia months later in December. Symons invited her to lunch and (so he thought) hit it off well with her – an impression that other star-crossed suitors would also soon receive. Initially he felt encouraged and was (fleetingly) convinced that she was about to bless his proposal to write a biography. He was surprised when she temporised, then demurred. In a refrain that would become familiar to future candidate biographers, she half-apologised that it was 'too early' for a biography and that she did not want to 'violate George's wishes'.

In hindsight, the timing of Symons's inquiries seems to have been cursed with horrid luck. He first wrote to her about the biography on 10 December 1954 – just two days before the BBC-TV adaptation of *Nineteen Eighty-Four*, a landmark of media history. That Sunday evening broadcast on 12 December triggered a firestorm of controversy that included weeks of debates in parliament and countless editorials, columns and letters in the British press. One viewer even suffered a heart attack during the broadcast and died the next day; several war veterans wrote letters to the press, protesting that the on-screen violence exceeded anything that they had witnessed in combat. Interviewed by the press and quite swept up in the hubbub, Sonia was mortified that the BBC adaptation – which, of course, she had approved – was evidently distorting and darkening her husband's legacy.

By the time that Symons wrote to her again about his book proposal on 30 December, in the wake of a second BBC-TV teleplay broadcast of the novel (on 16 December), the Halas-Batchelor cartoon adaptation of *Animal Farm* was about to enter British cinemas – and about to enter the political fray too.

The controversy was raging when the next applicant – another old Orwell friend, George Woodcock – entered the scene. Writing from Vancouver in February 1955, Woodcock was possibly aware of the BBC hullabaloo – yet certainly could not have anticipated the thunderstorm overhead with the approach of the *Animal Farm*

ARTICLE

JOHN RODDEN

adaptation. Released just days earlier in January, the *Animal Farm* animated film sowed bewilderment among viewers about the targets of Orwell's satire (e.g., porcine look-alikes of Senator Huey Long and recently deceased Labour leader Ernest Bevin? Old Major's Churchillian-sounding delivery?) and was widely savaged by the critics.

All this made Sonia more skittish than ever about the very idea of a biography, let alone a biographer. Cleverly (or so it seems in hindsight), she took the unexpected, apparently odd step of announcing publicly that she would overcome her hesitations, reverse herself, and authorise a biographer to proceed: Orwell's good friend, Malcolm Muggeridge, who had co-arranged (with Anthony Powell) Orwell's funeral and burial. Muggeridge, a BBC veteran, had been the most prominent spokesman about Orwell throughout the initial week of BBC-TV tumult and the long aftermath. On the Monday following the opening broadcast, he had joined the director of the BBC drama division on the highly regarded news show *Panorama* to defend the literary quality of the broadcast and explain Orwell's intentions to the public.

Although the selection of Muggeridge seemed to settle the matter, Orwell's friends and colleagues – and doubtless Sonia herself – regarded his appointment as a stalling tactic. Under the cover of the BBC-TV and *Animal Farm* turmoil, Sonia had seemed to 'give in' and recognise the need for a biography. In reality, she had evidently chosen Muggeridge merely to escape the pressure exerted by Orwell's publishers and friends for a biography.

Given her motives, Sonia had chosen the right man for the job. Like his professional colleagues, she suspected that Muggeridge would never get down to work. He was a raconteur, a *bon vivant*, a leader-writer and essayist. He was not a researcher. He lacked both the discipline and the drive to complete a project of this sort. Four years later, he had still barely begun, making only the feeblest gestures to interview people, ferret out uncollected pieces and gather scattered letters and other potentially valuable documents. 'The project defeated me,' he acknowledged in a memoir of Orwell, conceding that the defeat owed 'partly to my own indolence' (1972: 175).

In 1959, Muggeridge announced that he was bowing out. Questions about his selection, which puzzled other friends and scholars of Orwell, hang in the air to this day. Had Muggeridge originally accepted the commission with a certain understanding between him and Sonia as to his role, happily willing to collude in the charade and fully intended to be dilatory in his progress?[3] Did Sonia also choose him because – as London acquaintances of both parties later confirmed – they were conducting an affair in the mid-

1950s and end it once the affair cooled down by 1959? Or did the increased contact with Sonia occasioned by the literary commission lead to the affair? Either way, the story represents another interesting mini-chapter in the history of Orwell biography.

THE 'LIFE' ORWELL MAY HAVE HAD....

Now that Muggeridge was out of the picture, Orwell's British and American publishers – Fredric Warburg and William Jovanovich, respectively – took the initiative once again in late 1959. They proposed a biographer with impeccable credentials. Certainly he is the most illustrious biographer ever floated as a possibility – and the literary historian grieves about the missed opportunity and the might-have-beens.

The biographer was Richard Ellmann who was basking in the international acclaim accorded his new biography of James Joyce, published in September 1959 to universal praise on both sides of the Atlantic. Approached jointly by Orwell's publishers to do a biography of Orwell and offered a huge $25,000 advance, he pondered the offer seriously. Meanwhile, Warburg and Jovanovich urged Sonia to accept him. They contended that he would do a magnificent job, noting that the Joyce biography represented indisputable evidence and was destined to raise Joyce's standing even higher, both with the critics and the public. Nobody alive, they argued, was better qualified. And nobody could serve George Orwell's work and legacy better.

Indeed, the literary historian cannot help but wonder: what if Ellmann had written Orwell's life story? What if a biography of George Orwell had appeared in the mid-1960s, a biography of the scale and quality of the peerless Joyce biography – a biographical classic that stands (along with Boswell's *Life of Johnson*) as the greatest one-volume literary biography in the English language? Would it have pre-empted Sonia's four-volume edition of Orwell's largely uncollected work in 1968 – and all the biographies that have followed in its wake? Would it have turned Orwell into a literary figure highly respected in the elite echelons of the literary academy and a favourite in courses in the twentieth-century British literature, long before the professors began to accord him much respect during the 'countdown to 1984'?[4] Would a standout biography have largely settled the political claims to, and controversies about, Orwell's legacy that raged long after 1984 – and continue to this very day?

However fascinating it is to pose such questions of counterfactual history, we will never know. Rather, what we do know is that negotiations between the publishers and Ellmann dragged on, with both Warburg and Jovanovich pleading with Sonia to approve their candidate – and Ellmann becoming increasingly hesitant to sign on, notwithstanding the large advance. After a telephone conversation with Ellmann, she wrote to Warburg that 'no real proof of his desire to do the book' existed 'apart from money' or 'of his ability'. Both claims were preposterous; Warburg had just told her that Ellmann had 'half a dozen publishers' pursuing him and had raved that Ellmann was a 'superb scholar' and 'perceptive critic' ('thorough, careful, and exacting,' with 'imagination and grace of style') who would 'do justice' to 'the Orwell genius'. What more could a publisher possibly say?

Yet Ellmann must have gathered from that single phone conversation alone that Sonia harboured doubts about him. And it was Sonia's hesitation that provoked Ellmann's. Whatever she may have said in 1955 about her 'change of mind', she had now reverted to type. Sonia returned to her original position, telling Warburg that she was extremely uneasy about contradicting what she regarded as Orwell's last will and testament, however inconsistent that might seem with her recent actions. She added that she had reservations about authorising an American. Not long after Sonia's letter expressing doubt was forwarded to him, Ellmann withdrew in August 1960.

That Sonia professed to harbour reservations about Ellmann's qualifications was – to put it mildly – ironic. Not only did the Joyce biography refute them. So too did Ellmann's stellar biography and critical study of Yeats (*Yeats: The Man and The Masks*, 1948; and *The Identity of Yeats*, 1954). Who knew the British scene better? His subsequent biography of Oscar Wilde would further enhance his scholarly and critical stature.

Yet far more ironic and to the point: before Ellmann's name had been put forward, Sonia had pursued an American candidate of her own in mid-1959: the writer-editor Dwight Macdonald. Like Muggeridge, Macdonald was an engaging and iconoclastic essayist and intellectual journalist, but he was no scholar and had never written a literary biography – and worse, he was notoriously unreliable. In hindsight, once again, Sonia had been simply looking for an excuse to reject Ellmann, her publishers' hand-picked favourite.

Macdonald had been an editor of *Partisan Review* before and during World War Two, had founded his own journal *politics* (proudly lower-cased) during the war years, folding it as the decade closed. In mid-1959, he was residing in London, working as an editor on *Encounter* with Stephen Spender and others of Sonia's acquaintance. She met him, was impressed, and offered him the job to write the biography.

This time, however, it was the biographer – rather than the literary widow – who temporised, ruminating about the offer for eight months – by which time Sonia, taking heed of widely circulating reports in literary London of Macdonald's mercurial temperament, had changed her mind and explained that the publishers had developed cold feet. (If Sonia had a reputation for flakiness, it was exceeded by Dwight's fame on that account – and she had that impressed on her by Orwell's British friends from the moment they heard about her precipitous offer to him.)

The overtures to Macdonald and Ellmann in 1959-1960 represented the high water marks in the decades-long saga of a 'Sonia and Orwell biography'. It would be another dozen years before she anointed a candidate, but the intervening period – though the queue of suitors continued – never witnessed another candidate get close to a 'yes'. Names of prospective biographers were floated by the publishers throughout the 1960s. Among the prospects was John Gross, then teaching at King's College, Cambridge, and contributing regularly to the literary pages of many periodicals. He would go on to write the acclaimed *The Rise and Fall of the Man of Letters* (1969) and become the editor of *TLS* in the 1970s.[5] Yet his candidature, like the passing attention devoted for a few years in the late 1950s to Richard Hoggart, a highly regarded cultural critic who had just published *The Uses of Literacy* (1957) and was still only in his late 30s, was never seriously pursued.[6] Neither man was ever introduced to Sonia by Orwell's publishers. Probably the most accomplished prospective candidate was the critic and broadcaster Walter Allen, who did meet Sonia in 1964. Allen was a man of letters whom Orwell could have respected, having already published six well-received novels and written three critical-biographical studies of Orwell's predecessors (George Eliot, Arnold Bennett, Joyce Cary) as well as four analyses of the art and history of the novel itself. (It is quite possible that Orwell knew his literary studies of the late 1940s, *Arnold Bennett*, 1948, and/or *Reading a Novel*, 1949.) Allen was 'mad keen' to proceed with the Orwell biography (according to Warburg) – but Sonia decidedly was not. And so Allen's courtship also came to grief.

THE ORWELLIAN UNKNOWNS OF *THE UNKNOWN ORWELL*

I have tracked the strange odyssey of the failed biography-suitors in order to make clear that, by any ordinary measure, Peter Stansky and William Abrahams were speeding toward a Scylla and Charybdis, which most biographers would have avoided at the first signs of bad weather ahead. I also stress the vexatious prehistory in order to establish that Stansky's version (in *Twenty Years On*) of their dealings with Sonia does not seem at all exaggerated: before getting very far, virtually all his predecessors voiced similar frustrations. Sonia had become a caricature of the classic literary widow, erratic,

JOHN RODDEN

temperamental and overprotective. Stansky and Abrahams were rushing headlong into a decade-long ocean minefield of contorted complications and fond hopes blown to smithereens.

And so, after the Ellmann turndown in 1960, Stansky and Abrahams appeared on the scene in the mid-60s. Already in 1962, they had begun to conduct research for a projected study of four English writers' participation in the Spanish Civil War. Initially they received help from family members of all four of the principals (Julian Bell's brother, Quentin; John Cornford's brother, Christopher; Spender himself; and Sonia). The Americans sought to build on Stansky's senior thesis at Yale, but they quickly dropped Spender, who was still alive and skittish about being included. Not long thereafter, they also resolved that Orwell deserved special treatment in a separate study. So their first aim was to tell the story of the distinctive paths toward Spain of Julian Bell and John Cornford, whereupon the Americans deferred any attention to Orwell until 1966, after completing *Journey to the Frontier: Two Roads to the Spanish Civil War*.

And in an eerie repetition of the experience of previous literary suitors, the history of which was unknown to the Americans at the time, of course – which represents yet another dimension of the 'unknown' of *The Unknown Orwell* – an initial honeymoon period was soon succeeded by acrimony. After a couple of cordial early meetings with Sonia, which appeared to them as a vote of confidence to proceed with their plans, Stansky and Abrahams began to step on a series of landmines, each of which detonated with a blast.

Their plans had not originally entailed the writing of a biography, but rather merely a critical study of Orwell's participation in the Spanish Civil War. They requested that Sonia support their plans for interviewing friends and colleagues of Orwell. And she did so, even giving them the address of his sole surviving sister, Avril Blair. The drama of rising and falling action culminated in a crash – 'a confrontational dinner' in Paris in 1967 that 'grew quite emotional' as Sonia and Abrahams 'argued about what the book would look like', with Stansky looking on sheepishly as he 'ate my delicious and expensive chicken' and watched 'the disastrous evening' spiral downward into Sonia's regal ultimatums and Abrahams' indignant rejoinders. According to Stansky, Sonia dictated that 'we could go ahead and continue to use the archive *only* if we would show her the manuscript' and gain her 'approval'. In a subsequent communication with the would-be biographers, 'She repeated that perhaps good relations could be restored if we would show her the manuscript and give her total power over what might be included or excluded'. To both edicts, the biographers tersely replied that her conditions were 'unacceptable, of course' (115-116).

What aroused Sonia's wrath was the biographical approach that the Americans took in *Journey to the Frontier*, which, she contended, 'demonstrated that our line of approach to Orwell would also be biographical'. In reply, Stansky and Abrahams noted that Cornford and Bell were much less well known than Orwell. Nor had they written numerous autobiographical essays and documentaries. Nor, in addition, did anything like a 2,000-page collection of their nonfiction and correspondence already exist.

Sonia remained sceptical, not only because *Journey to the Frontier* was heavily biographical, but also because the Americans had taken her up on her (generous) offer to interview Orwell's family, friends and colleagues – which she now suspected, whatever their denials, had to do with gathering material for a biography after all.

In addition, as Sonia's familiarity with the materials of the Orwell Archive proceeded, her commitment to an edition of Orwell's uncollected work deepened, her conviction about having proprietary rights to potentially useful archival material developed, her conception of what constituted others' 'biographical' treatment of Orwell broadened and her resolve to fend off potential interlopers stiffened. Sonia told the Americans what she would later repeat on the book jacket for *The Collected Essays, Journalism and Letters of George Orwell* (*CEJL* 1968), which she co-edited with Ian Angus of the Orwell Archive, namely that the chronologically organised, 1,900-page collection was meant to 'stand in for a biography'. As a result, there would be no more need for a formal biography because Orwell already told the story of his own life in so many of his autobiographical writings.[7] And the previously uncollected material in *CEJL* would round off the story and fill in any missing gaps. Indeed, as the book jacket promised, readers would have the opportunity to hear Orwell tell it even more fully in these essays, journalism and letters that 'have thus far remained fugitive and uncollected'.[8]

The Americans refused to back down and grant Sonia the right to vet their book. So both sides retreated to their corners and remained at a standoff. Sharp letters (sent from Sonia, 'in her fury' alleging vaguely all manner of errors in *The Unknown Orwell*, as well as from her agent in charge of the George Orwell estate, Mark Hamilton at A. M. Heath) followed all the way up to publication of the biography (115-116).

The outcome of the contretemps was that Sonia forbade Stansky and Abrahams further access to the Orwell Archive. That was not such a great loss, Stansky recalls, because 'we had already seen everything and didn't really need to use the Orwell Archive any longer' (Rodden interview). Once it became clear to Sonia, however,

JOHN RODDEN

that the Americans intended to write not a critical study that would include some biographical material, but rather a thoroughly researched biography covering the life of Blair/Orwell through the years of his experience in Spain, her pique turned to 'rage', as Stansky remembers it. For now they were not only violating Orwell's last will and testament, they were also quite deliberately challenging the suitability of *CEJL* as a 'stand-in' for a biography and planning to compete with it.

As relations further deteriorated, Stansky and Abrahams were also refused permission to quote from all of George Orwell's writings – certainly a costly penalty, especially given the resonance of Orwell's voice as a writer and his fame as one of England's greatest prose stylists.

THE AUDACITY OF INNOCENCE, OR EAST COAST YANKEES IN QUEEN SONIA'S COURT

All these roadblocks and restrictions may well have intimidated most biographers and deterred them from moving ahead with a biography. The restrictions on quotation, for example, meant that they had to resort to paraphrase and elaborate description, all the while avoiding copyright infringement.

Yes, 'most' biographers may have hesitated – or halted. Here again, however, Sonia would find to her dismay that she was not dealing with Orwell's friends and colleagues, or with his publishers – all of whom felt that they had to pay court and then tiptoe around her. Rather, unlike the case with the deferential or diffident prospective biographers of previous years, she was dealing with a pair of determined East Coast Yankees who possessed a gritty can-do attitude in the face of all the obstacles.

And that fact raises quite explicitly two questions: Why did Stansky and Abrahams proceed when all previous candidates did not? What did they have that the other biographers did not possess?

First, a sense of independence. They were already well advanced on their initial goal – telling a compelling story of a generation's participation in the Spanish Civil War from a literary angle. Earlier biographers were not: they had come to Sonia hat in hand, for approval – and formal permission to proceed. Moreover, the pair had been gathering materials and interviewing sources for years, benefiting from the extensive research already conducted for *Journey to the Frontier*, some of which was not only relevant to the topic 'Orwell in Spain' but also had overlapped with their planned Orwell study.

Unlike earlier prospective biographers, therefore, Stansky and Abrahams sought Sonia's help – not her permission. Also unlike Orwell's colleagues and friends, they never felt that they were 'violating his will', let alone 'betraying George' if they undertook to write a biography in opposition to the express wishes of his literary widow. Letters in the Orwell Archive from Orwell's friends and colleagues attest to the unceasing efforts by those who had known him to reassure Sonia that, as Julian Symons had put it in 1954, 'I should value your advice and knowledge' and 'would be anxious not to disclose anything unjustifiably painful to anybody and particularly to you'.

Secondly, the American duo had the paradoxical advantage of being outsiders – and outliers. Stansky had the unusual freedom provided by a sabbatical year, supported by a Guggenheim Award to spend it unencumbered in England throughout 1966-1967. He also had an offer in hand to return to the US and take up a prestigious position in the history department at Stanford University. For his part, Abrahams was already well-established as an East Coast book editor for Atlantic Monthly Press. As a result of their success with *Journey to the Frontier*, published by Little, Brown in Boston, they were assured that they would get a contract, with no need to fear that legal threats would derail the project, no need to depend on Sonia's approval or the good offices of Warburg or Jovanovich. (As it turned out, Robert Gottlieb at Knopf edited both volumes of the biography, as we have noted.)

The biographers' outsider status as Americans unfamiliar with the London literary scene not only emboldened them; less obviously, it also inadvertently blessed them with a certain derring-do innocence – or willfully fortunate ignorance. That is to say, because they were neither generational peers of Orwell nor insiders to the London literary scene, they were unaware of the quagmire that they were stepping into – and so they plunged ahead with gusto, precisely how and where their cautious predecessors feared to tread. Although I believe that knowledge about their predecessors' failed entreaties to Sonia would not have proven a deterrent, the fact is that, by the time Stansky and Abrahams did begin to find out about the history of failed efforts to win Sonia's favour, they were already well along in their thinking about the book as well as in their research – and they never looked back.

They were self-starters too, and Peter was just 34 in 1966 when they first met Sonia. 'Billy' was 47 – exactly the same age as Sonia herself – but collaboration on an Orwell biography was evolving into a secondary pursuit for Abrahams. His literary career was giving way 'to the career in which he would achieve his greatest reputation: being one of the most prominent book editors of the twentieth century' (13). As co-author of *The Unknown Orwell*, he seems to have functioned primarily as an expert editor who helped conceptualise their overall approach; unlike Stansky, he was not a

JOHN RODDEN scholar or researcher, and the idea for a book on British writers in the Spanish Civil War had come from Stansky, who was returning to his Yale College thesis topic. True, when the pair had met at a Christmas party in 1960, Stansky was just 28 and Abrahams was already a published poet and the author of three novels. Even then, however, he was turning his attention to the publishing world. Having become an editor at Atlantic Monthly Press in Boston shortly before meeting Sonia, his professional identity was firmly centred in this latter capacity – specifically, as a book editor of serious fiction and nonfiction. His stable of authors would come to include Lillian Hellman, Joyce Carol Oates, Diane Johnson, Brian Moore, Thomas Flanagan and Pauline Kael. (Sonia was especially impressed to know that he edited the O. Henry Award volume every year – and even more so that he handled Hellman's work, and Sonia delighted in his stories about her.)

The larger point is that, unlike their failed predecessors, who felt constrained to proceed without Sonia's blessing, Stansky and Abrahams flung themselves full throttle into the research. As we have seen, they could pursue the Orwell biography with greater psychological freedom because they were outsiders; and they had no worries about 'what George might think' (or others on the London literary scene) and no dependence on any publisher as middle man (e.g., Harcourt or Secker & Warburg).[9]

Nonetheless, as the foregoing details suggest, it warrants emphasis that both Stansky and Abrahams had already accomplished much in their literary careers, both individually and in partnership. For his part, Stansky had already published his first scholarly monograph, a revised version of his Harvard dissertation, as *Ambitions and Strategies: The Struggle for Leadership of the Liberal Party in the 1890s* (1964). Moreover, during their research and writing of the biography, Stansky also edited two books devoted to earlier periods in British history (*The Left and War: The British Labour Party and the First World War*, 1969, and *John Morley: Nineteenth Century Essays*, 1970). Most importantly, by the time they were fully under way on *The Unknown Orwell*, the collaboration between Stansky and Abrahams had already proven itself: *Journey to the Frontier* had received sterling reviews on its publication in March 1966 and would be nominated for the 1967 National Book Award in history.

HOW THE BIOGRAPHY GOT WRITTEN

What precisely was the nature of this literary collaboration? How did these two talented men develop a working relationship that achieved consensus on a biographical approach and avoided ego battles?

The basic pattern had already been established during the research and composition of *Journey to the Frontier*, but the Orwell biography demanded efforts on a much larger scale (more sources, a wider geographical expanse, etc.) and far more difficult conditions (Sonia's lack of cooperation and restrictions on quotation).

Generally speaking, most of the research was done during Stansky's 1966-1967 sabbatical and the summers that he and Abrahams spent together. Most of the in-person interviews were jointly conducted. In the course of the Americans' fruitful meeting with Avril Blair, whom they noticed was decidedly cool about Sonia, it became clear to them that Sonia's antagonism towards them represented – another hilarious turn in the saga – an unanticipated asset. 'Plenty of people were willing to talk to us,' Stansky recalled, 'and, in fact, some of them regarded it as a distinct plus that Sonia's attitude toward us had turned negative – because they themselves were not on the best terms with Sonia. So that was rather amusing' (Rodden interview).

The biography was largely written during 1968-1972, in California, where Peter and Billy lived together. (Abrahams worked out an arrangement whereby he relocated as the West Coast editor for Atlantic Monthly Press.)

The practical division of labour – as I understand it from my conversations with Peter – emerged according to the strengths and skills of both men. Stansky assumed the role of main writer and head researcher, with Abrahams serving as sounding board and editor/reviser. Stansky corresponded with librarians, sources and potential interviewees. He also composed the first draft, which he would then hand off to Abrahams. Billy, however, was 'a bit of a procrastinator, and he had lots of irons in the fire, so I had to do some vigorous prodding occasionally to get Billy to keep up with the evolving manuscript' (Rodden interview).

Like so much else in the odyssey towards *The Unknown Orwell*, the apparent disadvantage of Abrahams' procrastination led to an unexpected and ultimately quite fortunate development. Stansky recalls that the initial plan had been to write the story of Orwell's life through his own 'journey to the frontier' of Catalonia in a single volume. They conceived the book as a counterpart to the Bell-Cornford story in *Journey to the Frontier*. By 1970, Peter realised that Billy's procrastination was delaying their progress – and that he would feel more strongly motivated 'to get on with it' if he 'glimpsed the light at the end of the tunnel' (Rodden interview).

As they progressed beyond the Eton and Burma years, a simple and attractive solution came into view: Why not end the book in January 1933, with the publication of *Down and Out in Paris and London*, with Eric Blair nearing the age of thirty and publicly

JOHN RODDEN

launching himself as a writer? Why not conclude with the logical milestone of 'Blair into Orwell'?

This was an inspired – and inspiring – reframing of the project. The pair realised that this solution would facilitate a quick ending to the contracted book and make it a compact study. They had amassed a wealth of material, certainly enough for two volumes. The sequel would take the story, as planned from the very start, through Orwell's return from Spain and the composition and publication of *Homage to Catalonia* in 1938. *The Unknown Orwell* would be about 'becoming a writer'. *Orwell: The Transformation* would be about 'becoming a socialist'.[10]

As Stansky recalled: 'We had never intended to write a full-scale biography. Just as we had always assured Sonia, our endpoint was Spain. That is, with the participation of Bell, Cornford – and now Orwell – in Spain'.

The trilogy of 'journeys to the frontier' told the stories of three English writers in Spain: the two poets died, the man of letters returned from the front and eventually became the world-famous author of *Nineteen Eighty-Four*. But the biographers were content to leave the later episodes of his journey – the story of Orwell's last dozen years – for other biographers to tell.

ACHIEVEMENT, INFLUENCE, LEGACY

The impressive achievement represented by *The Unknown Orwell* and *Orwell: The Transformation* is not just a matter of priority, though I should stress how revelatory both volumes seemed to their original audience, since they broke new ground, serving as the first substantial, well-documented, thoroughly researched biographical study.

Apart from the challenge of mapping the *terra incognita* of Blair's youth and Orwell's early development – and covering three continents in the process – the Stansky-Abrahams dual biography popularised a conception of Orwell so familiar today that we forget how stunning and original it was to readers of the 1970s: the complicated experience of the prep school boy, rather at variance with his self-reports in 'Such, Such Were the Joys'; the surprising glimpse of Eric Blair as a literary bohemian, even a 'dandy'; the crucial role of his first wife, Eileen O'Shaughnessy, in his maturation; the step-by-step advance of the emerging 'political writer' from Wigan to Spain and back to England. It is not that these views of Blair/Orwell originated with Stansky and Abrahams. Some Orwell friends and colleagues had already formulated all of them. But the biographers were the first to track down witnesses, gather stray or undiscovered documents, anatomise Blair/Orwell's growth, and weave it all into a coherent, sustained narrative. As a result, both volumes of the biography – and most especially *The*

Unknown Orwell – represent first-rate contributions that are not only richly detailed and still informative, but also offer themselves as enjoyable as well as edifying reading experiences.[11]

What are the distinguishing features marking a stellar biography? I believe that two characteristics are essential – and that *The Unknown Orwell* passes the test on both counts. I refer specifically here to the subgenre of the literary biography, since that is what Stansky and Abrahams wrote.

First of all, a biography – especially a literary biography – should ask: how did the life give rise to the art? It should show how an appreciation of the life enriches our understanding of the writer's *oeuvre*. Both *The Unknown Orwell* and *Orwell: The Transformation* do this, in the 'Life and Letters' tradition of literary/intellectual biography. Together they represent a portrait of the artist as a young man. They inspire us to want to know more, fill us with an intense desire to 'know this person', to grasp how his life gave rise to the masterpieces. A richly imaginative literary biography is not content to speak of 'intertextuality', or 'literary influence', as if masterpieces only exist in relation to one another in a canon of works by Great Authors. No, the biography shows that the life deeply influenced the work, and that appreciation of the work is enhanced by biographical knowledge. (For example, the Los Angeles screenwriter Christopher Angel has been so inspired by *Orwell: The Transformation* that he has written a five-part screenplay about Orwell's road to Spain and beyond, focusing on his months in the Spanish Civil War.) As they shed light on the interconnections between the life and the work, the best literary biographies send readers back to the author and to his work, stimulate them to rediscover (or discover for the first time) the author's achievement for themselves. As Stansky phrases it in *Twenty Years On*, 'the main reason for studying the life of a writer is to illuminate the work. To the extent that … we may have done so, we have achieved our purpose' (117).

Second, the compelling biography causes readers to ponder: how was the life shaped by 'an age like this'? (The phrase appears in a poem featured in Orwell's 1946 essay 'Why I Write'; Sonia Orwell and Ian Angus also chose it to title Volume 1 of *CEJL*.) That is, a distinguished biography enhances our understanding of the subject within history and society, in the tradition of the 'Life and Times' biography. Faced with Sonia's restrictions, Stansky and Abrahams compensated by pursuing all leads – both in the form of witnesses and documents – aggressively. Recognising that she had imposed a potentially stultifying limitation by her prohibition against quotation from Orwell's oeuvre, they parried, aiming to circumvent and even transcend the lack of Orwell's voice by furnishing an extremely enriched context of the time. In fact, both Christopher

JOHN RODDEN

Hollis and Cyril Connolly, in their sympathetic book reviews of *The Unknown Orwell*, praised the thoroughness of the research and the nuanced understanding of British schoolboy experience that emerged in the biography. Hollis, an Etonian schoolmate, marvelled: 'Their interviewing every variety of witness who had any connection with Blair's early life is beyond praise.' Connolly, who had attended both prep school and Eton with Blair, remarked that, except for a trivial detail or two, the Americans could have passed for Old-Etonians themselves.

These comments convince me that, redoubling their efforts in light of Sonia's restrictions, the biographers turned themselves into enterprising investigative reporters and inspired a generation of successors – such as the indefatigable Darcy Moore, who acknowledges how much his Burma research owes to them – to follow suit (Moore 2017: 109). Sonia's potentially crippling restrictions steeled Stansky and Abrahams to become both more determined to ferret out sources and more creative in the craft of portraiture. For instance, they interviewed Mrs Vaughan Wilkes (Blair's headmistress at St. Cyprian's), established contacts with the Rangoon Officers' Club, in Burma, and gained assistance from more than thirty of Orwell's acquaintances – several of whom were lost to subsequent biographers through death.

Looking back on the interdiction against quotation, Stansky recalled: 'We resolved that we would deal with the matter of quotation as best we could. We quoted less than we might have liked, but I think biographers frequently rely too much on quotations, and so I don't think the book suffered too much by that limitation' (115).

On rereading *The Unknown Orwell*, I am inclined to agree – and, therefore, to reconsider my judgement of thirty-odd years ago in *The Politics of Literary Reputation:* 'What George Woodcock had called the Americans' "proto-biography" was an album of others' memories, unfortunately deprived of the one voice which would have breathed life into it' (Rodden 1989: 149-150). Today, I would instead maintain that, by their skilful interlacing of narrative and description, the biographers themselves breathed life into their *Life*.

Third, the superior literary biography evinces a clear conception of the subject, which it promotes to clarify or combat the prevailing or erroneous interpretations. Both volumes of the Stansky-Abrahams biography convey a clear image of Blair/Orwell. Their biography is not at all a mere collection of the reminiscences of others (Woodcock's 'proto-biography'). Nor is it the subjective projection of the biographers' fancy about Orwell. By dint of careful research that marshalled solid and persuasive evidence, they showed how Eric Blair in *The Unknown Orwell* was a literary bohemian, even a dandy, who *became* the political writer George Orwell. Their dual biography thus depicted a double transformation: 'becoming the writer' and 'becoming the socialist'. In *The Politics of Literary Reputation*, I faulted *The Unknown Orwell* for pushing their thesis too hard:

> [T]he authors marked the Blair/Orwell division somewhat too sharply, implying that 'Orwell' suddenly came into being with his pen name. Their thesis that 'Blair was the man to whom things happened; Orwell the man who wrote about them' was an oversimplified dichotomy of the intricate relation between the man and the writer, neither of which was always or necessarily congruent with 'Blair' and 'Orwell' (1989: 150).

On re-reading both volumes, however, I think the authors' strong emphasis on the Blair/Orwell distinction was warranted, especially at that time. It is anachronistic to deny this fact: most readers in the 1970s and 1980s still had no clear idea of the differences between Eric Blair and George Orwell – and quite often had not even known that Eric Blair was his family name. In addition to the pleasure and honour of congratulating Peter Stansky on the happy occasion of his own and his biography's birthday milestones, I have also had the welcome opportunity to return to the path-breaking two-volume biography that he and William Abrahams gave us. And to appreciate more deeply than did a 'jejune' young scholar in his early 20s how successfully both men rose to meet the literary and interpersonal challenges facing them.[12]

And to glimpse today, as anyone can see with the hindsight of history, how they launched biographical scholarship on Orwell a half-century ago, providing a splendid framework and excellent foundation on which their scholarly heirs – all of us fellow workers in the field of Orwell Studies – have steadily built.[13]

NOTES

[1] The American edition of *Orwell: The Transformation* was published in 1980, which accounts for the date of the NBA nomination in 1981

[2] Gordon Bowker (2007) Orwell and the biographers, Rodden, John (ed.), *The Cambridge Companion to George Orwell*, Cambridge, Cambridge University Press p. 13. Bowker's well-researched essay covers Sonia's role in the history of Orwell biography. I have drawn on it for the specific dates of some correspondence between her, Orwell's publishers and the prospective biographers proposed by the publishers, and also (unless otherwise noted) for any quotations among them. I have gone well beyond Bowker, building on my earlier discussion of these matters in my 1989 essay in *Biography*, which was revised and expanded in *The Politics of Literary Reputation*

[3] Both Muggeridge and Sonia maintained links with British intelligence agencies; so too, apparently, did Fredric Warburg. What exactly was the nature of Orwell's relationship with the British intelligence services? The full story remains to be told. Scholars are still in dispute about the nature and extent of his connections. Whatever ultimately emerges from the ongoing biographical research, however, the relevant point is this: Muggeridge's intelligence background in Africa may

have further buttressed the rationale for his designation throughout the 1950s – when Cold War fears and the American 'Red Scare' peaked – as Orwell's 'official biographer'. Having served during World War Two in the intelligence corps in Mozambique and Algiers, Muggeridge would have been deemed 'reliable'. He could be counted on to keep any possible Orwell connections to MI5, the Information Research Department, and any other government propaganda or intelligence units from coming to public light – and Sonia's connections as well. Could it be, therefore, that Sonia was living out her own version of a Cold War thriller? Seeking both love and security, she had chosen an old Orwell friend and given him a 'cover role' as biographer. As her lover-confidant, shielding her from prying biographical eyes, he would become her secret 'dual' agent – until the late 1950s, when he became dispensable with the end of both the romantic affair and the extremes of Cold War hysteria. (Sonia remarried in 1958, to Michael Pitt-Rivers.) For an illuminating discussion of how Muggeridge's intelligence background bore on his role as Orwell's biographer, see Keeble 2021, especially pp 149-150

[4] On the inattention, uninterest and disrespect of the literary academy toward Orwell until the late 1980s and 1990s, see Rodden 1989 and Rodden 2020

[5] Interestingly, his wife Miriam Gross, then deputy literary editor of the *Observer*, would later edit an excellent collection of portraits, written by friends and colleagues of Orwell, *The World of George Orwell* (1972) – and it was a flattering review of that collection in September 1972 that impressed Sonia Orwell and induced her to select the reviewer as Orwell's biographer. The reviewer, of course, was Bernard Crick

[6] A tantalising clue as to what he may have written, at least in terms of his approach and emphasis, appeared even before *The Unknown Orwell*, namely Hoggart's essays on Orwell collected in the second volume of his collected essays, *Speaking to Each Other: About Literature* (New York: Oxford University Press, 1970)

[7] Only two items in *CEJL* predate the year 1930. That certainly left the impression that 'the unknown Orwell' remained largely unknown, *CEJL* notwithstanding. Writing in December 1968, just weeks after *CEJL*'s publication, Julian Symons pointed out to Sonia and Secker & Warburg's David Farrer that much of the story of Orwell's life remained to be told. Pleading his case as a suitable biographer yet again and no less eager to pursue than he was fifteen years earlier, Symons argued that a sensitive biographer would supplement the contents of *CEJL* and the first-person testimony provided by Orwell himself in it. (Sonia turned him down again in April 1969.)

[8] Essentially, Sonia was telling the Americans at their Paris dinner what she expressed in her *CEJL* introduction a year later. Sonia insisted that, while she did not aspire with *CEJL* to crown a 'Complete Works', let alone to have it misunderstood as the cornerstone of 'an academic monument', it should, nonetheless, be accepted as the final contribution to 'the definitive Collected Works' (Orwell and Angus 1968: xvii).

[9] The unique situation of the American pair applies not only to their differences from previous prospective biographers, but also to all the already-published critical-biographical studies that preceded *CEJL*: six books, published between 1953 and 1967, all of them written by men who had known Orwell. Except for Richard Rees (*Fugitive from the Camp of Victory*, 1961) and George Woodcock (*The Crystal Spirit*, 1967), the authors of the 1950s were no more than friendly colleagues, such as fellow *Tribune* socialist John Atkins, Orwell's predecessor as *Tribune*'s literary editor, and the intelligence officer assigned to the BBC'S Eastern Service while Orwell worked there from 1941-1943, Laurence Brander, or slight acquaintances such as *Picture Post* editor Tom Hopkinson and Eton schoolmate and Conservative MP Christopher Hollis. In fact, it is likely that Sonia's lack of objection to the four books of the 1950s – especially her tacit approval of Hollis's *George Orwell* (1956), which contained both his personal

recollections and substantial biographical material on Blair at Eton and in Burma – emboldened Rees and Woodcock to contribute their own studies, which they too combined with memoir and biographical information. Here again, Stansky and Abrahams were just as much in the dark about these six authors' behind-the-scenes maneuvering around Sonia as they were about the elaborate dance steps of previous prospective biographers. They did not realise the lengths to which all six authors felt obligated by Orwell's expressed public wishes – and intimidated by his widow's strong private wishes – for no formal biography. Orwell's will and 'Sonia's Will', as it were, acted as formidable constraints, checking an author's initiative and confining his range of inquiry

[10] Beginning in the 1980s, I sought to tell the later stages of the fascinating story, that is, the development from 'becoming Orwell' to becoming 'Orwell', the posthumous icon and talisman. I conceptualised the trajectory as a five-stage ascending movement: 1, becoming a writer (Orwell); 2, becoming a socialist (in Spain); 3, becoming a 'conscience' ('of his generation' upon his death); 4, becoming immortal (the canonical classroom staple since the 1950s who authored *Animal Farm* and *Nineteen Eighty-Four*); 5, becoming 'Orwell' (the bogeyman behemoth, the mythic figure confused and conflated since the mid-1950s with his 'Orwellian' Frankenstein creation, Big Brother).

[11] Nonetheless, Stansky notes that the sales of both volumes of the biography were disappointing. In *Twenty Years On*, he speculates on the cause – and his 'theory' surprised me: 'I've always held a theory why biographies of Orwell don't sell as well as one might hope – at least that has been my experience; perhaps other biographers have had better luck. My theory is that high school students don't believe that actual people have written the books they are required to read, and hence in later years they have little interest in their biographies'

[12] Speaking of 'jejuneness' and specifically of that young scholar's assessment of the Stansky-Abrahams biography, I vividly (and sheepishly) recall a long-ago conversation in the spring of 1980 with a visiting speaker who had also just read the American edition of *Orwell: The Transformation*. Our guest speaker was in his mid-40s and was known to us at the University of Virginia as a well-known Conrad scholar who had been attracting much attention for his more theoretically oriented recent work. A most engaging and affable fellow, he treated this 23-year-old graduate student who had not yet gained an MA degree with a surprising degree of (unearned) respect, as if we were virtually peers. He expressed admiration for the Orwell biography, remarking that both volumes gave him a richer and more nuanced understanding of Blair/Orwell's complex relationship to imperialism, which had been the topic of both the guest lecture and the recent book. When I voiced my qualms about the biography, he was surprised; I elaborated on my reservations, and he listened to this critique attentively, then paused. He looked quizzically at the student who was professing such high critical standards, then gently replied, in a quiet tone of genuine humility: 'Well, I thought it was better than that.' The man's name was Edward Said

[13] Shelves of books have addressed the work habits, professional challenges and personal battles of a major author such as George Orwell. Rightly so. For a writer who bequeaths humankind a magnificent work of world-historical significance – such as *Nineteen Eighty-Four* – understandably leaves readers insatiable for knowledge about his trials and triumphs. Yet how seldom do we learn much about the backstory of a work by a scholar-critic or nonfiction writer like ourselves. And how amazing that story sometimes may also be! The story of how *The Unknown Orwell* reached print illustrates that fact well. The play-by-play history (and pre-history) of *The Unknown Orwell* exemplifies how both personal and interpersonal struggles occur in the lives of scholars too. The saga of its 'becoming' reminds us that the adversities and adventures of a scholar-critic may also be absorbing – and instructive for us scholars personally. For we scholar critics can usually identify much more readily with the Sisyphean battles undergone by a fellow researcher than with the radically different, 'titanic' contests with 'the gods' in which a canonical literary figure such as Orwell

JOHN RODDEN

appears to engage. Whatever the differences between a brilliant imaginative writer's encounters with the blank page and our own, however, the real point is that we scholars typically find the long journey of our 'fellow workers' to bring a book to fruition – the ultra-marathon of gathering the research, studying the scholarship and coping with the army of archivists and legions of editors and publishers – highly relevant to (and even revelatory for) our own proletarian pilgrimages. At least that has been true for me: the epic 'inside story' of the Stansky-Abrahams 'journey to the frontier' – and back to the barricades! – has rewarded me with invaluable insights about my own star-crossed literary odysseys through the years

REFERENCES

Bowker, Gordon (2007) Orwell and the biographers, Rodden, John (ed.) *The Cambridge Companion to George Orwell*, Cambridge: Cambridge University Press pp 12-27

Connolly, Cyril (1972) 'Such Were the Joys', *New York Times Book Review*, 12 November

Crick, Bernard (1992 [1980]) *George Orwell: A Life*, Harmondsworth, Middlesex: Penguin

Hollis, Christopher (1972) Review of *The Unknown Orwell*, *Spectator*, 4 September

Keeble, Richard Lance (2021) Orwell and the important Muggeridge Archive revelations, *George Orwell Studies* Vol. 6, No. 1 pp 130-152

Moore, Darcy (2017) Stansky and Abrahams: Orwell's first biographers, *George Orwell Studies*, Vol. 4, No. 2 pp 104-13

Muggeridge, Malcolm (1972) A knight of the woeful countenance, Gross, Miriam (ed.) *The World of George Orwell*, London: Weidenfeld and Nicolson pp 166-175

Orwell, Sonia and Angus, Ian (1968) *The Collected Essays, Journalism and Letters of George Orwell, Vol. 1, An Age Like This*, Introduction, London: Secker & Warburg

Pritchett, V. S. (1980) Doomed for success, *New York Review of Books*, Vol. 27, No. 7, 1 May p. 3

Rodden, John (1989) Personal behavior, biographical history, and literary reputation: The case of George Orwell, *Biography*, Vol. 12, No. 3 pp 189-207. Revised and expanded as: Lives of independence: The history of Orwell biography, *The Politics of Literary Reputation*, New York: Oxford UP, 1989 pp 141-53

Rodden, John (2020) *George Orwell: Life and Letters, Legend and Legacy*, Princeton: Princeton University Press

Rodden, John (2022) Interview with Peter Stansky, 8 January

Stansky, Peter and Abrahams, William (1972) *The Unknown Orwell*, New York: Alfred A. Knopf

Stansky, Peter and Abrahams, William (1979) *Orwell: The Transformation*, New York: Alfred A. Knopf

Stansky, Peter (2020) *Twenty Years On: Views and Reviews of Modern Britain*, Hillsborough CA: Pinehill Humanities Press

Woodcock, George (1980) Review of *Orwell: The Transformation, New Leader*, Vol. 63, No. 11, 16 June p. 19

NOTE ON THE CONTRIBUTOR

John Rodden is the author of several books about George Orwell and his heritage, including *George Orwell: Life and Letters, Legend and Legacy* (Princeton, 2020).

ARTICLE

Retracing the Steps of Orwell and Dorothy Hare in Kent

The secretary of The Orwell Society, Neil Smith, has researched Orwell's connections with Kent including his hop-picking journey in 1931, unearthing some previously unknown information. Here he compares Orwell's account with the one he gives his central character, Dorothy Hare, in his novel *A Clergyman's Daughter* (1935). Neil worked with local historians in Kent including Terry Bird and Liz Gandon.

In the middle of the night of 14 March 1938, the 34-year-old George Orwell started hemorrhaging blood and may have died were it not for his wife, Eileen, and her brother, Eric. They arranged for an ambulance to take Orwell to Preston Hall tuberculosis sanatorium, near Aylesford, in Kent, where he stayed for almost six months. This was not Orwell's first time in Kent. As he recovered from his illness and explored the area (visiting Maidstone Zoo and an ancient burial mound called Kit's Coty House) he may have reflected on the time he spent, seven years earlier, hop-picking in the county. While tramping around the county looking for work, he and his fellow tramp, Ginger, had probably walked past the entrance to Preston Hall and then later been driven past it after they hitched a lift from a lorry.

Orwell's hop-picking diary, first published in 1968, is full of detail that can be used to work out, with some certainty, where he went. With the help of local historians, I have pieced together his journey and the fictional journey of Dorothy Hare, in *A Clergyman's Daughter* (1935). The timeline that follows shows how closely Dorothy's journey was based on Orwell's. It includes some interesting diversions from the main subject. I follow this with further detail regarding Orwell's other connections to Kent.

DOROTHY HARE'S TRAVELS IN *A CLERGYMAN'S DAUGHTER* WITH ORWELL'S CORRESPONDING REAL-LIFE JOURNEY AND ADDITIONAL INFORMATION ON TIME HE SPENT IN KENT.

Dorothy	**Orwell**[1]
Wednesday 21 August[2] Opening day of the novel. Dorothy is in her hometown of Knype Hill, described as an East Anglian parish with 2,000 inhabitants. Dorothy falls asleep after midnight that night.	Knype Hill is generally considered to be based on Orwell's hometown of Southwold, in Suffolk.
Thursday 29 August Dorothy wakes up on the New Kent Road in London, eight days after falling asleep at the Rectory. She walks to 'The Elephant' (Elephant and Castle) at the end of the New Kent Road (so only a few minutes' walk away) with Nobby, Flo and Charlie where they catch the tram to Bromley, 15 miles according to Nobby, but actually less than 10, even by the route the trams took.	Friday 28 August 1931 Orwell catches a tram to Bromley. The night before Orwell's tram trip he had stayed at a lodging house 'in the Southwark Bridge Road' which is a short walk to Elephant and Castle though he does not say where he caught the tram.

The only direct tram service from Elephant and Castle to near to Bromley in the 1930s was the 74 which (as at October 1934) ran from Victoria Embankment (Savoy Street) (Sundays only) via Blackfriars Bridge (John Carpenter Street) via Elephant and Castle to Downham (about 1.5 miles north-west of Bromley) with an extension Saturdays pm to Grove Park (a further 1.5 miles north-east along Downham Way and around 2 miles north-east of Bromley).[3] Given neither Dorothy nor Orwell travelled on a Saturday it is reasonable to assume that the tram terminated at Downham. The tram terminus at Downham was at the corner of Bromley Road and Downham Way.

Tram, Downham Way, 1933
© London Metropolitan Archives
(City of London Corporation)

A contemporary account from farnborough-kent-village.org.uk[4] says: 'On Downham Way, there were two sets of tramlines and at Bromley Road there were two sets of three tramlines. This was because, on Downham Way, the trams got their electric power from the overhead cables and, on Bromley Road, the power was in a conduit under the third track. When the trams reached Bromley Road, the driver would get out of the tram and manually disconnect the overhead power and then slip a large electrical conductor, which was called the "shoe", under the tram and connect it to the middle track. When the driver did that the locals called it the "changeover". Trams were not comfortable to ride in. They rocked from side to side and to get on a tram one had to walk into the middle of the road in order to board.'

London's first generation trams were decommissioned in the 1950s. The current 136 bus route follows a similar route to the 74 tram from Elephant and Castle to Grove Park.

| Dorothy and the others '"drummed up" on a horrible, paper-littered rubbish dump, reeking with the refuse of several slaughter-houses, and then passed a shuddering night, with only sacks for cover, in long wet grass on the edge of a recreation ground'. | Orwell '"drummed up" on a rubbish dump … and had to spend the night in long wet grass at the edge of a recreation ground'. He says that 'there were houses all round; we were also lying on a slope, so that one rolled into the ditch from time to time'. |

Downham did not exist until 1924. Before then, the tram terminus was at the village of Southend, half a mile north on Bromley Road. Between 1924 and 1930 the Downham Estate, with around 6,000 dwellings, was built on former farmland.

The new estate at Downham was named after Lord Downham (William Hayes Fisher), a former chairman of London County Council (L.C.C.), who had taken his title from his birthplace, Downham, in Cambridgeshire. It was built between 1924 and 1930, one of a number of large estates built after the First World War to alleviate a housing shortage and improve conditions for the working classes ('Homes for Heroes' as Lloyd George described them). In early 1927, King George V and Queen Mary opened the L.C.C.'s 17,000th dwelling. During their visit, a tree was to be planted at the dwelling, 165 Downham Way, but due to a half-day holiday being given to all council workers, the tree was unfortunately locked away with the ceremonial spade in a council hut.

The Downham Tavern was the only public house built on the area owned by the L.C.C., all the others being technically outside its boundaries. It was for some years the world's largest pub, containing a dance hall, beer garden, two saloon bars, a public lounge, a lunchroom (with flats above) and service was by waiter only.

NEIL SMITH

London County Council plan, 1934, from www.ideal-homes.org.uk

A 1934 map of the Downham Estate shows the main part, as completed in 1930. The tram route is shown coming in down the Bromley Road in square A3, turning left into Downham Way in A4 (the 74 service Orwell – and Dorothy – probably used terminated at the turning) and continuing to the line terminus at Grove Park Station in F2.

Downham Recreation Ground is mainly in C3 and D3. The Ordnance Survey Map shows a contour line signifying a slope and it was surrounded by housing, thereby fitting Orwell's descriptions as to where he and Dorothy slept. It was a 10-minute walk from the tram stop. It is not clear where the rubbish dump was.

In 1926, a seven-foot high wall, capped with broken glass, was built across the street to the adjacent private estate, intended to prevent Downham's residents using the street as a short-cut to Bromley town centre. Such walls became known as 'class walls'. The wall remained until 1950. It was across Valeswood Road at its junction with owner-occupied Alexandra Crescent (C5 on the map). It is quite possible that Orwell and Dorothy had to take a slightly longer route than they would otherwise have had to were it not for this wall. (The current day optimum walking route from the recreation ground to Ide Hill goes down Valeswood Road according to Bing Maps).

Friday 30 August	Saturday 29 August
Dorothy and the others walk 20 to 25 miles, zig-zagging across the county (Kent), heading for the hop fields and Sevenoaks.	Orwell walks to Ide Hill (about 4 miles south-west of Sevenoaks), at least a 15-mile walk. He passes Ide Hill spike after deciding not to go in.[5] He 'kipped on the edge of a park near the church'. He eats sausages tapped from the local butcher.

Ide Hill spike was the Kent County Council Poor Law Institution, formerly the Sevenoaks Union Workhouse. It was on the road towards Ide Hill, about 1.5 miles north of the village. Orwell and Ginger would have walked south, up the long hill, past the spike, to Ide Hill and its church, stopping at the village butcher's shop on the way. The butcher's shop was attached to a pub to its north and to its south a large house, Prospect House, lived in by the butcher and his wife, Mr and Mrs Underwood. The shop, which went out of business after a rival opened in the village, is now the garage of Prospect House. St. Mary's Church is the highest church in Kent. Locals think that the location for the 'edge of a park near the church' where Orwell and Ginger kipped might well have been the churchyard itself – in 1931 no graves had yet been dug on the south side of the church.

It was probably not too far from the church and vicarage because the next morning (Sunday), 'the clergyman coming to early service caught us and turned us out, though not very disagreeably'. The vicar at the time was Rev. Charles Alder Stubbs who had taken over from the Rev. Cross in May of that year. The *Sevenoaks Chronicle*, on Friday 15 September 1933, reported: 'Ide Hill loses Vicar and friend of all. The news that the Rev. Charles Alder Stubbs had passed away suddenly on Thursday cast gloom over the village of Ide Hill where he had been Vicar since May 1931.'

A current resident of Ide Hill, Mrs. Leigh (then Freda Cole), remembers moving to Prospect House in 1934 and says that tramps often used to come to the Prospect House front gate and her family, the Coles, always filled their drums, or billycans as she called them.[6]

Saturday 31 August	Sunday 30 August
Walks 20 to 25 miles.	After being turned out by the vicar, he walks through Sevenoaks to Seal, 2 miles north-east of Sevenoaks. Then 'three miles further on' to Mitchell's farm where no work is available.

ARTICLE

NEIL SMITH   Today there is a Foxbury Farm, 2 miles south-east of Seal, which has been in the Mitchell family since 1909.[7]

Sunday 1 September	
Walks 20-25 miles. Meets Irishwoman Mrs McElligot in Wale, described as a 'little village'.	Orwell then walks on to Kronk's Farm where, again, no work is available. After visiting Kronk's, Orwell and Ginger start off towards Maidstone (i.e. heading east) and then meet an Irishwoman who is working at Mitchell's.

There is no such place as Wale though it could be based on the village of Seal, visited by Orwell on his Sunday, near Sevenoaks, and near where he met an Irishwoman and with a place name that sounds like another aquatic mammal. Kronk's is actually Cronk's, either deliberately or accidentally misspelled by Orwell. According to 'Visit Kent', the farm is at 'Newbarns, West Malling'. There is a New Barns, just outside West Malling which has existing oast houses. However, this is about 9 miles from the presumed location of Mitchell's Farm which seems too far to fit the narrative, especially since after heading west from Cronk's, Orwell meets the Irishwoman who was working at Mitchell's – placing Mitchell's and Cronk's quite close together. A more likely candidate is Fullers Hill Farm, near Seal.[8] This was also owned by Cronk. It is 1.5 miles north-west from the presumed location of Mitchell's and less than a mile from Seal.

	That night they sleep in an empty house after getting some hot water from a cottage and having tea with the Irishwoman. They had earlier been turned away by a farmer whom they ask for shelter and they had then tried to shelter in a church lychgate beside the farmhouse. They buy and steal provisions from the grocers.

Orwell and Ginger may have stayed the night in or near to Seal. St. Peter's Church, in Seal, has a lychgate marked as such on the 1930s Ordnance Survey Map and it is next door to Church Farm.

Monday 2 September	Monday 31 August
Dorothy and Charlie try to get work at Chalmers's Farm, 5 miles from Wale. They wait there for four hours before being told there is no work. They then try several other farms.	Orwell and Ginger meet the Irishwoman in a nearby wood then walk 1-2 miles to Chambers's Farm where they are kept waiting from 8am to 1pm before being told there is no work.

Chambers farmed at Greatness Farm, just over 1 mile west of Seal.

	They then start along the Maidstone Road (the A25) heading for Maidstone, walking around two hours and stopping for dinner at 3 pm. Near here they are refused cold water at two houses and are given butter and money by a gentleman in a car picnicking. They then walk a few miles more before deciding to head for West Malling spike, described as 'about eight miles distant'. They get a lift from a lorry and are set down about 2 miles from the spike.

It is about a 10-mile walk heading east from Chambers's Farm to West Malling spike. For Orwell and Ginger to walk east from the Seal area on the Maidstone Road and end up 8 miles away from the spike they must have walked through a point not too far from the spike, then continued east towards Maidstone, perhaps walking up to 15 miles in the day. This would explain Orwell not feeling 'equal to another night in the open'. If they did walk to somewhere close to Maidstone then the lorry could have taken them back along the Maidstone Road for about 6 miles dropping them off on that road at a point 2 miles north of the spike (thereby fitting the eight miles distant') at 8 o'clock in the evening.

	They stay in West Malling spike.

There is an Orwell plaque in West Malling.[9] West Malling spike was the Kent County Council Poor Law Institution (formerly the Malling Union Workhouse), originally built in the 1830s. It was on King Hill, about 1 mile south-west of West Malling. In the 1990s, five large houses were built on the site and the cul-de-sac was named Orwell Spike.

Tuesday 3 September	Tuesday 1 September
Dorothy and Nobby try to get work at 11 farms before being taken on at Cairns's in the village of Clintock that evening. They work there for several weeks.	The next day Orwell gets a job at Blest's, 3 miles from West Malling spike. He works there for nearly three weeks.

Dorothy's journey is clearly based on elements of Orwell's journey and Cairns's farm is clearly based on Blest's farm. Differences in their journeys include that Dorothy spends all her nights on the road sleeping outdoors (whereas Orwell has a night in the spike) and she takes a less direct route to the Sevenoaks area (probably walking more than 50 miles over two-and-a-bit days versus Orwell's 15 mile walk in one day).

NEIL SMITH

'Blest's was farmed by Frank Blest (age 44 in 1931) who owned or rented several other farms making up 'probably the biggest single hop-growing business at that time.'[10] His farms included Canon Farm and Home Farm, in Wateringbury, and Brewers Hall Farm and Bull Farm, in Mereworth. Frank Blest's grandsons are not certain which farm Orwell worked on. However, they think it is highly probable that it was one of his Mereworth farms and probably Brewers Hall Farm, which is about 2 miles from the spike and 2.5 miles from Wateringbury railway station, fitting Orwell's description.

Winifred and Frank Blest in the 1940s or 1950s
with permission of Jan Blest

Orwell describes washing his shirt and socks in a stream. Wateringbury Stream runs through Brewers Hall Farm. The stream continues its way across the road from the farm and into the grounds of Mereworth Castle. As he washed his socks did Orwell realise that he was so close to this Palladian country house where his great great grandmother, Lady Mary Fane, grew up before marrying Charles Blair, in 1765? Lady Mary's portrait can be seen in the background of several of the Vernon Richards' photographs of Orwell and his son Richard at his Canonbury Square flat.

Mereworth Castle. Source: Wikipedia public domain

A description of pre-First World War hop-picking in Mereworth (called Fladmere in the book) is provided in *A Boy in Kent*, by C. (Clarence) Henry Warren (1937) in a chapter titled 'The Gay Invaders'. No hops are now grown in Mereworth or Wateringbury.

Frank's grand daughter-in-law, Jan Blest, has spoken to Frank's niece, Sylvia, and writes: 'We do have an interesting anecdote which was provided by Sylvia Spooner, who was the niece of Frank and the first cousin of John. She, now approaching her 100th birthday later this year, recalls that in possibly 1933*, or thereabouts, Orwell, having published his accounts of hop-picking, was invited by the family to join them for Sunday lunch at [the family home] Broomscroft. This does not appear to have been a very rewarding experience for either the family or Orwell! The conversation was apparently dominated by [Frank's wife] Winifred and would no doubt have been of mundane matters probably of interest only to the family and no one seems to have engaged in any deep questioning of Orwell and his time hop-picking. So, the memorable thing for Sylvia was sitting next to him at the dining table, but that, to a 13-year-old, he appeared to be a rather dour and somewhat boring person! He didn't seem interested in his hosts and they were not particularly bothered about him.'

* Author note: The hop-picking essay was published in October 1931 so 1933 is possible though perhaps 1931 or 1932 more likely.

Wednesday 4 to Friday 27 September	Wednesday 2 to Friday 18 September
During her time on the farm, Dorothy pays several visits to the general shop or post office in the village (described as being 1.5 miles away) to buy notepaper and then to check whether she has had a reply to the letters she has sent to her father. On the last visit she hears the bells from the 'village church round the bend of the road'.	During his time on the farm Orwell helps a fellow hop-picker carry her belongings to Wateringbury station, described as being 2.5 miles away.
	Orwell says there is a pub in the village where the 'people who had money used to get well drunk, and it needed the police to get them out of the pub'.

It is about 1.5 miles from Bull Farm and about 2 miles from Brewers Hall to the site of the former post office on Bow Road, in Wateringbury, near to the junction with the A26 Tonbridge Road. The post office was around 700 yards from the church.

It is not clear whether Orwell is referring to the village of Mereworth or Wateringbury. Both had a number of pubs in 1931, including The Torrington Arms, in Mereworth, and The King's Head, in Wateringbury.

Saturday 28 September	
Hop-picking comes to an end.	
Sunday 29 September	Saturday 19 September
Dorothy gets the hoppers' train from West Ackworth station, 4 miles away. This is probably a fictional name for West Malling. It takes 'six hours to do thirty-five miles' to London. That night she stays with the Turles 'in a tenement house not far from Tower Bridge Road'.	Hop-picking comes to an end. Orwell and Ginger walk to Wateringbury stopping off 'to buy tobacco, and as a sort of farewell to Kent, Ginger cheated the tobacconist's girl of fourpence, by a very cunning dodge'. Orwell gets the 'hop-pickers' train' from Wateringbury station. It takes 'nearly five hours to get us to London – 30 miles. At about 10 at night the hop-pickers poured out at London Bridge station'. He goes into 'the nearest pub' with Deafie and Ginger, 'the first beer I had had in three weeks'. So, Orwell did not attend the Saturday night visits to the pub in Wateringbury or did not drink beer if he did (the latter seeming unlikely). Orwell stays overnight at a kip in Tooley Street (which runs past London Bridge station).

Tower Bridge Road is half a mile from London Bridge station and since Orwell's train comes into London Bridge we can assume Dorothy's train does as well. Orwell's diary notes the 'queer game of catching the women and putting them in the bins'. He says that 'very likely there will be something about this in *The Golden Bough*'. He is partly right. In *The Golden Bough: A Study in Comparative Religion* (12 volumes published between 1890 and 1915 by Sir James George Frazer); in a chapter titled 'Killing the Corn-spirit', it says: 'In hop-picking, if a well-dressed stranger passes the hop-yard, he is seized by the women, tumbled into the bin, covered with leaves, and not released until he has paid a fine.'

In 1970 Bridge Books of Wateringbury published a limited (300 copy) edition of Orwell's *Hop-Picking Diaries* (excluding the part of the diary covering the period after he returned to London). The diaries had first been published in the 1968 *Collected Essays, Journalism and Letters*, edited by Sonia Orwell and Ian Angus. The Bridge Books edition, called *George Orwell in Kent*, includes a critical introduction by Medway Fitzmoran and a postscript by John Blest, son of Frank Blest.

ORWELL IN KENT – OTHER REFERENCES

DOWN AND OUT IN PARIS AND LONDON[11]

Orwell describes visiting several casual wards (or 'spikes') in *Down and Out in Paris and London* including three which are in Kent (or described by Orwell as being in Kent). This journey through the county is probably earlier than the hop-picking journey since 'The Spike' essay (see below) was published in April 1931, before the hop-picking journey – unless the *Down and Out* Kent trip is a mix of experiences with some of them being later.

After a 16-mile walk from London starting down the Old Kent Road, he stays at 'Cromley' spike. Cromley is a fictional name, probably taken from a mixture of Bromley and Croydon. The book strongly suggests that Cromley spike is in Kent[12] making it more likely based on Bromley (which is in the traditional county of Kent) than Croydon (which is in the traditional county of Surrey). The Kent County Council Poor Law Institution (formerly the Bromley Union Workhouse) was in Locksbottom, 3 miles south of Bromley on the site of the modern-day Princess Royal University Hospital. The only surviving building is the chapel.

After Cromley spike, he walks to the fictionally named Lower Binfield spike where he has to stay two nights because it is a weekend (since those who stayed had to do a day's work but couldn't work on a Sunday). The description of his stay in Lower Binfield spike is similar to the description in his 1931 essay 'The Spike' (see below). Lower Binfield is also the fictional name of George Bowling's hometown in Orwell's novel *Coming up for Air* (1939).

Lower Binfield is probably Godstone spike, on the site of the Clerks Croft Mental Deficiency Institution (formerly the Godstone Union Workhouse). The site was redeveloped in the 1980s and is now the Clerks Croft housing estate.[13] Godstone is in Surrey though Orwell says it is in Kent.[14] It is the most likely candidate for being Lower Binfield because it is a 14-mile walk from 'Cromley' spike (assuming this to be Locksbottom) and a 12-mile walk to Ide Hill spike. No other spike fits the geography anything like as well.

After Lower Binfield spike he mentions other tramps going to Ide Hill spike and says that he stayed in it subsequently. He does not stay in it when hop-picking either. We do not know when he stayed there but it means there was (at least) a third trip to Kent during his tramping days. He sets out north for London, staying another night at Cromley on the way.

'THE SPIKE' ESSAY[15]

'The Spike' essay is similar to the description of Lower Binfield spike in *Down and Out in Paris and London* though the spike is not named in the essay. After leaving the spike Orwell says that he 'set out for Croydon'.

NEIL SMITH

SANATORIUM

Orwell was a patient at Preston Hall tuberculosis sanatorium, known as the British Legion Village, in Aylesford, Kent, for five-and-a-half months. He was admitted on 15 March 1938, discharged the same day and readmitted on 17 March, remaining until 1 September.[16] The sanatorium was outside Aylesford, on the A20 between Maidstone (3 miles away) and West Malling spike (5 miles away). Part of the site is still used by the Royal British Legion. The hall itself is now housing. Orwell may have walked and/or been driven past the sanatorium seven years earlier on his hop-picking journey.

He spent part of his time working on the attached farm. Orwell mentions visiting the zoo at Maidstone at least twice. Around 1.5 miles from Preston Hall, it was opened in 1934 and closed in 1959. It is now Kent Life Heritage Farm Park. He also visited Kit's Coty House, the chamber of a long barrow (an ancient grave mound) about 3 miles north-east of Preston Hall. On 25 August, while at the sanatorium, he mentions the 'Gipsies beginning to arrive for the hop-picking'.

There is one other brief mention of Kent in relation to a sanatorium in Orwell's works. On 2 February 1949, Orwell writes to Anthony Powell asking him to thank Malcolm Muggeridge for suggesting a sanatorium in Kent for Orwell. He does not take up the suggestion.

1921 CENSUS

The 1921 census reveals that Orwell (aged 17) was in Kent on census day, 19 June. He was at Cousins Farm, Smarden, West Ashford. The census has him as a visitor along with several others – not obviously connected to him. It is not clear why he visited.

- A summary version of this article was first published in The Orwell Society *Journal*, edition 18, Spring 2021.

NOTES

[1] Orwell called himself Eric at least part of time (hop-picking diary)

[2] The opening day of the novel is Wednesday 21 August. We know this because we are told that Holy Communion and the Mothers' Union meeting are both that day, a Wednesday, in Chapter One. In Chapter Two we are told that Dorothy fell asleep on 21 August. This was a Wednesday in 1935. The novel was written in 1934 (with amendments made in early 1935) and published on 11 March 1935. Orwell's own visit to the hop fields started on Friday 28 August 1931. It is possible that Orwell drew up a timeline of days and dates to give the novel internal coherence without considering a specific year for these to correspond to

[3] Historical edition of *The Greater London Bus Map 3rd October 1934*, by Mike Harris from https://www.busmap.co.uk/

[4] https://www.farnborough-kent-village.org.uk/transport_bromley_district.html

[5] Orwell tells us in *Down and Out in Paris and London* that he did once stay at Ide Hill spike

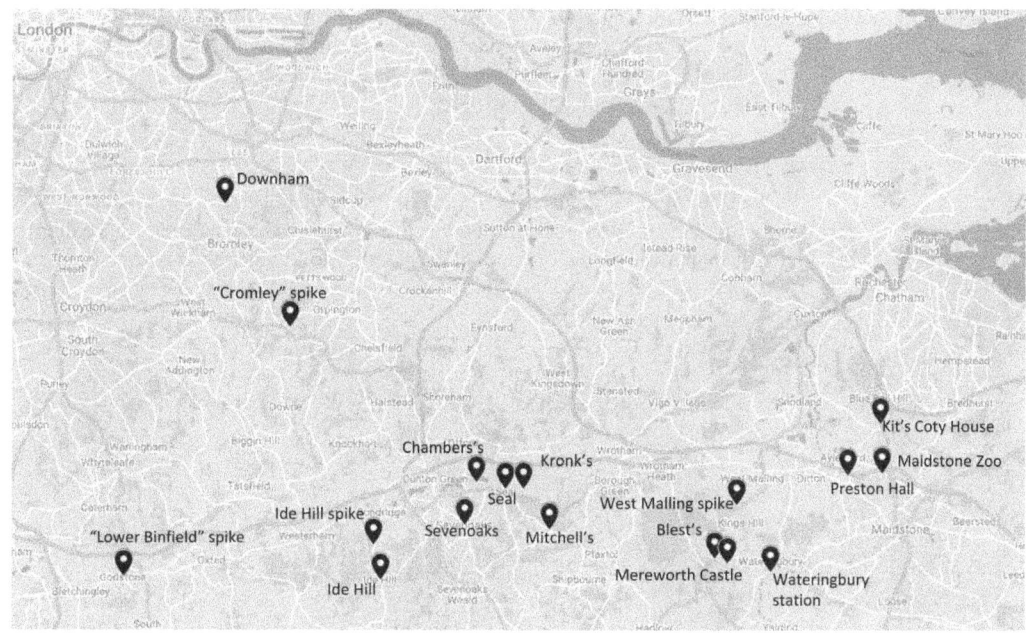

Map © Google

[6] Email from Liz Gandon from Ide Hill, 18 October 2020

[7] Profile of Robert Mitchell on The English Apple Man website: http://www.theenglishappleman.com/profile_robert_mitchell_mbe.asp

[8] *Kent & Sussex Courier*, of Friday, 1 June 1934, shows Capt. W. D. Cronk selling cherries from farms in West Malling and Seal. The 1911 census shows family living at Fuller Street, Seal, the location of Fullers Hill Farm

[9] https://www.visitkent.co.uk/malling-blue-plaques/#Orwell

[10] Obituary of Frank Blest's son, John, *Rostrum*, the parish magazine for the village of Wateringbury, in Kent, November 2018. https://0501.nccdn.net/4_2/000/000/06b/a1b/2018--November.pdf

[11] Published on 9 January 1933

[12] The tramps set out down the Old Kent Road which they would be less likely to do if heading for Croydon. After reaching Cromley, a tramp, Bill, says: 'I ain't goin far in [unknown swearword censored in original publication] Kent'

[13] workhouses.org.uk. http://www.workhouses.org.uk/Godstone/

[14] As they leave Lower Binfield spike, Orwell says, in relation to two tramps, William and Fred: 'This was the second spike in Kent that they had made too hot to hold them', having earlier described them cheating the Tramp Major at Cromley

[15] 'The Spike', published in *The Adelphi*, April 1931

[16] *The Complete Works of George Orwell, Vol. XI: Facing Unpleasant Facts 1937-1939*, Item 432 pp 127-128, letter from Eileen Blair to Jack Common

REFERENCES

Orwell, George (1998a) *The Complete Works of George Orwell, Vol. III: A Clergyman's Daughter*, Davison, Peter (ed.) London: Secker & Warburg

Orwell, George (1998b) *The Complete Works of George Orwell, Vol. X: A Kind of Compulsion 1903-1936*, Peter, Davison (ed.) London: Secker & Warburg, item 111, Hop-Picking Diary, 25 August-8 October 1931 pp 214-226

NEIL SMITH

Orwell, George (1998c) *The Complete Works of George Orwell, Vol. XI: Facing Unpleasant Facts 1937-1939*, Davison, Peter (ed.) London: Secker & Warburg, Appendix 1, item 518, Domestic Diary pp 264-268

Orwell in Kent, Bridge Books, 1970

NOTE ON THE CONTRIBUTOR

Neil Smith is an accountant who spent most of his career working for a large energy utility, latterly responsible for the company pension scheme. His interest in Orwell was sparked by reading *Down and Out in Paris and London* at the age of 19. He has been secretary of The Orwell Society since 2013 with a two-year 'break' as treasurer.

ARTICLE

Orwell's Status as Political Prophet on the Wane

Despite Orwell's continuing cultural ubiquity, Nicholas Harris argues that the ever-increasingly imprecise use of Orwell's work in political debate, most recently in our 'culture wars', may indicate that the status he enjoyed as a 20th century political prophet is on the wane.

In his essay on Rudyard Kipling, published in the February 1942 edition of *Horizon*, George Orwell writes that Kipling had reached 'the peculiar position of having been a by-word for fifty years', that parts of his work had been 'given almost Biblical status' and that he was 'the only English writer of our time who has added phrases to the language'. He concludes the essay with a typical Orwell construction: a long, precise and evocative list tracking Kipling's dissemination beyond the literary-minded to a broad popular audience:

'In his own lifetime, some of Kipling's poems travelled far beyond the bounds of the reading public, beyond the world of school-prize days, Boy Scout singsongs, limp-leather editions, pokerwork and calendars and out into the yet vaster world of the music halls' (Davison 2020a: 313-314). Orwell's famous thumbnail description of Dickens's visage – a 'nineteenth-century liberal, a free intelligence' who nonetheless seems 'generously angry' – has often been taken as an unconscious self-portrait (Orwell 2000: 78). But this description of Kipling's legacy, along with his 1931 aside about the 'large vague renown' that Thomas Carlyle still then enjoyed (Hitchens 2002: 45), far more accurately sketches the status Orwell retains today, seventy-two years after his death.

The posthumous fame and reverence George Orwell still commands is extraordinary, unknown to any writer but Shakespeare, and outstripping even him in political applicability. He has been a by-word for far longer than fifty years, his name now transformed into a versatile signifier for anything construed as bleak or authoritarian, and his phrases and coinages still echo through the English language. His twin masterpieces, *Animal Farm* (1945) and *Nineteen Eighty-Four* (1949), have sold around 50 million copies since his death and – through the turbine of post-war mass media: television, film, advertising and now the internet – have disseminated Orwell's image and ideas to an even greater audience (Rodden 2007: 8). As various scholars of Orwell's reception have shown, this incredible post-war reputation is largely explicable. The corpus of George Orwell – man and work rolled into one in the minds of many – came to be seen as the intellectual and literary reportage on the key decade when the Second World War was fought and the Cold War began, required reading for, as Timothy Garton Ash put it in 1998, anyone 'who wants to understand the twentieth century' (Garton Ash 1998).

The themes of Orwell's work (significantly truncated in the broad popular imagination to the totalitarian novels and the essays read as studies for those books like 'Notes on Nationalism' and 'Politics and the English Language') aligned so closely with the global twentieth century conflict between totalitarian ideologies and liberal capitalism that he was transformed into a political prophet. But he also captured the moral landscape at a more granular level. The importance of honesty and reason in an age of mass media, the role of the individual within a nightmarishly collectivised society, the threat of bio-surveillance and the potential for violent abuses of power under authoritarian governments – these were hallmarks of the 20th century's presiding ideologies and Orwell's work features them all. In short, as Christopher Hitchens hyperbolically put it fifty years on, Orwell was 'the man who confronted three of the great crises of the twentieth century [imperialism, fascism and communism] and got all three of them, so to speak, "right"' (Davison 2020b: ix).

ORWELL'S 'INTELLIGENCE OF PERCEPTION AND COURAGE OF PRINCIPLE'

Hitchens's typically forthright summary here introduces the parallel side of Orwell's main popular legacy: the received understanding of his character. Beginning with the obituaries after his death, it was established that to have seen so deeply into the currents of his time, Orwell must have possessed a clear-sightedness, an intelligence of perception and a courage of principle that made him personally worthy of special respect and emulation. V. S. Pritchett's 1950 encomium for 'the wintry conscience of a generation which in the thirties had heard the call to the rasher assumptions of political faith' set the tone for much that followed by emphasising Orwell's moral independence, apart from his easily led contemporaries (Meyers 1975: 294).

Of course, there was plenty of truth in this image. Orwell pursued the manipulation of the historical record around events in the Spanish Civil War relentlessly (and probably to the detriment of his own journalistic career) and he wrote early and forcefully about the crimes of the Soviet Union at a time when such talk was not at all fashionable (see Davison 2020a: 31-34; Davison 2020b: 216-272). But after his death, friends and then votaries magnified this capacity for frank confrontation, this 'power of facing unpleasant facts' as Orwell himself called it (Orwell 2000: 1), into the governing aspect of his personality. Famously for Lionel Trilling, Orwell represented 'the virtue of not being a genius, of fronting the world with nothing more than one's simple, direct, undeceived, intelligence', and this is the model he became for many of the 20th century's leading writers, journalists and intellectuals (Davison 2020b: x).

When Timothy Garton Ash finished his studies at Oxford, he spent the summer reading Orwell's work and then set off to Eastern Europe in search of a suitably Orwellian subject for his own writing (Collini 2016: 267-290). Orwell was the touchstone of Christopher Hitchens's entire career, and his study *Why Orwell Matters* is a gushing tribute to Orwell's intellectual fearlessness, arguing that the 'first thing to strike any student of Orwell's work and Orwell's life will be its *independence*' (Hitchens 2002: 8, emphasis in the original). John Rodden's chapter in the *Cambridge Companion to George Orwell* which he edited consists almost entirely of a list of rules for 'good thinking' that he has derived from Orwell's work (Rodden 2007: 179-189). And Tony Judt's polemic, *Ill Fares the Land*, takes Orwell's line that to 'see what is in front of one's nose needs a constant struggle' for its epigraph (Judt 2010: 11). All these writers sought to understand the 20th century and confront its threats with Orwell's courage, using the tools that they found, seemingly uniquely, in his work.

HOW COULD ORWELL REMAIN SO CENTRAL WHEN THE THREATS WERE CHANGING?

But following the end of the Cold War, even some of these most devoted disciples found themselves adrift. Before 1989, the grey, paranoid, rubber-truncheoned form of totalitarianism practised in the Soviet bloc which Orwell understood so instinctively had been an existential issue for the thinkers and populations of the West alike. But how could he remain so central when the threats and circumstances of the age were changing? Introducing an edition of Orwell's political writings at the turn of the millennium, Garton Ash pondered why should we 'still read Orwell on politics? Until 1989, the answer was plain. He was the writer who captured the essence of totalitarianism. ... Yet the world of *Nineteen Eighty-Four* ended in 1989' (Davison 2020a: xi). From the 1990s, when such ideological conflict was thought to be consigned to history, to the new conflicts of our time, it has become clear that we have

NICHOLAS HARRIS

evolved beyond and away from the 20th century's pathologies of communism, revolutionary ideology and political violence. At the start of the 'War on Terror' (also around the time of Orwell's centenary) there was a revival of Orwelliana by writers like Hitchens who attempted to lend the conflict a specious sense of Cold Warrior credibility; opponents of the wars, instead, targeted the 'Orwellian' rhetoric of its commanders-in-chief.

But certain assumptions of Orwell have clearly become dead anachronisms. Throughout Orwell's political life the most dynamic political movements in Europe were fascism and communism, and he consistently extrapolated from this that the state would command an ever-increasing role in human affairs. He always thought that the liberal capitalism of the late 19th and early 20th centuries was dead, leaving a political battle to take place over whether the authoritarian states of the future would be utilised to bring about totalitarianism or democratic socialism (see Davison 2020a: 415-435).

We now live in an era when the state has for some time seemed a notably supine institution, held hostage by multinational companies and terrorists independent of territory or culture. And, in general, the political nightmares of 21st century life have developed beyond Orwell's imagination and have thus necessitated new dystopias. Neil Postman's influential 1985 book *Amusing Ourselves to Death* (2010 [1985]) argued that it was Huxley's *Brave New World* (1932) which more accurately anticipated the late capitalist West, and there has been a revival of popular interest in Postman's work in the age of social media, the lyrics of the Arctic Monkeys' 'Tranquillity Base Hotel and Casino' referencing him much as Bowie's 'Diamond Dogs' once name-checked Orwell. And the satires of the modern world, from David Foster Wallace's *Infinite Jest* (1996) to Charlie Brooker's Channel 4 television series *Black Mirror* (2011-2014) and Dave Eggers's *The Circle* (2013), show that what we fear most today are dystopias of consumer excess facilitated by the forces of private capital, not the austere authoritarianism of Orwell's Ingsoc (Lynskey 2021: 254-256).

Though Orwell remains quotable in discussions of surveillance, Shoshana Zuboff, one of the leading scholars on the subject, has argued that the state-mandated telescreens he imagined (a crude technology inspired by the early television) bear little resemblance to the complex algorithms that tech companies use to indulge, and then track and exploit, our digital lives (Zuboff 2019). Ultimately, Orwell's analysis of totalitarianism is distinctly 20th century, a product of his own understanding of National Socialism and Stalinism, and his reading of once-modish thinkers such as James Burnham. As various critics have argued, at both the level of politics as well as detail, Orwell's visions in *Nineteen Eighty-Four* are satirical exaggerations of the 1940s, not a fantasy which anticipates our present concerns any longer (see also Meyers 2010: 136-140).

HOW ORWELL REMAINS ALIVE AND WELL

But this is not to say that Orwell's presence in contemporary discussion has substantially faded. While perhaps not nearly the diagnostician of the age he once was, the Orwell who served as inspiration to Hitchens and Judt, the unyielding intellectual who champions the unbreakable bond between freedom and truth, is alive and well. In order to maintain his relevance, the reference points to his work have shifted to mirror our contemporary concerns, most recently on the matter of free speech. 'If liberty means anything at all, it means the right to tell people what they do not want to hear' is certainly the line of Orwell's with the most currency in our present culture wars (see for instance Doyle 2021).

But he is most generally deployed to signify a diligent commitment to intellectual honesty in opposition to ideological obfuscation. For this modern usage at its most kitsch, see a video from Dr Jordan Peterson's *YouTube* channel entitled 'On Free Thought and Speech in London' (2018). Featuring a segment filmed alongside Orwell's statue outside the BBC's Broadcasting House in central London, Peterson praises Orwell as 'one of the first intellectuals in the West to sound the alarm about [totalitarianism] especially in the Soviet Union' and calls him one of his 'intellectual heroes'. Elsewhere, in part of a lecture entitled 'Identity politics and the Marxist lie of white privilege', Peterson (2017) speaks of Orwell's prescience about the USSR, and uses sections of the second half of *The Road to Wigan Pier* (1937) to present him as a shrewd analyst of the hidden *ressentiment* behind Soviet-sympathising Marxist activists. The not-too-subtle implication is that Peterson is on a similar mission today, exposing the pernicious influence of neo-Marxist intellectuals with Orwell's moral vigour.

More recently, in the culture wars on this side of the Atlantic, Orwell's usage has even extended to the vitriolic debates between gender-critical feminists and trans activists. In 2020, shortly after winning the Orwell Prize, Janice Turner wrote a column in *The Times* on this issue and concluded: 'Unlike the woke left, George Orwell didn't spend his life scrabbling to be on the "right side of history": he believed that telling the truth is in itself a revolutionary act' (Turner 2020). And when J. K. Rowling tweeted to her 14 million followers about changes to how the Scottish police record the gender of rapists with quotations from *Nineteen Eighty-Four*, she was making use of Orwell's reputation as someone who sees to the truth behind linguistic opacity (Horne 2021).

NICHOLAS HARRIS

These are just a few examples of Orwell's recent political deployments; see the afterword to paperback edition of Dorian Lynskey's *The Ministry of Truth* for his thoughts on other contemporary issues like statue-toppling (Lynskey 2021: 271-280). But when we witness Orwell being deployed in this way, one wonders exactly what authority is being appealed to. Of course, Orwell's writings do have some bearing on culture war concerns like freedom of speech, and he wrote particularly well about how the bounds of public debate can be narrowed voluntarily when writers and intellectuals do not face up to the truths that confront them (see Davison 2020a: 306-315). But his views were complex, and a few years before his most famous remarks on free speech, he wrote that the self-serving influence of newspaper owners was as great a cause of this narrowing of acceptable ideas – an argument one doesn't see repurposed today by well-paid newspaper columnists harking in the culture war (see Davison 2020a: 35).

More relevant for our purposes is why Orwell, above other thinkers from John Stuart Mill to Rosa Luxemburg who also wrote powerfully on free speech, is invoked in these debates; why was it to Orwell that the American commentariat turned during the presidency of Donald Trump? Is it because Orwell still anticipates our present predicament so well that his ideas are simply unavoidable? Or is it because having got these great 20th century questions right, he is still treated and taught as the supreme model for political reasoning, even as he becomes increasingly anachronistic? More cynically put, is it because his accumulated status as a 20th century political prophet provides useful rhetorical authority in any political discussion, so long as he can be shoehorned into it?

Imagine, for sake of discussion, a 19th century writer of similar dates to Orwell but a hundred years removed, a composite perhaps of Thomas Paine, William Hazlitt and William Cobbett. To borrow Hitchens's soundbite that Orwell 'got imperialism, fascism and communism right', imagine that this Victorian Orwell (a nineteenth century liberal, a free intelligence) had got three contentious, numinous issues right in his own time: slavery, democracy and industrialisation. It is perhaps harder to see what being 'right' in all these cases would look like, but one can at a stretch imagine a figure producing essays excoriating the evils of the slave trade, novels satirising hereditary rule and pamphlets warning of the rapid social change the Industrial Revolution might portend.

What role might such a figure have in our contemporary debates? Would they, like much of the writings of Paine, Cobbett, along with more famous figures of the day such as Thomas Carlyle, be regarded as of chiefly historical interest? Or would they still be held up as exemplary political thinkers, with much to tell us about how to confront the divisions that beset us decades hence? Are, in fact, many contemporary applications of Orwell the hollow echoes of a fading 20th century idolatry?

Orwell's posthumous reputation has been remarkable, indeed unique. But chiming so deeply with your time is not itself a guarantee of longevity. Rudyard Kipling, whose cultural penetration Orwell treats as a given in the essay with which we began, dated quickly in the second half of the 20th century and, such is his current infamy, that even previously anodyne pieces of his popular verse are now stripped from university buildings (*BBC News* 2018). Thomas Carlyle, whose status Orwell still acknowledged as late as 1931, is perhaps more comparable in having once been treated as a key political thinker as well as a popular phrase-maker (though we still unknowingly use his coinages 'environment', 'the cash nexus' and 'the dismal science'). In 1906, a poll of newly-elected Labour MPs showed that, after Ruskin and Dickens, Carlyle was still one of the main writers from whom they drew inspiration (none mentioned Marx) (Hunt 2006).

For a Labour MP to cite Carlyle in a speech today would confuse most of their listeners and disconcert the minority who are aware of his current, very faint popular reputation, mainly for his racism and support for autocratic politics. The reputations of even the most revered writers and thinkers can develop in ways previously unimagined, and though it is very difficult to imagine Orwell's undergoing quite such a metamorphosis, it is certainly possible. Much popular historical discussion currently involves the fundamental reassessment of previously adored figures from Orwell's time, like Churchill who, rather than a national hero, is nowadays regarded by many young people as a racist and crypto fascist. Indeed, I have had conversations with people my age who, thanks to his deployment by the political right as a free speech fundamentalist, regard Orwell as essentially a conservative figure and are unaware of his committed socialism. The judgement of time has a tendency to kick the pedestals away from many once-adored cultural ubiquities, while distorting and transforming the reputations of those who do endure.

ORWELL'S REPUTATION AT A CROSSROADS

Orwell's reputation, then, stands at something of a crossroads. Its first period, during which Orwell helped to define an entire political age and language, is very clearly over. Since the 1990s though, we have witnessed various attempts to draw a more universal set of principles from Orwell's work and apply them to contemporaneous contexts. But the roles of Noughties neocon and now free speech culture warrior have never managed to recapture Orwell's 20th century status. Orwell has found himself increasingly wrenched onto matters on which he has no real bearing, such as contemporary gender politics, one issue, I think it's fair to say, Orwell did not anticipate whatsoever.

That his legacy and reputation has become so diffuse is gradually emptying his figure of any grounded meaning, minimising, as John Rodden has recently argued, the actual Orwell of Jura, *Horizon*, the Spanish Civil War, Eileen, and Burma, in favour of 'Orwell', a versatile phantom summoned by anyone and everyone to serve their political ends (Rodden 2020).

Sometimes political texts formed in the heat of a historical moment contain such profundity that they long outlive their time of writing, such as Milton's call for freedom of expression in *Areopagitica* (1644) from which Orwell himself drew inspiration (Orwell 2000: 328). Over the coming years and decades, it will become more apparent whether Orwell's work is fated for the same timelessness, durable through several centuries. But the noise and confusion around his reputation at present is only further distorting what that work could mean.

Perhaps this is part of the process by which Orwell is forgotten, at least as a major popular figure, and becomes historical, as Carlyle and so many other thinkers who were colossal in their time have faded from view. But allowing the large vague renown of 'Orwell' to perish may, in fact, ensure that a less grand, but more genuine Orwell lives on, before the name they share bursts into a meaningless blaze of ambiguity.

REFERENCES

BBC News (2018) Manchester students deface poem by 'racist' Kipling, 19 July. Available online at https://www.bbc.co.uk/news/uk-england-manchester-44884913, accessed on 23 January 2022

Collini, Stefan (2016) *Common Writing*, Oxford: Oxford University Press

Davison, Peter (ed.) (2020a) *Orwell's Politics*, London: Penguin Classics

Davison, Peter (ed.) (2020b) *Orwell in Spain*, London: Penguin Classics

Doyle, Andrew (2021) Your right to think and act freely is CANCELLED, *Daily Mail*, 25 February. Available online at https://www.dailymail.co.uk/news/article-9301389/ANDREW-DOYLE-right-think-act-freely-CANCELLED.html, accessed on 23 January 2022

Garton Ash, Timothy (1998) Orwell in 1998, *New York Review of Books*, 22 October. Available online at https://www.nybooks.com/articles/1998/10/22/orwell-in-1998/, accessed on 23 January 2022

Hunt, Tristram (2006) Labour goes back to its roots, *Guardian*, 5 February. Available online at https://www.theguardian.com/politics/2006/feb/05/education.schools, accessed on 23 January 2022

Horne, Marc (2021) Gender code akin to *1984*, Harry Potter creator J. K. Rowling says, *The Times*, 30 December 2021. Available online (behind a paywall) at https://www.thetimes.co.uk/article/gender-code-akin-to-1984-harry-potter-creator-jk-rowling-says-stqr9gzj9, accessed on 23 January 2022

Judt, Tony (2010) *Ill Fares the Land*, London: Allen Lane

Lynskey, Dorian (2021) *The Ministry of Truth: A Biography of George Orwell's 1984*, London: Picador, second edition

Meyers, Jeffrey (1975) *George Orwell: The Critical Heritage*, London: Routledge and Kegan Paul

Meyers, Jeffrey (2010) *Orwell: Life and Art*, Urbana, Illinois: University of Illinois Press

Orwell, George (2000) *Essays*, London: Penguin Modern Classics

Peterson, Jordan (2017) Identity politics and the Marxist lie of white privilege, *YouTube*, 13 November 2017. Available online at https://www.youtube.com/watch?v=PfH8IG7Awk0&t=3345s accessed on 23 January 2022

Peterson, Jordan (2018) On free thought and speech in London, *YouTube*, 31 October. Available online at https://www.youtube.com/watch?v=XKadDgpq5nU, accessed on 23 January 2022

Postman, Neil (2010 [1985]) *Amusing Ourselves to Death*, London: Methuen

Rodden, John (ed.) (2007) *The Cambridge Companion to George Orwell*, Cambridge: Cambridge University Press

Rodden, John (2020) *Becoming George Orwell*, Princeton, New Jersey: Princeton University Press

Turner, Janice (2020) The woke left is the new Ministry of Truth, *The Times*, 11 July 2020. Available online (behind a paywall) at https://www.thetimes.co.uk/article/the-woke-left-is-the-new-ministry-of-truth-vmrgt823b, accessed on 23 January 2022

Zuboff, Shoshana (2019) The surveillance threat is not what Orwell imagined, *Time*, 6 June. Available online at https://time.com/5602363/george-orwell-1984-anniversary-surveillance-capitalism/, accessed on 23 January 2022

NOTE ON THE CONTRIBUTOR

Nicholas Harris graduated with a degree in History from the University of Cambridge, in 2020, and with a Master's in Magazine Journalism from City, University of London, in 2021. He is now an editorial trainee at *UnHerd*, and he has also contributed features and book reviews to *Prospect*, the *Literary Review*, the *Mail on Sunday*, the *Daily Telegraph* and the *Spectator*. In May 2020, he won The Orwell Society's Young Journalist Award, and he thanks the Orwell Society for their generous support in the writing of this article.

Beyond the 'Nancy Poet' Jibe: Orwell and Auden

Richard Lance Keeble.

Orwell's relationship with the poet W. H. Auden is fascinating and constantly evolving. Both begin their UK careers as teachers; both have some of their first writings published in the *Adelphi*, edited in the early 1930s by Richard Rees. And both go to the Spanish Civil War. Orwell damns Auden over a line in his poem 'Spain' and mocks his circle of poets in *The Road to Wigan Pier* and in his essay 'Inside the Whale' (the subject of Ian McEwan's Orwell Memorial Lecture in London, on 26 November 2021).[1] Yet Auden does not take offence, changes the line and then removes the poem altogether from his collected works – and later goes out of his way to praise Orwell.

INTO THE SPANISH CAULDRON

Orwell leaves for Spain just before Christmas 1936 with the intention of fighting on the Republican side in the civil war which has erupted on 19 July after a part of the army under General Franco attempts to seize power from the Popular Front Republican government. Impressed with the revolutionary fervour he witnesses in Barcelona, he joins the POUM militia. After a spell on the frontline, Orwell and some of his Independent Labour Party comrades return to Barcelona where, in May 1937, he witnesses the street fighting between the communists (determined to take control of the Republican cause) and the anarchists and Trotskyists. Back on the Huesca front, Orwell is shot in the neck by a sniper on 20 May and narrowly escapes death. After recovering in hospital, he and his newly-wed wife, Eileen, who has joined him in Spain, decide to escape. And with the communists hard on their heels, determined to capture - and maybe even torture and kill - them, they escape into France and safety (Bowker 2003: 225).

Auden departs for Spain on 11 January 1937 determined to serve as an ambulance driver for the Republican cause. He is by this time already a media celebrity and his departure is covered in both the communist *Daily Worker* and *Sunday Times*. In Barcelona, he meets Cyril Connolly and they go for a walk in the gardens at

Montjuich. When he disappears behind a bush to urinate, he is immediately arrested by two militia men and is only released after Connolly produces a letter of recommendation from Harry Pollitt, general secretary of the British Communist Party (Lewis 1998: 287). Failing to find work in both Barcelona and Valencia as an ambulance driver, Auden ends up broadcasting propaganda for the Republican government. Biographer Charles Osborne comments: 'But as his broadcasts were in English and were transmitted over a radius of not much more than fifty miles, they cannot have been of the slightest practical use. … Disillusioned, he remained in Spain for several weeks returning to England early in March' (1995 [1980]: 135).

WRITING FOR THE REPUBLIC

Soon after arriving in Spain, Auden sends a report which is published in the *New Statesman and Nation* under the title 'Impressions of Valencia' on 30 January 1937 (ibid: 137-138). It begins rather poetically: 'The pigeons fly about the square in brilliant sunshine, warm as a fine English May.' Then it suddenly shifts its focus: 'In the centre of the square, surrounded all day long by crowds and surmounted by a rifle and fixed bayonet, 15ft high is an enormous map of the Civil War, rather prettily illustrated after the manner of railway posters urging one to visit Lovely Lakeland or Sunny Devon. Badajoz is depicted by a firing party; a hanged man represents Huelva …' Auden comments on the somewhat gruesome posters: one, a photomontage, shows a bombed baby lying on a field of aeroplanes. He continues: 'Today a paragraph in the daily papers announces that since there have been incidents at the entrances to cabarets, these will in future be closed at nine pm. … Since the Government moved here the hotels are crammed to bursting with officials, soldiers and journalists. There are porters at the station and a few horse-cabs, but no taxis, in order to save petrol. Food is plentiful, indeed an hotel lunch is heavier than one could wish. There is a bullfight in aid of the hospitals; there is a variety show where an emaciated looking tap-dancer does an extremely sinister dance of the machine-guns.'

Finally, celebrating the ways the revolutionary spirit is allowing people to finally taste true freedom, he writes: 'For a revolution is really taking place, not an odd shuffle or two in cabinet appointments. In the last six months these people have been learning what it is to inherit their own country, and once a man has tasted freedom he will not lightly give it up; freedom to choose for himself and to organize his life. … That is why, only eight hours away at the gates of Madrid where this wish to live has no possible alternative expression than the power to kill, General Franco has already lost

RICHARD LANCE KEEBLE

two professional armies and is in the process of losing a third' (ibid).

Back in England, Orwell finds many of the men he had been fighting alongside are being falsely accused of seeking to undermine the revolution. So he composes his first-hand frontline account, *Homage to Catalonia*, in a state of 'white hot anger' during the second half of 1937. And this helps account partly for the extraordinary freedom of his writing, its flair, outspokenness, its creative, imaginative, literary richness – and its use of an eclectic range of fictional techniques. Victor Gollancz, his usual publisher, objects to his links with POUM and the anarchists so it is eventually published by Fredric Warburg on 25 April 1938. While generally well reviewed, it sells only 700 copies during Orwell's life and there is no US edition until 1952 (Keeble 2015).

ORWELL AND THE AUDEN CLIQUE

While in Spain, Orwell's account of his two months in early 1936 investigating the plight of the miners, the poor and the unemployed in the north of England, *The Road to Wigan Pier*, is published. Early on, after describing in graphic detail his experience going down a coal mine and witnessing the men, nearly naked, toiling underground, he writes: 'More than anyone else, perhaps, the miner can stand as the type of the manual worker, not only because his work is so exaggeratedly awful, but also because it is so vitally necessary and yet so remote from our experience. … It raises in you a momentary doubt about your own status as an "intellectual" and a superior person generally. For it is brought home to you, at least while you are watching, that it is only because miners sweat their guts out that superior persons can remain superior. You and I and the editor of the *Times Lit Supp* and the Nancy poets and the Archbishop of Canterbury and Comrade X, author of *Marxism for Infants* – all of us really owe the comparative decency of our lives to poor drudges underground, blackened to the eyes, with their throats full of coal dust, driving their shovels forward with arms and belly muscles of steel' (1980 [1937]: 138-139).

The 'Nancy poets' jibe is clearly directed at Auden and his circle many of them known to be homosexuals. According to biographer Jeffrey Meyers, Orwell actually experiences guilty homosexual feelings and uses the 'Nancy boy' condemnation as a way 'to distance himself from these feelings' (Meyers 2000: 38).

In the second section of the book, Orwell, idiosyncratically and provocatively, explores his own background and the current state of socialism in Britain. In the process, he delights in mocking socialist supporters: 'As with the Christian religion, the worst advertisement for Socialism is its adherents' (1980 [1937]: 203). As a result, he argues, artists of any note can never be persuaded to join the

Socialist fold. Next follows another jibe at Auden and his circle: 'A whole generation has grown up more or less in familiarity with the idea of Socialism; and yet the high-water mark, so to speak, of Socialist literature is W. H. Auden, a sort of gutless Kipling, and the even feebler poets who are associated with him. ... It is certain that in Western Europe Socialism has produced no literature worth having. ... The real Socialist writers, the propagandist writers, have always been dull, empty windbags – Shaw, Barbusse, Upton Sinclair, William Morris, Waldo Frank etc.' (ibid: 208-209).

Moreover, when approached by Nancy Cunard to contribute to her *Authors Take Sides on the Spanish Civil War*, Orwell's response, according to biographer D. J. Taylor, is 'one of the most intemperate paragraphs he ever committed to paper':

> Will you please stop sending me this bloody rubbish. ... I am not one of your fashionable pansies like Auden and Spender, I was six months in Spain, most of the time fighting, I have a bullet-hole in me at present and I am not going to write blah about defending democracy or gallant little anybody (Taylor 2003: 245).

In contrast, Auden wrote for Cunard:

> I support the Valencia government in Spain because its defeat by the forces of International Fascism would be a major disaster for Europe. It would make a European war more probable; and the spread of Fascist Ideology and practice to countries as yet comparatively free from them, which would inevitably follow upon a Fascist victory in Spain, would create an atmosphere in which the creative artist and all who care for justice, liberty and culture would find it impossible to work or even exist.[2]

Significantly, Orwell is at pains to retract the 'gutless Kipling' comment in his essay 'Inside the Whale', of 1940. He writes: 'As a sort of criticism this was quite unworthy, indeed, it was merely a spiteful remark' (1980 [1940]: 507). But this retraction does not stop him from engaging in a new attack on the Auden Circle (incorporating figures such as Stephen Spender, Cecil Day-Lewis, Louis MacNeice, Christopher Isherwood, Arthur Calder-Marshall, Edward Upward, Alec Brown and Philip Henderson) which Philip Bounds describes as 'one of the most scathing Orwell ever wrote' (Bounds 2016 [2009]: 112).[3] The leading writers of the Joyce-Eliot 1920s generation were of very varied origins, few of them passed through the ordinary English educational mill (the best of them, bar Lawrence, were not English) and most of them had had at some time to struggle against poverty, neglect and even downright persecution. 'On the other hand, nearly all the younger writers fit easily into the public school-university-Bloomsbury pattern. The few who are of proletarian origin are of the kind that is declassed early in life, first by means of scholarships and then by the bleaching tub of "London culture"' (1980 [1940]: 507).

To a certain extent, Orwell spoils his argument against Auden by criticising the poem 'You're leaving now, and it's up to you boys' for being 'pure scout-master, the exact note of the ten-minutes' straight talk on the dangers of self abuse' (ibid). In fact, it's from Day-Lewis's early volume of poetry, *The Magnetic Mountain*.[4]

But Orwell is intent on damning Auden & Co: 'Marxized' literature, he suggests, has moved no nearer to the masses. 'Even allowing for the time-lag, Auden and Spender are somewhat farther from being popular writers than Joyce and Eliot, let alone Lawrence.' Above all he suggests that Auden's Circle is using communism to express a range of notions which are largely reactionary. Thus, their support for the USSR is basically a manifestation of displaced patriotism. As Bounds summarises: 'Raised in their bourgeois homes and their public schools to put love of country before everything else, people like Auden, Spender and C. Day-Lewis longed to be the loyal servants of a nation state. The only problem was that they could no longer give their loyalty to England, since the inglorious history of the post-war period had gone a long way to shattering their illusions about it. Their solution was to transfer their allegiance to Stalin's Russia' (Bounds 2016 [2009]: 112).

Orwell is not alone in his criticisms of the Auden Circle. But many communists insist that their essential commitment is to fascism. Edgell Rickword, in the first issue of *Left Review*, in October 1934, argues that the young writers of the left have, in fact, been gripped by a mood of irrationalism. The fascist regimes in Germany and Italy provide a focus for their patriotism and their adolescent hunger for violence (ibid: 114). While in *Partisan Review*, the US leftist journal to which Orwell is to contribute during the war years, F. W. Dupee (1938) acknowledges that Auden is the leader of his group but continues: 'He lacks a critical intelligence; and one cannot be sure whether the hub is turning the spokes or the spokes the hub. At present we may guess that Auden is captive of his friends' reformist gentility; their politically fostered blindness, the rationalized prudence of their democratic front against fascism – as though fascism were a respecter of prudence, of democracy.'

'WAR OF WORDS' OVER 'SPAIN'

Orwell follows up his own comments in 'Inside the Whale' with a blistering attack on Auden's poem 'Spain', published in May 1937, by Nancy Cunard, in her series of poems in English, French and Spanish – with the royalties donated to Medical Aid for Spain.[5] A longish poem of almost 100 lines, it was acclaimed by critics of the day as one of the best to have come out of the conflict. As Osborne comments: 'It is a mature, complex and moving poem not so much about Spain as about political struggle and moral choice. To some extent it is an abstract and rather cold examination of its subject' (Osborne 1995 [1980]: 139). The poem contrasts the hoped-for glories of the socialist future with the hum-drum tasks needed to bring about that future. A line to which Orwell takes particular exception goes: 'The conscious acceptance of guilt in the necessary murder' which seems to imply that one of the 'necessary' tasks is that of committing political assassinations.

Orwell typically balances his critique, beginning by acknowledging that the poem 'is one of the few decent things to have been written about the Spanish war' (Orwell 1980 [1940]: 510). He continues:

> … notice the phrase 'necessary murder'. It could only be written by a person to whom murder is at most a *word*. Personally I would not speak so lightly of murder. It so happens that I have seen the bodies of numbers of murdered men – I don't mean killed in battle, I mean murdered. Therefore I have some conception of what murder means – the terror, the hatred, the howling relatives, the post-mortems, the blood, the smells. The Hitlers and Stalins find murder necessary, but they don't advertise their callousness, and they don't speak of it as murder; it is 'liquidation', 'elimination' or some other soothing phrase. Mr Auden's amoralism is only possible if you are the kind of person who is always somewhere else when the trigger is pulled. So much of left-wing thought is a kind of playing with fire by people who don't even know that the fire is hot (ibid) (italics in the original).

Orwell concludes: 'On the whole, the literary history of the thirties seems to justify the opinion that a writer does well to keep out of politics' (ibid: 512). Samuel Hynes comments (1976: 387): 'This is an odd conclusion to get from the author of *The Road to Wigan Pier* and *Homage to Catalonia*, but it became a commonplace of the Thirties Myth: for a decade, so the Myth goes, young writers were seduced into political actions that they didn't understand, and both politics and literature suffered.'

Initially, Auden responds defensively to Orwell's critique of the 'necessary murder' phrase, saying: 'I was not excusing totalitarian crimes but only trying to say what, surely, every decent person thinks if he finds himself unable to adopt the absolute pacifist solution. (1) To kill another human being is always murder and should never be called anything else.[6] (2) In a war, the members of two rival groups try to murder the opponents. (3) If there is such a thing as a just

RICHARD LANCE KEEBLE

war, then murder can be necessary for the sake of justice.'[7]

To the consternation of many of his admirers, Auden accepts the King's Gold Medal for Poetry from George VI. Then, leaving – very controversially – with his friend Christopher Isherwood for America in January 1939, Auden converts to Christianity in the following year. Significantly, he changes the controversial line in 'Spain' (now renamed 'Spain 1937') in his collection *Another Time* (1940), to read: 'To-day the inevitable increase in the chances of death;/The conscious acceptance of guilt in the fact of murder.' Another passage referring to the 'people's army' is also dropped. Edward Mendelson argues that Auden's revision is published a month before 'Inside the Whale' so he could not have been reacting to Orwell's criticisms (Mendelson 1977: 424-425; Crick 1980: 615 n.1).

During the 1950s, Auden comes to believe that writers hold no responsibility to promote political causes. He crosses out the two lines of Cyril Connolly's copy of 'Spain' and scribbles in the margin: 'This is a lie' while copies of other friends are treated in a similar way (Osborne 1995 [1980]: 140). In 1967, when Auden's *Collected Shorter Poems 1937-1957* are published, the entire poem is excluded. When Alan Bold approaches Auden to include the poem in his *Penguin Book of Socialist Verse* (1970), he replies: 'As you know, I disapprove of my poem "Spain", in particular the last two lines which assert that immoral doctrine (it may be Marxist, but it certainly isn't socialist) that whoever succeeds historically is just.'[8]

The historian E.P. Thompson, author of *The Making of the English Working Class* (1963), takes issue with both Orwell and Auden. The phrase 'necessary murder', he suggests, has nothing to do with 'political murders': 'The volunteers who joined the Spanish Republican cause (of whom Orwell himself was one) were committed, as soldiers, to the activity of "murder"; Auden no doubt chose the word with care to emphasise, exactly, that soldiering, in whatever cause, is not "all very edifying" and that killing entails an "acceptance of guilt"; but this "murder" Auden then believed was "necessary" because – as the entire structure of the poem in its first version worked to establish – he believed that the Spanish War was a confrontation of critical historical importance' (Thompson 1978). Thompson continues: 'Orwell, by indicting the cause as a swindle *and* by ridiculing the motives of those who supported it, unbent the very "springs of action". He sowed within the disenchanted generation the seeds of a profound self-distrust. Socialist idealism was not only discounted, it was also *explained away*, as the function of middle-class guilt, frustration or ennui' (ibid, italics in the original).

William Empson is also very critical of Auden's decision to cut the poem. He writes, in the *United Review* of August 1940: 'He [Auden] has also, very oddly, cut out the best verses, the comparisons of aspects of suburban fretfulness with the machine of war which they are supposed to have engendered. And the "conscious acceptance of guilt in the necessary murder".'[9] And the poet, polymath, television critic and wit, Clive James, comments on the decision to cut 'Spain' from his corpus: 'Auden was denying the pluralism of his own personality. It was his privilege to do so if he wanted to, but it was remarkable how tamely this crankily simplistic reinterpretation of his own creative selfhood was accepted.'[10]

AUDEN'S PRAISE FOR ORWELL

Soon after the controversy over the 'Spain' poem, Auden and Isherwood contribute an article to *Vogue* magazine (of all outlets) on 'Young British writers on the way up' (Auden and Isherwood 1939). Before moving on to (the now sadly forgotten) Ralph Bates[11] and Arthur Calder-Marshall, the focus falls on Orwell. Auden and Isherwood write:

> Orwell's career has been extraordinary. Educated at Eton he has become a voluntary exile from his own class, preferring to inhabit the bitter and sordid world of the unemployed. A period of service with the Burmese police produced *Burmese Days*, a brilliant attack on British imperialism in the East. *Burmese Days* is the only novel that can bear comparison with Forster's *Passage to India*. Orwell lacks Forster's humanity. His irony is coarser, his satire less delicate. But *Burmese Days* is, nevertheless, a thrilling and moving story of one man's failure in his struggle with the official machine. Returning to Europe, Orwell wandered about, acquiring the terrible experiences which are recorded in *The Road to Wigan Pier*, *The Clergyman's Daughter* and *Down and Out in Paris and London*. Not since Jack London's *People of the Abyss* has anyone written so frankly about the Lower Depths of English life and its inhabitants, the miserable, huddled figures in their bundles of rags whom you can see any evening trying to snatch a few moments of police-disturbed sleep on the benches of the Embankment and Trafalgar Square. When the Spanish civil war broke out, Orwell went to fight on the Loyalist side. While operating a machine gun he was severely wounded in the throat and for some time almost lost the use of his voice. Another book, in some ways his best, has been the result.

Auden clearly holds no grudges against Orwell and is keen to praise him when given the chance. Orwell, when literary editor of *Tribune*, which he joins after quitting the BBC in November 1943, displays a similar inability to sustain personal hostilities over a long period and reprints an article on Kipling by Auden (whose wartime departure for America he deplores) (Bowker 2003: 304).

Much later in his career, just two years before his death in 1973, Auden uses a review in the *Spectator* of the four volumes of *The Collected Essays, Journalism and Letters of George Orwell*, edited by Sonia Orwell and Ian Angus, to compose what amounts to a very moving, somewhat idiosyncratic and (in places) misguided, 1,700-word tribute to the author of *Nineteen Eighty-Four*.[12] He writes:

> Among the writers of this century, he stands out, like Hilaire Belloc, as a master of unadorned English prose. Even when one disagrees with what he is saying, one has to admire the vigour and lucidity with which he says it. Like the Austrian, Karl Kraus, he knew that corruption of the language must corrupt society: hence his admirable essay on 'Politics and the English Language' (I wish he had written one on political and military euphemisms). As a novelist, he is, I think, most successful when he is least 'fictional', that is to say, when he narrates what he himself has personally felt and witnessed. Though I am very glad for his sake that he wrote *Animal Farm* and *1984*, since they freed him from financial anxieties, neither, in my opinion, quite comes off. When one compares his encounters with the poor in the early nineteen-thirties with those of his great predecessor, Henry Mayhew, in the eighteen-fifties, one is struck, and saddened, by the decline in their powers of verbal expression. Compared with the Dickensian exuberance of Mayhew's interviewees, Orwell's seem almost inarticulate. I rather fear the cause may be universal elementary education, which has destroyed their instinctive native speech, but not trained them to do more than read the cheaper newspapers.

He continues: 'About other writers he shows keen insights and astonishing fair-mindedness. Though himself a man of strong political and moral convictions, he is always ready to recognize aesthetic merit in those of whose politics and morals he disapproves …'

He goes on to criticise Orwell for failing to understand the poets of the 1930s – including himself. They were, Orwell wrote, didactic, political writers, aesthetically conscious but more interested in subject-matter than technique. Auden writes:

> To this, I can only say, that all my life I have been more interested in poetic technique than anything else. What is true is that I am technically more conservative, more conscious of my debt to the nineteenth century (Yeats was too, for that matter) than poets like Eliot and Pound. Then, aside from a few plays, very little of the poetry I wrote in that decade

was overtly political: basically I have always thought of myself as a comic poet. More seriously, he charges us with refusing to admit that we were bourgeois. The term bourgeois, like proletariat, has no meaning in English-speaking countries, but if he means that I was ashamed to be, like himself, professional upper middle class, I have never thought of myself as anything else. At times, to be sure, I wrote satires about my class, but one can only satirise what one knows at first hand.

He next challenges Orwell's views on socialism: 'What Orwell seems to have hoped for was a Socialist (non-Communist) party which would be elected by an overwhelming majority and, like the Swedish Socialist Party, stay in power for decades, so that it would have nothing to fear from rival political parties. It will crush any open revolt promptly and cruelly, but it will interfere very little with the spoken and written word. Political parties with different names will still exist, revolutionary sects will still be publishing their newspapers and making as little impression as ever.'

Orwell is too optimistic. 'As a commentator on the contemporary political and social scene, he reminds me of Cobbett: he exhibits the same independence of party and the same vigour. Both of them, too, were not under the illusion that political action can solve all problems.'

Auden still misses Orwell: 'Today, reading his reactions to events in the war and the immediate years after the war, my first thought is: O how I wish Orwell were still alive, so that I could read his comments on contemporary events.' Given Auden's conversion, it is not surprising that he moves on to question Orwell's views on Christianity:

> He did, I think, have one blind spot. His fanatic, essentially religious hatred of Christianity, prevented him from seriously studying the subject. Thus, while I am sure he was well read in Communist literature, I very much doubt if he had read much theology or ecclesiastical history. He seems to have imagined that Christianity, like Manicheism and Buddhism, is an 'other-wordly' religion. In fact, from the accession of Constantine to the present day, the charge which all too often can justly be brought against the Churches, both Catholic and Protestant, is that they have been all too 'worldly', all too willing to make shady deals with temporal powers that would protect their power and wealth. The English Catholic apologists of this century, Belloc, Chesterton, Beachcomber etc., all had very definite views about politics, society, history. One may disagree with them – I do myself – but the one thing one cannot accuse them of is a lack of concern for the things of this world.

RICHARD LANCE KEEBLE

He suspects the cause for his hatred of Christianity probably lies in his experiences at his 'nasty' prep-school, St Cyprian's. 'I also suspect that his upbringing in early childhood had more effect on his sensibility and character than he realized.'

Yet he ends the review on a surprising and paradoxical note: 'If I were asked to name people whom I considered true Christians, the name George Orwell is one of the first that would come to my mind.'

CONCLUSION

The Orwell/Auden relationship is particularly interesting since it shows how two writers can fundamentally disagree on a topic and yet later graciously acknowledge the other's personal and literary qualities. Orwell regrets using the 'Nancy poets' jibe at Auden, Spender and Day-Lewis and after Spender, on the suggestion of Cyril Connolly, visits Orwell while he is recovering from an attack of TB at Preston Hall Sanatorium, in Kent, in 1938, the two men become friends. He apologises for making 'offensive remarks' about 'parlour Bolsheviks such as Auden and Spender' (Shelden 1991: 322; Crick 1980: 361) and he is never again to use the phrases 'Nancy' or 'pansy' poets. As Orwell later tells Connolly about Spender: 'Funny, I always used him & the rest of that gang as symbols of the pansy Left ... but when I met him in person I liked him so much & and was sorry for the things I had said about him' (Bowker 2003: 236). And while working for the BBC as a talks producer from 1941-1943, he praises Auden's poem 'Spain' as a 'very good' war poem (Taylor 2003: 314).

Likewise, Auden, despite the spat over 'Spain', maintains a constant (though critical) admiration for Orwell – praising him in print when the opportunity arises.

- The author thanks L. J. Hurst for his comments on a draft but remains solely responsible for all the contents. An early version of this article was published at https://orwellsociety.com/beyond-the-nancy-poet-jibe-orwell-and-auden/.

NOTES

[1] In his excellent, wide-ranging talk – and in the Q and A afterwards – McEwan highlights Orwell's 'generosity' towards Henry Miller's passivity and apolitical attitudes – and compares Orwell's views on the political engagement of the writer with those of Albert Camus. He makes only a passing reference to Orwell's critique of the Auden Circle (to whom he is not quite as generous) towards the end of the Q and A. See https://t.co/fviIW9uqCi?amp=1. The lecture appears as Outside the whale: George Orwell, politics and the role of the imagination in a time of crisis, *New Statesman*, 10 December 2021-6 January 2022 pp 36-42

[2] See Calver, Katherine Elizabeth (2014) *Authors Take Sides on the Spanish Civil War: A Dossier*. Part of a PhD thesis, Boston University. Available online at https://open.bu.edu/bitstream/handle/2144/15314/Calver_bu_0017E_10741.pdf p. 63

[3] Samuel Hynes comments: 'The only surprising names here are the last two. Alec Brown was a Marxist who had written *The Fate of the Middle Classes* (reviewed unfavourably by Orwell in the *Adelphi*), and a novel, *Daughters of Albion* (described by Orwell as "a huge wad of mediocre stuff"); Henderson was a Marxist literary critic, author of *The Novel Today* which Orwell had called "badly written and thoroughly dull" in a review in the *New English Weekly*). The two are inserted here for an obvious reason – to increase the communist content of the list, and to do so with two obviously inferior writers' (Hynes 1976: 388)

[4] L. J. Hurst comments: 'Davison correctly attributes this to Day-Lewis, but he fails to note that Orwell's confusion was understandable since Day-Lewis's poem is almost identical to Auden's earlier "Since you are going to begin to-day". Contemporary readers probably would have made the mental correction, keeping up with Orwell's argument. (It also indicates the breadth of Orwell's reading that he should have been able to quote poets who were only being published in small magazines and in slim collections.)' (in email to author, 27 November 2021)

[5] See Calver, Katherine Elizabeth (2014) *Authors Take Sides on the Spanish Civil War: A Dossier* pp 364-366

[6] Patrick Hamilton makes the same point (controversially) in his 1929 play *Rope*. Significantly, when Alfred Hitchcock directs a film version in 1948 this aspect of the drama is missing. Perhaps so soon after the war, it is difficult for many to consider all killing (even of Nazis) as 'murder'

[7] See https://c20poetry.wordpress.com/2013/03/28/auden-orwell-and-murder/

[8] See Auden's 'Spain': A close study, by Ramkrishna Bhattacharya. Available online at https://www.academia.edu/12367161/Audens_Spain_A_Close_Study p. 5

[9] Ibid p. 3

[10] Ibid p. 10

[11] Bates's *Lean Men* (1936), about olive growers in Spain, has been hailed as a pioneering 'proletarian' novel. He fought for a while with the International Brigades during the Spanish Civil War. He later moved to America where he became professor of creative writing and English literature at New York University. Details of MI5 surveillance of Bates is included in Richard Knott's *The Secret War Against the Arts: How MI5 Targeted Left-Wing Writers and Artists 1936-1956* (Pen and Sword, Barnsley, 2020)

[12] See http://archive.spectator.co.uk/article/16th-january-1971/18/w-h-auden-on-george-orwell

REFERENCES

Auden, W. H. and Isherwood, Christopher (1939) Young British writers on the way up, *Vogue*, 15 August. Available online at https://archive.vogue.com/article/1939/8/young-british-writers-on-the-way-up

Bounds, Philip (2016 [2009]) *Orwell & Marxism*, London: I. B. Tauris

Bowker, Gordon (2003) *George Orwell*, London: Little, Brown

Crick, Bernard (1980) *George Orwell: A Life*, Harmondsworth, Middlesex: Penguin

Dupee, F. W. (1938) The English literary left, *Partisan Review*, Vol. 5, No. 3 pp 11-21. Available online at http://www.bu.edu/partisanreview/books/PR1938V5N3/HTML/files/assets/basic-html/index.html#18

Hynes, Samuel (1976) *The Auden Generation: Literature and Politics in England in the 1930s*, London: Bodley Head

Keeble, Richard Lance (2015) Orwell and the war reporter's imagination, Keeble, Richard Lance (ed.) *George Orwell Now!* New York: Peter Lang pp 209-224

Lewis, Jeremy (1998) *Cyril Connolly: A Life*, London: Pimlico

RICHARD LANCE KEEBLE

Mendelson, Edward (1977) *The English Auden*, London: Faber & Faber

Meyers, Jeffrey (2000) *Orwell: Wintry Conscience of a Generation*, London and New York: W. W. Norton & Company

Orwell, George (1980 [1937]) *The Road to Wigan Pier*, in the *Collected Non-Fiction*, London: Secker & Warburg/Octopus pp 123-232

Orwell, George (1980 [1940]) Inside the Whale, in the *Collected Non-Fiction*, London: Secker & Warburg/Octopus pp 494-520

Osborne, Charles (1995 [1980]) *W. H. Auden: The Life of a Poet*, London: Michael O'Mara Books

Shelden, Michael (1991) *Orwell: The Authorised Biography*, London: Heinemann

Taylor, D. J. (2003) *Orwell: The Life*, London: Chatto & Windus

Thompson, E. P. (1978) Outside the Whale, in *The Poverty of Theory and Other Essays*, London: Merlin. Available online at https://www.marxists.org/archive/thompson-ep/1978/outside-whale.htm

NOTE ON THE CONTRIBUTOR

Richard Lance Keeble was the chair of The Orwell Society 2013-2020. His latest book, *Orwell's Moustache*, has just been published by Abramis, of Bury St Edmunds.

ARTICLE

Orwell, Radio and the Propaganda War

Orwell's association with wartime radio is most commonly referenced in connection with his propaganda work for the Indian Section of the BBC's Eastern Service. The background events that resulted in his BBC appointment and the propaganda work that he did for the corporation is an interesting, although seldom told story. Moreover, in working for the BBC, did Orwell betray his principles? Ron Bateman assesses the arguments.

Following the declaration of war in September 1939, the British government did not have to wait long to discover where India stood in terms of supporting the national effort. A statement on behalf of the Indian National Congress Independence Party was presented to the war cabinet by the secretary of state for India on 27 September, indicating that 'India was in full sympathy with the allies, but any co-operation would be withheld until a full statement from the British government of their war aims in their application to India was forthcoming'. The cabinet unanimously agreed that it would be undesirable to enter into any formal commitments at this early stage, and responded that without Britain's help India was virtually defenceless against external aggression (National Archive 1939).

The government was more worried that the BBC had ceased to transmit news bulletins to India, and criticised the corporation's indifference towards the listening public in Britain's most treasured imperial possession. There was a critical need to keep subject peoples informed through regular news broadcasts and commentaries, and the BBC needed to up its game considerably if it were to avoid stinging criticism from MPs that it had ceased to relay news to India at the start of the war, essentially giving Germany a free run. Such criticism was inevitable; Berlin was speaking to India in half a dozen languages including Hindustani, and immediate action was required to put the BBC on at least an equal footing with Germany. In November 1939, the Empire Service was renamed the Overseas Service and, thereafter, it continued to expand as the number of staff required to keep the various channels ticking over rose significantly. The India Service resumed broadcasting in May 1940, typically countering the Nazi broadcasts by focusing on British culture and music, along with occasional news bulletins.

Unfortunately, the reception to the newly-revived service was lukewarm. In July 1941, the journalist Kingsley Martin launched a bitter attack on the Ministry of Information and the corporation in an editorial for the *New Statesman*, citing the solemnity of the service and of failing to appreciate that Indians despised European dance music. He said 'plenty of Indians would welcome serious talks on literature and other topics which recognise their equality of interests'. German propagandists had studied Indian tastes and susceptibilities while war news from Berlin had proved to be a great attraction for Indian listeners. Programmes typically featured classical music selections, coupled with the aim of promoting German culture as being more highbrow than the British. The BBC countered this by emphasising the cultural links that already existed between the two countries and later by allotting time at the microphone to broadcasters sympathetic to the aims of the National Congress.

As the war spread into the Far East, the 'war of words' raging over the question of on which side India's interest might be better served could not be won without a considerable programme of expansion. This resulted in the Eastern Service swiftly outgrowing its space allocation and, in June 1942, it was transferred to a disused department store in Oxford Street. By that time the service had increased the number of languages for its broadcasts to India to include Marathi, Gujarati, Tamil and Sinhala. With over 250 million Indians being fluent in Hindustani, the BBC had originally prioritised that language, with Bengali having been introduced a year later in 1941.

A DIFFICULT RELATIONSHIP BETWEEN RULER AND RULED

The business of formulating propaganda directed towards the people of the empire presented a different and very challenging undertaking for the BBC when compared with other forms of political warfare. Unlike in the enemy and enemy-occupied territories where the intention was to spread disaffection, undermine the enemy and to motivate and provide guidance for resistance groups, the aim of the India Service propaganda was to appeal to subjugated peoples to side with their oppressors over the 'common enemy'. This was a difficult task given the delicacy of wartime relations between Britain and India, particularly when the independence movement was in the ascendency. The corporation had to reflect the views of the pro-independence National Congress Party, even though many of its staunchly anti-British leaders, including those of the Quit India Movement, had been slung in jail. Reflecting on the task that faced them, one former employee, Donald Stephenson, remembered that 'nobody pretended that broadcasts from London could dissipate the fog of India's political troubles, but it can project a beam of light into the gloom and consolidate common misunderstandings'.[1]

The chances of successfully disseminating radio propaganda to India was also hampered by the fact that barely one in every 4,000 Indians possessed a radio, and the department laboured away, unsure of whether they were having any real effect on the hearts and minds of the Indian intelligentsia. The Germans certainly believed it to be worthwhile; Axis propaganda to the subcontinent was ramped up significantly in 1941 when the former president of the Indian National Congress, Subhas Chandra Bose, arrived in Berlin, having escaped from house arrest in British India. Bose was received warmly by the Nazis, who took an opportunistic line of sympathy to the independence cause, and furnished him with funds to set up the Free India Radio Service that enabled him to direct propaganda against the British Raj.

CLEARED FOR OVERSEAS BROADCASTING

Orwell was recruited on to the staff of the BBC in August 1941, and even though there was a specific need to broadcast a more highbrow selection of programmes to Indian listeners, his selection for a job organising propaganda was a strange one; especially given his deep anti-imperialism was evident in his first published novel, *Burmese Days* (1934). Orwell's sense of revulsion over what he witnessed in Burma had underpinned the social conscience that shaped his early literary development. He knew where he stood and was no longer averse to going against the establishment on sensitive issues.

Details of Orwell's security check, before being accepted on to the staff of the BBC, also make for interesting reading: 'Blair [Orwell] came under notice of the Wigan Borough Police in February 1936 in connection with his Communist activities in Wigan,' and it was noted that previously 'he seems to have eked out a precarious living as a freelance journalist in France'. Another report notes that he worked at a bookshop for a man called Westrope, who 'holds Socialist views' and considers himself an 'intellectual' (National Archive n.d.) Regardless of Orwell's 'questionable past', his report stated 'nothing recorded against' and he was effectively cleared for overseas broadcasting. Orwell had likely captivated his new employers with his particular interest in the Far East and his experience of being amongst the Burmese people. Taken alongside his proven literary abilities and impressive connections, he was considered to be the perfect fit to head up a highbrow staff aiming to reach Indians of superior educational grounding. While Indians were already the target of German propaganda questioning whether

RON BATEMAN   enslaved people should willingly die for their masters, Orwell, who was a committed anti-imperialist and a voice for pro-independence, was now under contract to direct radio propaganda that would involve promoting the British view rather than his own. He had only recently expressed an opinion about the BBC to the editors of the American quarterly *Partisan Review* that 'In spite of the stupidity of its foreign propaganda and the unbearable voices of its announcers, it is very truthful, and generally regarded here as more reliable than the press' (Davison 1998a: 472).

A little over five months after writing that letter, Orwell signed up to become a contributor to the BBC's 'stupid foreign propaganda' he had previously derided. Throughout a period of well over two years, he worked firstly as talks assistant, then later as talks producer, for the India section of the Eastern Service. An enormous body of work that Orwell did for the station, running to over 2,000 pages, has survived and has since been published in *The Complete Works*. His work included editing more than 200 newsletters on the war situation for broadcast to India, Malaysia and Indonesia in English and translated for broadcast in Gujarati, Marathi, Bengali and Tamil. Additionally, he organised a number of cultural, educational and political programmes on general issues including propaganda. In his introduction to the vast collection of Orwell's BBC papers, Peter Davison regards the Indian Service's attempt at distance teaching as the most remarkable aspect of his propaganda work. Orwell inherited this project almost as soon as he arrived at the BBC and immediately set about expanding the range of courses to incorporate an additional thirteen on a wide diversity of subjects. The courses were supplemented by talks involving many distinguished speakers from the worlds of literature and science. Orwell also wrote numerous propaganda talks of the 'government advice' type on subjects such as 'paper rationing' before he noticeably moved away from all that to a much more sophisticated kind of propaganda embedded within his cultural and educational programmes.

DID ORWELL BETRAY HIS PRINCIPLES?

Edward Stourton, in *Auntie's War*, believes that Orwell's propaganda work placed him in difficult territory – leading him into 'a betrayal of everything he stood for' (Stourton 2017: 313). At the time, Orwell would have been acutely aware of the possible damage to his reputation that he was exposing himself to; after all, much of the Axis propaganda *and* the BBC's counter-propaganda involved ignoring passages in Nehru's speeches. In his *War Diary* in April 1942, he refers to the betrayals and contradictions that working for the BBC had forced upon him, especially after his friend and

Horizon editor Cyril Connolly had reminded him of a passage he had written in *Homage to Catalonia* about war propaganda being the most horrible feature of war – 'all the screaming lies and hatred come inevitably from people who are not fighting' (Davison 2010 [2009]: 328). Orwell concluded that 'sooner or later we all write our own epitaphs' (ibid). Having said that, a committed anti-imperialist he may have been, Orwell was at pains to inform the subject peoples not to believe the assurances of liberty for the conquered peoples being churned out by the Nazi propaganda machine, including high-sounding promises of freedom being directed towards the 'coloured peoples' now under British rule. Orwell emphasised this point in his 1941 essay 'All Propaganda is Lies':

> This comes, it should be noticed, from men who only yesterday were openly describing the coloured races as the natural slaves of the white, and who described negroes, for example, in Hitler's own words as 'semi-apes'. And even while the German wireless woos its Indian listeners with promises of independence, it woos the British public by declaring that Germany has no wish to break up the British Empire, and praises the British for the civilising work they have done in India (Davison 1998b: 93).

This was typical of the tone Orwell adopted in his efforts to keep Indian subjects onside in his radio broadcasts; he acknowledged that he was rapidly becoming 'propaganda-minded' and developing a cunning he did not previously have. He was also quick to counter criticism coming his way, particularly from the literary critic and pacifist, George Woodcock, who accused him of using radio propaganda to 'fox the Indian masses'. 'Does Mr Woodcock really know what kind of stuff I put out in the Indian broadcasts?' Orwell began. He pointed out that most of his broadcasts were aimed at Indian left-wing intellectuals, some of them bitterly anti-British. The intention was not to 'fox the Indian masses'; rather it was to present an awareness of what a fascist victory would mean to the chances of India's independence. Orwell was at pains to make it clear that radio actually had the effect of making war a more truthful business, and felt that critics should actually find out what he was doing at the BBC before attacking his good faith.

In 1943, Orwell edited a book, *Talking to India,* which contained transcripts of a selection of broadcasts, alongside examples of the Axis propaganda being broadcast by Chandra Bose reproduced for comparison. In his Introduction, he asserts that most Axis propaganda to India is poor; however, he regarded Chandra Bose to be 'the high water mark' and noted that for propaganda purposes 'Bose is reduced to pretending that the Axis powers have no imperialist aims' and that 'the enemy consists solely of Britain and the USA' (Orwell 1943: 8-9). After an illuminating comment reflecting how Bose had been obliged by his position to change tack on his view of the Sino-Japanese War (despite having been prominent on various 'aid China' committees), he then focuses on aspects of the war deliberately omitted by Bose. This included any admission that Germany was at war with the Soviet Union, the fact that both Italy and Japan possessed subject empires, or that the Germans were forcibly holding down some 150 million people in Europe; 'none of which fitted in with his general propaganda line' (ibid: 9). It was clear to Orwell that Bose was obliged by his Berlin masters to avoid mention of certain major issues of the war affecting a vast percentage of the human race. To suggest that Orwell's propaganda was in some major way a betrayal of his ideals is to ignore the distinction between honest and dishonest propaganda. Little wonder Orwell was more than happy to allow samples of his own BBC broadcasts to stand alongside those of the Axis.

ORWELL AND PROPAGANDA – KEEPING OUR CORNER CLEAN

Aside from his frequent outbursts of frustration, Orwell took his work seriously and worked diligently in what he regarded as a small and remote outpost in the radio war. 'He knew how important radio propaganda could be, if intelligently organised,' remembered Laurence Brander, the intelligence officer at the BBC Eastern Section while Orwell worked there (Brander 1954: 8-9). Peter Davison uncovered a plethora of interesting information on Orwell's time at the BBC that suggests he tended to follow his own propagandist agenda, rather than one that may have been prescribed by the BBC. A good example are the broadcasts he organised on the subject of prison literature at a time when India's future leaders including Gandhi and Nehru were in prison, insisting that it was something he particularly wanted to put across in India so far as it is possible. Additionally, he commissioned the writer K. S. Shelvankar, whose 'Penguin Special', *The Problem of India*, had recently been banned in the country, to deliver a number of talks and, despite protests from above, these all went ahead. Orwell also arranged talks on what Indian culture had given to the West, citing E. M. Forster's *My Debt to India* and two talks on philosophy by C. E. M. Joad – a household name in Britain courtesy of the BBC programme *The Brains Trust* (launched in 1941). Davison indicates that none of these could be classed as 'lying propaganda'. Talks arranged on the subject of great books such as *The Social Contract*, *The Koran* and *Das Kapital*, as well as discussions on major social problems such as 'Moslem minorities in Europe' and 'The status of women in Europe' can be seen as an enlightened form of propaganda that went right over the heads of the 'higher-ups'. There were other talks by Indian intellectuals in various Indian languages that could be construed as having been a much more innocuous form of propaganda – tackling such subjects as *The Beverage Report*, the history of fascism and the Japanese threat to Asia.

In October 1942, Brander suggested to Orwell that he begin broadcasting as George Orwell, rather than Eric Blair – essentially putting his literary reputation on the line. In doing so he was able to extract considerable licence from the BBC to conduct the programmes on his own terms. Not only did this give him a much greater freedom of speech, it also afforded him greater political licence when he insisted that his commentaries always followed 'what is by implication a left line'. How could he not at a time when he was also under contract to supply regular contributions to the American, communist-backed quarterly *Partisan Review*. The downside to this extension of his freedom was that it brought Orwell back on to the radar of the security service when he applied for clearance to Allied HQ shortly before he resigned from the BBC, in November 1943. However, the authorities were more concerned about the people he was mixing with, rather than the content of his broadcasts. A security file contains tales that gossiping BBC informants had reported about him to Special Branch. 'He has a good many Indian friends and has offered employment to K. S. Shelvankar [whose books were banned], and he is telling some of his friends that his department was trying to get Mulk Raj Anand on the staff.' Anand was a socialist writer and propagandist who had been active in the Indian Independence Movement. The India Office was strongly opposed to his appointment, but Orwell somehow managed to get his friend on board. Orwell was also described by his colleagues as being 'a bit of an Anarchist', 'a man of advanced Communist views' and 'a man in touch with extremist elements' who had 'thrown in his lot with Victor Gollancz', the left-wing publisher. He was also described as 'dressing in a Bohemian fashion', both at his office and during his leisure hours (National Archive n. d.)

In April 1943, Orwell seized an opportunity to put on record his belief that the task of broadcasting propaganda to India was considerably more difficult than that of the propagandists working for the European service of the BBC who, he felt, were operating 'on an easy wicket'. 'The harsh penalties for listening, ensures that the broadcasts are accepted as true' he wrote when reviewing a book about the service.[2] In the same review, he asserts that propaganda can only be effective in speeding up processes already in operation, a claim that the events leading to the capitulation of Italy would later verify (Davison 1998c: 84-86). 'Propaganda cannot fight against the facts,' he wrote. And he kept his own corner clean by refraining from the added colour and distortion of the type of propaganda he despised. Because the corporation was rigidly committed to truthfulness, telling big lies would have proved to be counter-productive anyway, as the negative effects of early attempts to use the BBC broadcasts to deceive the German High Command had previously shown.[3]

A HOPELESS TASK

Despite his readiness to fend off critics who questioned his motives for directing propaganda to India, Orwell increasingly found the task both tedious and exasperating. When he finally decided to call time on his stint at the BBC, his resignation letter reflected his frustration over wasting so much time and public money on doing work that produced no result. 'I believe that in the present political situation, the broadcasting of British propaganda to India is an almost hopeless task,' he concluded. Given his critical comments about the BBC and his work there that Orwell recorded in his war diaries, it is surprising that he did not resign earlier. Six months after joining the corporation he famously described the atmosphere as 'something halfway between a girls' school and a lunatic asylum'. A short while later, in June 1942, he inveighed against the 'moral squalor and futility' of the job and 'the impossibility of being able to plan any wireless campaign whatever when policies were so ill-defined and disorganisation so great' – complaining that anything worthwhile was typically 'watered down' or 'cancelled from above'. The final straw came when it was discovered that there were plenty of Indians with short-wave sets who had no idea that the BBC were broadcasting to India, which merely served to reinforce his opinion that the broadcasts were simply 'shot into the stratosphere, and not listened to by anyone' (Davison 2010 [2009]: 354).

It is difficult to assess Orwell's remarks when there is so little evidence to prove or disprove his assumption. The service certainly continued to expand during his time, with twelve Asiatic languages being incorporated within the forty-seven being broadcast by the BBC shortly before his resignation. Orwell had always been acutely aware that it was the English speakers who were most likely to have access to short-wave radio sets, and that the most important broadcasts were the three-quarter-hour transmissions aimed at the English-speaking Indian population, rather than the European population or the British troops in India. In terms of the literacy figures, Orwell records in *Talking to India* that there were five million Indians literate in English and several millions more could speak it – a figure that added up to only 3 per cent of the population (Orwell 1943: 7). He could only console himself with the fact that no attempt was ever made to boycott listening to the BBC in India.

SUBJUGATION BY TERROR

Finally, on the question of whether Indians, with their aspirations for independence, had anything to fear from a Nazi victory, it is worth consulting the memoirs of Ivone Kirkpatrick, the former controller of the BBC's European Service, who recalled an incident that occurred during his time at the foreign office. As first secretary at the British Embassy in Berlin, Kirkpatrick effectively had a ringside seat throughout the critical discussions before the Munich Crisis, in September 1938, and accompanied foreign secretary Lord Halifax and British ambassador Neville Henderson during their respective interviews with the volatile and unpredictable Führer. At the very mention of India, Hitler had been quick to air his views on British policy:

> He could not understand, he said, why we tolerated disorder, or wasted time in parley with Congress. The remedy was quite simple: 'Shoot Gandhi,' he said in his sharp staccato accent. 'And if that does not suffice to reduce them to submission, shoot a dozen members of Congress, and if that does not suffice, shoot 200 and so on until order is established. You will see how quickly they will collapse as soon as you make it clear that you mean business' (Kirkpatrick 1959: 97).

As Hitler continued his tirade – a clear indication that he intended to massacre countless hundreds of India's National Congress until they cowered to his will – Kirkpatrick looked across at the foreign secretary and studied his expression. 'Halifax gazed at Hitler with a mixture of astonishment, repugnance and compassion.' The feeling that it would have been a complete waste of time to argue had long taken hold.

CONCLUSION

Having been rejected for military service on medical grounds, Orwell was always determined to find some type of war work that would make use of his particular talents. The fact that he ended up at the India Service of the BBC was the result of a specific need to direct a certain type of propaganda that would appeal to Indian listeners. There is a certain irony here given that it was the savage criticism of the service by Kingsley Martin at the *New Statesman* that likely led to Orwell being recruited by the BBC. Orwell had harboured a personal grudge against Martin after the latter had rejected his review of Franz Borkenau's *The Spanish Cockpit* on political grounds. He later described Martin as 'a bloody fool who seems to think war is a cricket match' (Davison 1998d: 223).

Finally, I do not subscribe to the view that Orwell betrayed his principles in any significant way in the course of his propaganda

RON BATEMAN

work for the service. It is much fairer to say that he used his position, his name and his influence to keep the propaganda as close to the corporation's policy of truthfulness as he could and, furthermore, he used his name to facilitate opportunities for members of India's pro-independence movement to have a voice over the airwaves.

NOTES

[1] Donald Stephenson, in *India a Picture? BBC Yearbook*, 1945 pp 88-89

[2] The book Orwell reviewed was *Voices in the Darkness*, by Edward Tangye Lean

[3] During the Norwegian campaign in 1940, the BBC was given false news by the government regarding military movements in an effort to deceive the German High Command. The Germans were not deceived, but the public were, and the BBC's reputation nosedived, taking many months to recover

REFERENCES

Brander, Laurence (1954) *George Orwell*, New York: Longmans Green

Davison. Peter (ed.) (1998a) *The Complete Works of George Orwell, Vol. XII*, London: Secker & Warburg

Davison, Peter (ed.) (1998b) *The Complete Works of George Orwell, Vol. Xlll*, London: Secker & Warburg

Davison, Peter (ed.) (1998c) *The Complete Works of George Orwell, Vol. XV*, London: Secker & Warburg

Davison, Peter (ed.) (1998d) *The Complete Works of George Orwell, Vol. XI*, London Secker & Warburg

Davison, Peter (ed.) (2010 [2009]) *George Orwell Diaries*, London: Penguin Modern Classics

Kirkpatrick, Ivone (1959) *The Inner Circle*, London: Macmillan

National Archive (1939) War cabinet minutes, 27 September: reference CAB 65/1

National Archive (n.d.) Orwell's security file: reference KV-2-2699

Orwell, George (ed.) (1943) *Talking to India*, London: Allen & Unwin

Stourton, Edward (2017) *Auntie's War*, London: Black Swan

NOTE ON THE CONTRIBUTOR

Ron Bateman is an alumnus of the Open University, a founder member of The Orwell Society and former editor the society's *Journal*. He is the author of *The Radio Front: The BBC and the Propaganda War 1939-45*, published by The History Press on 7 May 2022. Previous full-length works include *The End of the Line: The Last Ten Years at Swindon Works* (2020) and *Rifleman of the Raj: A Soldier's Journal British India, 1919-20* (2018).

ARTICLE

In Search of Máirín Mitchell

Martin Tyrrell

Máirín Mitchell is remembered, if at all, as the author of the travel memoir *Storm Over Spain* (1937). And *Storm Over Spain* is remembered chiefly because it is one of a number of books on Spain and its civil war that Orwell reviewed around the same time that he was working on *Homage to Catalonia*. In a relatively brief notice in *Time and Tide*, he praised Mitchell for the way she reported on the anarchists in particular. Unlike almost all English writers on Spain, he commented, she gives them a fair deal (Orwell 1998a [1937]: 102). In Orwell's view, this was a useful corrective when 'the average English person still retains his eighteen-ninetyish notion that Anarchism is the same thing as anarchy'. He recommended that anyone who wanted to understand what the Spanish anarchists had achieved should read the book's seventh chapter, while at the same time noting with regret that much of this achievement had by now likely been undone. Shortly after, Mitchell wrote to thank him for his review, but also to put him right – 'unlike almost all English writers', she said, she was Irish[1]. She was particularly pleased Orwell had given her such a positive review since, judging by *The Road to Wigan Pier*, she doubted they were in the same place politically.

Mitchell does not say what parts of *Wigan Pier* she disagreed with. It could have been Orwell's hostility to Catholicism (Mitchell was a committed, if somewhat unconventional, Catholic) or his sweeping dismissal of people who lived unconventionally – vegetarians, fruit-juice drinkers, people who wore pistachio-coloured shirts and sandals. Mitchell, who writes in *Storm Over Spain* that the radical fringe – the fringe of the fringe – had been important to her in her formative years, was something of an eccentric herself. And Tinka Hérányi, her travelling companion on the Spanish trip, seems to have been a kind of proto-New Ager. Reflecting on the books that influenced her most she lists the unusual trio of Hardy's *Jude the Obscure*, James Connolly's *Labour in Irish History* and *Gleanings from the Buddha's Fields* by Lafcadio Hearn, a writer of mixed Greek-Irish ancestry who spent most of his life in Japan. He is mentioned by Orwell in *Notes on Nationalism* where he is cited as an example of transferred national loyalty – a nationalist who 'does not even

MARTIN TYRRELL

belong to the country they have glorified. ... For the past fifty or a hundred years, transferred nationalism has been a common phenomenon among literary intellectuals' (Orwell, 1998f [1945]: 146). Mitchell, it transpires, was herself something of a transferred nationalist.

I had not heard of Máirín Mitchell before I read Orwell's review of her book on Spain and when I began researching her, it seemed that she had been largely forgotten. Katrina Goldstone's *Irish Writers and the Thirties* (2020) gives perhaps the fullest account of her, describing Mitchell as 'an acute observer of the London Irish community' whether in her published writings or her correspondence, notably with the author Desmond Ryan, his journalist father William (the dedicatee of *Storm Over Spain*) and Irish feminist Hanna Sheehy-Skeffington (whose obituary Mitchell would write for the *Irish Democrat* in 1946).[2] Regarding *Storm Over Spain*, Goldstone comments that it is 'one of just a few texts of witness by an English-speaking woman, who also happens to be a fluent speaker of Spanish' but not 'a committed Leftist … not actively involved in campaigns for Republican Spain…' That Orwell's is 'the only reference it now receives in literary histories of the Spanish Civil War' Goldstone attributes, in part, to Mitchell's lack of profile and connections. (So private was her life, and so disconnected from mainstream literary circles, that I have been to date unable to track down a photograph of her). 'I decided to leave Bloomsbury,' she writes in the closing pages of *Storm Over Spain*, saying that she is repulsed by the spread there of what she calls 'the war mentality' (p. 243). In leaving, she may have left, as well, her chances of literary prominence.

MÁIRÍN MITCHELL – THE TRANSFORMATION

Máirín Mitchell was born Marion Houghton Mitchell in England in 1895 to an Irish father and an English mother. Her father, Thomas Houghton Mitchell, was an Irish Protestant who came of age at a time when the Irish Protestant ascendancy was in marked political decline. The rise of Irish nationalism – the campaign for Home Rule – was a sign of this decline. In Ireland, Protestants tended to identify as British and support maintaining Ireland within the United Kingdom – they were Unionists. Catholics, on the other hand, typically identified as Irish and backed self-government (either Home Rule or – initially a minority campaign – outright independence). They were Nationalists or Republicans. This correspondence of religious to political identity was not rigid. There were some Catholic Unionists and significant Protestant enthusiasm for Irish nationalism – Charles Stewart Parnell, 'the most gifted leader Ireland ever had', thought Orwell (1998e [1944]:

188), W. B. Yeats, Constance Markiewicz, Roger Casement. And the poet Susan Langstaff Mitchell with whom Máirín Mitchell had a family connection. This was via a branch of the Mitchell family that was prominent in the Irish legal profession and lived in what was then Parsonstown in King's County but is now Birr in Offaly. Susan Mitchell stayed for a time in the Mitchell's house at Oxmantown Mall but was unhappy with the family's politics (Pyle 1998). A chapter of *Storm Over Spain* opens with a quotation from one of Susan Mitchell's poems.

> Bring back the people of my heart again
>
> With me to dwell upon the lovely plain
>
> Human as I once knew them.

Only one Mitchell is named in Máirín Mitchell's will – a James Mitchell of Oxmantown Mall, to whom she bequeathed a signet ring.

By the time of Máirín Mitchell's birth, in 1895, her father had been living in England for some years, had married an Englishwoman, Gertrude Pease, and was rising in the medical profession, eventually establishing a successful general practice in Ambleside in the Lake District. Mitchell attended St Winifred's, a private boarding school in Wales, and subsequently studied at Bedford College in London, now part of the University of London. Her brother, Edward, attended St Bees School, a private school whose alumni include Rowan Atkinson, and then Sandhurst, becoming first a lieutenant in the Border Regiment, then a pilot in the Royal Flying Corps/Royal Air Force. He died in an accident in May 1918, aged 20, while serving in Egypt.

I take from this albeit limited information that Thomas Houghton Mitchell was a somewhat British Irishman (he attended Trinity College, Dublin, when it was still very much an Ascendancy institution and in parallel to his rise in the medical profession, he rose through the grades of the Masonic Order, an organisation markedly more popular among the British Irish than the Irish Irish). The culture shock in moving islands may not have been that great for him, and his family appears to have lived a conventional English middle class life.

This was the life that the former Marion Houghton Mitchell chose to exit. She could have remained English but opted, instead, to emphasise her Irish background and to identify herself as Irish. She gaelicised her name and enrolled for lessons in the Irish language. For a time she used the Irish language versions of both her forename and her surname – Máirín Ní Mhaol Mhiceil – and in the old Irish alphabet.[3] As for her politics, she described herself,

MARTIN TYRRELL

in 1933, as 'rather conventionally republican'. Her writings of the time, including *Storm Over Spain*, bear this out ('An Englishman's home is his castle,' a visit to Gibraltar prompts her to write, 'but it is so often somebody else's castle,' op cit: 162). She is critical of past British policy in Ireland, of the partition of Ireland, Irish Unionism and the Unionist devolved administration in Northern Ireland (both of its very existence and of the policies it is pursuing). Éamon de Valera, a leader of the Irish independence movement, later to be Taoiseach on three different occasions, has her qualified approval.

In addition to becoming Irish, both culturally and politically, Mitchell became a Catholic, thus adopting the religion of the majority of Irish people and the majority of Irish nationalists and she would remain a Catholic for the rest of her life.

All of these changes – to her nationality, her politics and her religion – are likely to have distanced her from her family, maybe causing some estrangement. Although she dedicated her first book, *Traveller in Time* (1935), to her mother and although *Back to England* (1942a) hints at a positive relationship with her father, there are also some signs that the relationship may have been troubled. The Mitchells of Ambleside were wealthy – Thomas Mitchell was successful and from a prominent and privileged family; Gertrude Pease was the daughter of a very rich business owner; their family home in Ambleside, Rothay Garth, is now an up-market hotel. All in all, Marion/Máirín had an advantaged upbringing. Yet when she died in a Catholic care home in 1986, she did so with just a few thousand pounds to her name. And, as I said earlier, only one Mitchell, and he back in Ireland, was named in her will.

London may have been the turning point. It could be that living there was, for Mitchell, both formative and transformative, and that it was not so much Bedford College as the counter cultural circles in which she began to move that most affected her. 'I … would not have missed those days,' she writes in *Storm Over Spain*, 'among people who were not content with things as they were. Better in youth the endless talk, even the "isms", that divine discontent, than the young who do not question, who never rebel. … The veterans were generous in opening their minds to us, and releasing the rich garnering of years of experience, reflection and contacts' (op cit: 133).

Charles Lahr seems to have been central to this experience. Lahr was a German expatriate who ran the Progressive Bookshop (from premises described by his friend, the writer H. E. Bates, as 'no more than a cubicle', quoted in Taaffe 2014) on Red Lion Street, in London, for around twenty years – the original shop was destroyed in an air raid in 1940 and several attempts to start up elsewhere were unsuccessful. Mitchell may have lived with the Lahrs, who were reputedly hospitable, and she was certainly close enough to the family to be asked to be godmother to Lahr's daughter, Sheila, sometime in the late 1920s. The circumstances here were unusual. The Lahrs were Jewish, Charles Lahr by conversion and his wife, Esther, by birth. Esther had attended a Church of England school and had felt self-conscious at being exempted from religious education. For some reason this decided her that her own daughter should be raised as a Catholic and sent to Catholic schools – as Sheila Lahr records in *Yealm: A Sorterbiography* (2015). Sheila Lahr mentions Mitchell (whose name she writes as 'Maureen Mitchell') only briefly but says that Mitchell had previously acted, appearing as the Nurse in an early film version of *Romeo and Juliet*.[4] It seems to have been through the Lahrs and their circle that Mitchell came to know Hanna Sheehy-Skeffington, the suffragette and Irish nationalist, and William and Desmond Ryan, not to mention other Irish writers and political activists. It is, perhaps, in this environment and in this company that she herself decided to become Irish and Catholic. In her obituary of Hanna Sheehy-Skeffington, Mitchell recalls Hanna saying to her: 'I think we Irishwomen have a double dose of anarchism in our make-up' (Mitchell 1946). In the same piece, she goes on to say that, at this time, readers of the anarchist paper *Freedom* met at the Emily Davidson Club in Holborn Street and that the paper itself was printed in Ossulston Street 'by a sturdy friend of the Irish independence movement'. This would date Mitchell's time with the Lahrs to before 1927 since that was the final year *Freedom* was printed at Ossulston Street.

AN UNRELIABLE NARRATOR

Máirín Mitchell can be a most unreliable narrator. I get the sense that she tried, particularly in the 1930s, to convey herself as foreign, bohemian, unconventional and, thereby, more exotic and more writerly. In *Back to England*, for instance, she strongly hints that she grew up in Ireland or at least lived there some considerable time – which was not the case as far as I can see.

Writing to Desmond Ryan, she refers to her background as being Catholic 'complicated by Quakerism' and to be of 'Catholic-Quaker stock'. But Mitchell's Quaker ancestry was distant. Her maternal great-grandfather, Thomas Pease, had been a Quaker, indeed a member of a very prominent Quaker family. But he had broken with both the Society of Friends and his teetotal Quaker family in order to become an importer of wines and spirits, and had joined the Church of England (Lloyd 2020).

By any standards, Mitchell was an extensive traveller, but particularly by the standards of her time. Also a perceptive visitor with a keen and generally open-minded interest in the people and

MARTIN TYRRELL

places she visited. In Canada, she says, she was made an honorary Iroquois – 'for a service rendered, Grand Chief American Horse had initiated me ... with ritual of eagle feathers' (Mitchell 1942a: 23). But she was not the leisured traveller her writings sometimes suggest. Instead, she seems to have taken conventional employment to cover the costs of her travels or to have worked at jobs that would include travel such as becoming a stenographer on a Canadian Pacific ship, the Belfast-built SS *Minnedosa*. (This would date her transatlantic travels to before 1931 when the *Minnedosa* was sold to an Italian shipping company.) In her preface to *Storm Over Spain*, Mitchell implies that Vaduz, in Liechtenstein, is her eccentric place of residence when, in fact, she was simply visiting[5]. She was there as a tourist not a resident in August 1937, several months after *Storm* had been redrafted and accepted for publication. At most she put some finishing touches to the book while she was in Liechtenstein.

Storm Over Spain itself is based on a visit to Spain that began and ended before the civil war, which is why, as Orwell noted, the book was not primarily about the war so much as about Spain and its instabilities. Mitchell was in Spain in April and early May 1936. She had left by the 10 May, the date of her letter to William Ryan in which she says she has just returned home. In her letter, she mentions the poverty of southern Spain, nuns being prohibited from wearing their habits and a Malaga hotel manager locking 'us all' in the hotel on May Day, a story that appears in *Storm Over Spain*. But she does not, in this pre-war letter, suggest that anything she saw in Spain hinted that war was imminent.

I do not believe Mitchell was in Spain at any time during the civil war or that she left the country in the autumn of 1936 as she claims in the book. From her letters to Desmond Ryan, she was in London most of the second half of 1936 aside from a visit to Stockholm. In suggesting that her time in Spain coincided with the war, I believe that she was being somewhat economical with the truth, perhaps so as to make the book that little bit more marketable – it may well have been a publisher or an editor's suggestion. *Storm Over Spain*, from all the evidence available to me, began as a regular travel book that became potentially more of a commercial prospect on account of the war. Its coverage of the conflict is drawn mainly from newspaper reports, including the paper *Spain and the World*, which was published by British anarchists – the group associated with *Freedom* – who obtained their reports of the war from their Spanish counterparts. In *Storm Over Spain*, this second-hand war content sits somewhat awkwardly alongside the memoir material which is, by a long way, the better part of it.

STORM OVER SPAIN

Judging by her correspondence, Mitchell had completed the book that would become *Storm Over Spain* by the summer of 1936. She first mentions it in a letter to Desmond Ryan in August 1936, around a month after the start of the war and, by my reckoning, two or three months after her return from Spain. Towards the end of that month, there is a further letter to Desmond in which she says that her Spain book was rejected by Arthur Barker (whom Ryan may have suggested to her as Barker had published his own *Unique Dictator*, a study of de Valera) on the grounds that it was already dated. Rich and Cowan also thought the book was dated but said that they would have accepted it had they seen it earlier. The manuscript had further troubles in 1937 when it was rewritten at least once, and accepted then rejected at which point Mitchell was on the verge of throwing in the towel. Instead, however, there followed a further rewrite which Secker & Warburg accepted in just three days. Fredric Warburg later said that he had published it because he felt there was a gap in the market for a pacifist account of the war (Warburg 1959). 'I'm glad they are bringing it out,' wrote Mitchell to Desmond Ryan in April 1937, 'as they are courageous, and see beyond the L. Bk. Club.' Secker & Warburg would, of course, go on to publish *Homage to Catalonia* the following year. Both books sold badly.

It is remarkable, I think, that Orwell did not pick up on Mitchell's Irishness. In *Storm Over Spain*, as in her earlier *Traveller in Time*, she appears to go out of her way to emphasise that she is Irish, with the zeal of the convert. All but one chapter of *Storm Over Spain* – the anarchism chapter – is headed with a quotation from an Irish writer or political activist: W. B. Yeats, Patrick Pearse, James Connolly. Mitchell also draws frequent parallels between Spain and Ireland likening Spain's rural poor to their Irish equivalents of a century or so before – the 'croppies of Enniscorthy' and 'the pikemen of Wexford'. Parallels – perhaps not so commonplace in 1937 as they would later become – are also drawn between Euzkadi, the aspirant nation state of the Basque country, and Ireland. It is ironic, says Mitchell, that the Irish volunteers on the Francoist side are almost to a man Irish nationalists, some of them former combatants in the Irish War of Independence. Yet here, in Spain, these onetime liberationists are suppressing their Basque and Catalan counterparts. Similarly, many of the Irishmen fighting for Franco were the veterans or the beneficiaries of Ireland's lengthy agitation over land ownership in the late 1800s, and yet here they were fighting Spain's own beleaguered rural poor.

MARTIN TYRRELL

Orwell notes not Mitchell's nationality but her religion – '*Storm Over Spain*,' he comments by way of commendation, 'written by a Catholic but very sympathetic to the Spanish Anarchists' (Orwell 1998b [1938]: 114). It was, indeed, odd that a Catholic might write positively about Spain's anarchists given their anti-clericalism. Anti-clericalism, in fact, seems too mild a term. The anarchists were intent, not so much on discouraging the Catholic Church as removing all trace of it. Orwell mentions the many church burnings and is broadly in sympathy with them, his main regret being that Gaudí's *Sagrada Família* Cathedral proved resistant to attempts to raze it. He mentions fleetingly that people have been killed in this widespread anti-clerical binge but gives no sense – may not even have known – the extent of the violence or the number of fatalities.

Mitchell, too, comments on the church burnings and harassment of Catholic clergy while alleging that the Church, by its actions, has brought a considerable part of this on itself. 'Had the Church as a whole in Spain been the friend of the poor,' she writes, 'had the Catholic priests in general supported the social advancement of the toiling masses, it seems unlikely that the clergy would have suffered in the Civil War as they did' (Mitchell 1937: 59). Instead, she alleges that the Church was often conspicuously wealthy, noting that it was stated in the Cortes in 1931 that the Jesuit order owned around a third of Spain's total wealth.[6] If she has sympathy, it is for the Basque Church which she regards as a more humble affair than the Spanish Church in general – and more admired by its people. At the same time, she distances the anarchists from the violence waged against the Church. If anarchists were involved, then it was not, she alleges, with the sanction of the wider anarchist movement. The church burnings, she claims, were spontaneous rather than part of some general anarchist policy. Her depiction of the anarchists is as public-spirited community activists working in areas such as child and adult education. She also admires the anarchists for their free-spiritedness and their resistance to what Belloc famously called the servile state. We should not, she suggests, let the odd bad apple make us dismiss this otherwise benevolent movement. Her ideal society is one comprising a series of mutually tolerant anarchic communes. If she sees a problem with anarchism, it is that we are not yet sufficiently civilised to live anarchically. Not being up to the anarchist ideal, we must be governed.

While Mitchell concedes that anarchists have been violent, she writes that this violence has been 'in proportion to the oppression of the workers' (Mitchell 1937: 148). Or she excuses it as the work of nominal anarchists out of step with the wider movement. This is one area where her not having experienced the war, and her sometimes over-reliance on accounts of it that are sympathetic to the anarchists, weakens her account. The abuses attributed to the anarchists by the likes of John Cornford and John Langdon Davies (and fictionalised by Ernest Hemingway in *For Whom the Bell Tolls*) were wartime abuses. Marshall (2007) contrasts the programme agreed by the anarchist-dominated union, the Confederación Nacional del Trabajo (CNT), in Zaragossa, in May 1936, which aspired to a society based on communes free to pursue their preferred lifestyle, however anomic, to that of the more doctrinaire Federación Anarquista Ibérica (FAI), which took a harder line. Marshall describes the FAI on the eve of the war as having among its members criminals as well as a faction that advocated church burning as well as the killing, not just of priests but also male prostitutes. Mitchell, like Orwell, makes little mention of the physical attacks on Catholic clergy and quite possibly did not know of them.

She does, however, note the 'splenetic hate' she has found in England towards the Spanish Catholic Church or, at best, a concern at the destruction of churches more because these are heritage buildings than places of worship. Mitchell, in contrast, considers how the destruction of their churches must have affected the communities that used them. 'To take away from sorrowing people the one comfort they know, is no minor tragedy of modern revolutions' (Mitchell 1937: 60). There is here an appreciation, often overlooked, that the Church was not universally unwelcome or alien throughout Spain but a valued part of civil society. Many people in Spain, including many poor and disadvantaged communities, cherished the Church which they regarded as theirs. That Mitchell recognised this may, in part, reflect her awareness of the cultural importance of Catholicism in Ireland. Peadar O'Donnell, who had been central to Ireland's left-wing and secularising Republican Congress in the early 1930s (and included by Orwell on the notorious list of communist fellow-travellers he compiled for the government's secret propaganda unit, the Information Research Department, in 1949), recalls in his memoir *Salud! An Irishman in Spain* (2020 [1937]: 49) witnessing a church being vandalised and feeling only outrage: this 'cold act of bitterness by a few, dishonestly defended by false arguments, was an ugly business'. (Mitchell admired *Salud*, which she thought was sensitively written, though she was otherwise no great admirer of O'Donnell or others on the Irish far left.)

IRELAND AND THE SPANISH CIVIL WAR

The war deeply divided opinion in Ireland. The Catholic Church was overwhelmingly in favour of Franco and the rebellion and shrill clerical denunciations of the Republic and its Irish supporters meant that many of the latter were obliged to keep a low profile at home. Writing to Desmond Ryan on 30 September 1936, Mitchell says that a piece she wrote on Spain that was so mildly left as to be 'pale pink' nonetheless incensed a priest to the extent that he said he wanted to drown her. As a result, the periodical in which the offending article had appeared had told her it would not publish anything further of hers on Spain until Professor Hogan (a conservative academic) had published something on the same subject to counter-balance it.

In recent years, there has been considerable interest in Ireland and those Irishmen who fought for the Spanish Republic, among them O'Donnell, Charles Donnelly and Frank Ryan.[7] But many Irishmen volunteered to fight for Franco, establishing an Irish Brigade (so named in conscious homage to the Irish Brigades in the French, Spanish and Hapsburg armies in the eighteenth and nineteenth centuries, brigades formed by Irishmen who had left Ireland following defeat and conquest in the 1600s). Many of the members of this latter-day Irish Brigade were veterans of the Army Comrades Association, usually called the 'Blueshirts', which, in the early 1930s, provided paramilitary muscle to the Fine Gael party. Although the Blueshirts looked, marched and saluted like authentic fascists, some contemporary historians have questioned the extent to which they were fascist in ideology. While General Eoin O'Duffy, the organisation's leader, was a *bona fide* fascist who participated in European fascist networks, the commitment of the wider membership was less clear-cut although this was likely to have been the case in all fascist movements in Europe (and, indeed, all political movements of any kind). O'Duffy left the organisation in 1934 to establish the National Corporatist Party, taking a faction of Blueshirts with him. These quite literally restyled themselves the Greenshirts and were among the volunteers whom O'Duffy brought with him to Spain. His Irish Brigade's military performance in the civil war was by most accounts underwhelming, if not farcical, to the extent that it was eventually stood down. O'Duffy's memoir of his time in Spain, *Crusade in Spain* (1938) would be the subject of a panning review by Orwell in the *New English Weekly*. 'General O'Duffy's adventures in Spain,' wrote Orwell, 'do seem to have resembled a crusade in that they were a frightful muddle and led to nothing in particular…' (Orwell 1998c [1938]: 235). This prompted the former general to write an indignant letter to the editor and cancel his subscription.

Mitchell is more charitable than Orwell in her treatment of the Irish Brigade. While, as I have said, she notes the irony in their siding with Franco, she also remarks that many were motivated to do so primarily by their religious beliefs, which Mitchell herself shares but which she says secularists would have difficulty comprehending. Her general distaste for the business of war, for taking sides and for propagandising also makes her less critical of O'Duffy and his brigade. There is ultimately nothing moral about soldiering, Mitchell alleges. No volunteer – left or right – is above the ultimate criticism that warfare is an immoral business. Writing to Desmond Ryan, she said that Irish volunteers in Spain regardless of which side they took, would ultimately 'make Spanish children fatherless'. To Mitchell, the war is, at base, a matter of Spanish workers killing each other and that 'anyone who has been to Spain and seen these lovely people in the workers' quarters, and thinks of them now, can never be happy again'.

'I cannot rejoice,' she comments, 'when I hear of disasters overtaking the "Right" (any more than I can when I hear of "Left" reverses) when I think of workers' lives being lost. Nor those of the b— bourgeoisie among whom are such splendid people.' The Irishmen on both sides, she says, were courageous whereas English critics who 'meanly attacked' O'Duffy 'would run from a pop-gun'. Irish volunteers of the left and the right have been courageous, she tells Ryan, but have also 'added to the hate in the world' by their actions.

A similar even-handedness informs Mitchell's respectful attitude towards Spain's Arab heritage. And having acknowledged and celebrated that massive cultural influence, she goes on to call out the hypocrisy of some on the left regarding the Moroccan soldiers in Franco's army: 'Some very uncomplimentary things about the colour and social status of the Moors. They were "black barbarians", "semi-savage natives" – terms a little strange perhaps to be used by the people who at other times were loudest in proclaiming the virtues of the Moors during the Riff wars, and loudest in their calls for the liberation of subject peoples' (Mitchell 1937: 188). It is the kind of hypocrisy Orwell himself may have highlighted.

THE ENDURING TRAVEL BOOK

Storm Over Spain retains something of the travel book it started out as. Here and there, for example, there are hints of the vanished world of the late 1930s. Torremolinos – here 'Torre Molinos' – is still a fishing village. It 'reminded us of the old Claddagh in Galway, lime-washed thatched cabins … hooded mules with crimson trappings walking out of the houses … the whole shore front by the village was an animals' playground' (ibid: 31-32). By chance, Mitchell sees the Hindenburg, 'a great silver fish … sailing over the Straits' (ibid: 179).

A certain stress seems to have worked its way into Mitchell's relationship with her friend Tinka over the course of their journey,

MARTIN TYRRELL

Tinka's interest in botany trying the author's patience a little further than it can comfortably go. 'Tinka's room … looked like a bedding-out place. All over the floor, in rows, were those abominable plants, and pieces of plants. Tinka was tending something lovingly that looked like a dead dandelion. And she was far from being packed. … At that moment my feelings towards Tinka were not those of a friend' (ibid: 172).

A little later, Tinka decides she does not want to see Almargen. But Mitchell does. And Mitchell gets to see it anyway by telling a drowsy Tinka they are in Osuna ('It was dark, the odds were in my favour').

'What happened to us in Almargen,' she writes, 'belongs to another book. In the day and a half we were there, incidents happened which, if I were to relate them here, would give an air of unreality to the rest of this sober narrative. To this day, however, I have never discovered if Tinka really did know, before we reached the town, what its name was. … She picked her flowers and that is all I can say about that amazing day and a half in the extraordinary town of Almargen' (ibid: 182-183). Alas, there was no sequel to *Storm Over Spain*. The world war and, in all likelihood, the economics of the book business, got in the way.

RECEPTION

With publication at last secured, Mitchell seems to have been beset by anxiety over *Storm Over Spain*'s merit. Writing to William Ryan in October 1937, she comments: 'I know only too well its faults, and how irritating it must be in parts. … I did feel that a book something on these lines needed to be written and I wish someone properly qualified had done it.' Having dedicated the book to Ryan, she hopes that he 'won't feel embarrassed by all the bad press notices the book is sure to get from many quarters'. (In fact, his only concern with the dedication was that it was accompanied by a quotation from the anarchist, Peter Kropotkin: 'The beautiful, the sublime, the spirit of life itself, are on the side of those who strive for light, for humanity, for justice.' Innocuous enough, but it was perhaps not so much the message as the man, Kropotkin, to whom Ryan senior objected.

Mitchell worried that *Storm Over Spain* might be overshadowed by Kate O'Brien's *Farewell Spain* (1937). While she regarded O'Brien as the more mature author, she also thought her guilty of over-simplifying the Spanish conflict into a melodrama of authoritarians versus democrats. This was a view of the war Mitchell, like Orwell, dismissed, associating the 'defend democracy' slogan with the communists whose motives she thought as base as those of the Spanish right. She expected bad reviews from Peadar O'Donnell and Leslie Daiken,[8] but only good from Hanna Sheehy-Skeffington. In the event, Kate O'Brien wrote to Mitchell to commend her for *Storm Over Spain*. This was high praise, a relieved Mitchell could be gracious. O'Brien, she advised Desmond Ryan, was in her view 'a sounder "left" than some of the people are who will revile my effort'.

Mitchell does not mention Orwell's positive review of *Storm Over Spain* in any of the correspondence I have been able to access aside from when she lists, for William Ryan, the good notices she has received that could be used in publicity. Indeed, the only mention of Orwell that I can find in her writings is in a letter to Desmond Ryan from November 1945. This appears to have been prompted by Orwell's scathing dismissal in the *Observer* of Seán O'Casey's *Drums Under the Window*: '… there is no real reason why Cromwell's massacres should cause us to mistake a bad or indifferent book for a good one' (Orwell 1998g [1945]: 332).

Mitchell tells Ryan that she agreed with some of what Orwell had said. 'It didn't surprise me that Orwell wrote thus, to tell you the truth I thought it very Orwellish. That gentleman seems to have become increasingly flexible, or variable. But I think he has some English inhibitions and a streak of puritanism like so many English leftist writers have.'

MITCHELL'S LATER WRITINGS

Mitchell's subsequent *Atlantic Battle and the Future of Ireland* (1941) defends Ireland's wartime neutrality, in which context she cites Sebastian Haffner's *Offensive Against Germany* which had come out earlier the same year as a Searchlight book, the series edited by Orwell and Tosco Fyvel and published by Secker & Warburg. There were rumours at the time (subsequently discredited) that German U-Boats had been refuelling in neutral Irish ports. Haffner writes: 'Whether it is true or untrue that the German U-boats … refuel in Irish harbours, it is indisputable that Ireland excludes British destroyers from these ports and thereby renders valuable help to the German submarines. That is sufficient reason for taking control of their harbours' (quoted in Mitchell 1941: 31-32). Mitchell does not quote further, but Haffner goes on to say: 'If the Irish should resist, so much the worse for them. What is England waiting for? Perhaps an invitation from De Valera? Or a German landing as in Norway?' (Haffner 1941: 90[9]). Orwell, in his diary entry for 14 March 1941, writes: 'In his book which we have just published, Haffner explains that it is folly on our part to let the Irish withhold vitally important bases [the three former Royal Navy bases in Ireland] and that we should simply take these bases without more ado. He says that the spectacle of our allowing a sham-independent country like Ireland to defy us simply makes all Europe laugh at us' (Orwell 1998d [1941]: 44).

Mitchell, for her part, writes that Northern Ireland, which she suggests is based on a questionable democratic rationale, sours British Irish relations and is a barrier to meaningful co-operation. Were the partition of Ireland to be addressed, she argues, then some kind of mutual defence agreement would be possible, her preference being a defensive alliance of Ireland, Britain and the United States.

Mitchell's view of Germany is similar to that of, say, Robert Vansittart, the British diplomat and Germanophobe: that it is an inherently aggressive nation aiming for world domination and, therefore, implacably hostile to peace. British naval supremacy, she proposes, is fundamental to stability and should be accepted by all nations. The subsequent *Back to England* sets out a similar argument and there is the same or more so in both *The Red Fleet and the Royal Navy* (1942b) and *We Can Keep the Peace* (1945).

FINAL REFLECTIONS

Mitchell would continue writing until the 1970s, focusing on naval history (including a history of the Russian Navy) and on Basque and Spanish subjects (*Elcano: The First Circumnavigator*, 1958; *Berengaria: Enigmatic Queen of England*, written in the 1970s but published in 1986).

Máirín Mitchell died at the Holy Cross Priory in East Sussex on 5 October 1986 aged 91. Her will suggests that she died, not impoverished, but with little enough to show for a lifetime of writing. What she had, she bequeathed to acquaintances in England, Ireland, Spain and the Basque Country. Most of her books had sold badly and are today difficult to obtain. *Storm Over Spain*, for example, was, according to Fredric Warburg, a commercial failure (a 'flop' as he put it), even Orwell's endorsement not managing to give it a second life. In Spain, however, and in the Basque Country, there is currently considerable interest. There are at least two groups of researchers interested in her life and writings with plans underway for a first Spanish edition of *Storm Over Spain*. Surely an English edition cannot be far off.

- The author wishes to thank Katrina Goldstone, Jose Francisco Fernandez Sanchez, Amaia Lopez de Munain, Pamela Holway and Darcy Moore but remains entirely responsible for the contents of the essay.

NOTES

[1] Undated letter from Mitchell to Orwell, mentioned in footnote to Orwell (1998a [1937])

[2] Mitchell's surviving correspondence with both Ryans is held by the James Joyce Library at University College, Dublin. I am grateful to the staff there for making it readily available to me

[3] I have throughout spelt 'Máirín' the way it is usually spelt in Irish with accents on the relevant vowels. (The name in Irish is pronounced something like 'my-reen' but would have an entirely different pronunciation if the accents were removed). That is how Máirín Mitchell spelt her name in her correspondence in the 1930s. In her published writings, however, the accents are generally missing. I am not sure why this was so. It may be because, until the 1950s, Irish (like German) used a different alphabet and in moving Irish names from one alphabet to another, they lost their distinctive accents

[4] There were several film adaptations of *Romeo and Juliet* before the late 1920s but I can find no reference to Mitchell in any for which the cast details are available

[5] The visit to Liechtenstein is described in Mitchell (1942a) in a chapter entitled 'In Lilliputland' and comes between visits to Provence and Switzerland. In a letter to Desmond Ryan dated 17 August 1937, Mitchell writes, 'As far as the folk in this inn know, I'm the only Irish person who's stayed in Vaduz'

[6] Writing to Ryan on 24 February 1938 Mitchell mentions that she has received 'a very nice letter' from Edgar Allison Peers (Professor of Hispanic Studies at Liverpool University – Orwell reviewed his *Catalonia Infelix* in the same December 1937 *Time and Tide* review as *Storm Over Spain*) who challenged this claim. She responded with a source. Peers had been contesting the view that the Church was as wealthy and as extensively engaged in the Spanish economy as was being claimed

[7] O'Donnell, as noted, wrote his own account of the Spanish Civil War. Charles Donnelly was killed in action near Madrid in 1937; O'Connor (1992) gives an account of his short life. Accounts of Frank Ryan's interesting life include Cronin (1980) and McGarry (2002). McLoughlin and O'Connor (2020) is a comprehensive account of Irish engagement in the war

[8] Leftist Dublin author Daiken had given Mitchell's *Traveller in Time* a stinging review. Mitchell is critical of Daiken and O'Donnell in her correspondence

[9] Haffner is referring here to three former British naval bases in Ireland. These had been retained by Britain following the establishment of the Irish Free State in 1922 but were placed under Irish control in 1938

REFERENCES

Cronin, Seán (1980) *Frank Ryan: the search for the Republic*, Dublin: Repsol

Katrina Goldstone (2020) *Irish Writers and the Thirties: Art, Exile and War*, Abingdon: Routledge

Haffner, Sebastian (1941) *Offensive Against Germany*, London: Searchlight Books/Secker & Warburg

Lahr, Sheila (2015) *Yealm: A Sorterbiography*, London: Unkant

Lloyd, Chris (2020) *Secret Darlington*, Cirencester: Amberley

Marshall, Peter (2007) *Demanding the Impossible: A History of Anarchism*, London: HarperCollins

McGarry, Fearghal (2002) *Frank Ryan*, Dundalk, Ireland: Dundalgan Press

McLoughlin, Barry and O'Connor, Emmet (2020) *In Spanish Trenches: The Minds and Deeds of the Irish who Fought for the Spanish Republic in the Civil War*, Dublin: University College Dublin Press

Mitchell, Máirín (1935) *Traveller in Time*, London: Sheed and Ward

Mitchell, Máirín (1937) *Storm Over Spain*, London: Secker & Warburg

MARTIN TYRRELL

Mitchell, Máirín (1941) *Atlantic Battle and the Future of Ireland*, London: Frederick Muller

Mitchell, Máirín (1942a) *Back to England*, London: Frederick Muller/The Right Book Club

Mitchell, Máirín (1942b) *The Red Fleet and the Royal Navy*, London: Hodder and Stoughton

Mitchell, Máirín (1945) *We Can Keep the Peace*, London: Grout

Mitchell, Máirín (1946) A great Irishwoman, *The Irish Democrat*, 19 July p. 4

Mitchell, Máirín (1958) *Elcano: the first circumnavigator*, London: Herder

Mitchell, Máirín (1986) *Berengaria: Enigmatic Queen of England*, Burwash, East Sussex: Audrey Wright

O'Brien, Kate (1937) *Farewell Spain*, London: Heinemann

O'Connor, Joseph (1992) *Even the Olives are Bleeding: The life and Times of Charles Donnelly*, Dublin: New Island Books

O'Donnell, Peadar (2020 [1937]) *Salud! An Irishman in Spain*, Friends of the International Brigades in Ireland, Dublin: Connolly Books

O'Duffy, Eoin (1938) *Crusade in Spain*, London: Hale

Orwell, George (1998a [1937]) Review of Mairin Mitchell, *Storm Over Spain*, Davison, Peter (ed.) *The Complete Works of George Orwell, Vol. XI: Facing Unpleasant Facts*, London: Secker & Warburg

Orwell, George (1998b [1938]) Letter to *Time and Tide*, 5 February 1938, Davison, Peter (ed.) *The Complete Works of George Orwell, Vol. XI: Facing Unpleasant Facts*, London: Secker & Warburg

Orwell, George (1998c [1938]) Review of Eoin O'Duffy, *Crusade in Spain*, Davison, Peter (ed.) *The Complete Works of George Orwell, Vol. XI: Facing Unpleasant Facts*, London: Secker & Warburg.

Orwell, George (1998d [1941]) Diary entry 14 March 1941, Davison, Peter (ed.) *The Complete Works of George Orwell, Vol XII: A Patriot After All*, London: Secker & Warburg

Orwell, George (1998e [1944]) Review of *Parnell* by St John Ervine, Davison, Peter (ed.) *The Complete Works of George Orwell, Vol XVI, I Have Tried to Tell the Truth*, London: Secker & Warburg

Orwell, George (1998f [1945]) Notes on Nationalism, Davison, Peter (ed.) *The Complete Works of George Orwell, Vol XVII: I Belong to the Left*, London: Secker & Warburg

Orwell, George (1998g [1945]) Review of Seán O'Casey, *Drums Under the Window*, Davison, Peter (ed.) *The Complete Works of George Orwell, Vol XVII: I Belong to the Left*, London: Secker & Warburg

Pyle, Hilary (1998) *The Red-headed Rebel: Susan Langstaff Mitchell, Poet and Mystic of the Irish Cultural Renaissance*, Dublin: The Woodfield Press

Taaffe, Carol (2014) The strange career of Charles Lahr, *Dublin Review*, Vol. 55

Warburg, Fredric (1959) *An Occupation for a Gentleman*, London: Hutchinson

NOTE ON THE CONTRIBUTOR

Martin Tyrrell teaches literature and creative writing at Open Learning, Queen's University, Belfast. He writes regularly on literature, history and psychology and is currently under contract to Athabasca University Press to complete a book on Orwell's wars, from class war to Cold War.

BOOK REVIEWS

Writing in the Dark: Bloomsbury, the Blitz and *Horizon* Magazine

Will Loxley

Weidenfeld & Nicolson, 2021, pp 388

ISBN: 978 1 4746 1570 9 (hbk); 978 1 4746 1571 6 (pbk)

For those interested in Britain's World War Two literary scene, *Writing in the Dark* is compulsively readable. The book is not academic. Nor is it fiction. It is not solely a biography – though that is its closest genre – nor is it a literary study, despite the discussion of poems and novels throughout. Loxley's book falls into an emerging category of novelistic biographies: biography that is written and reads like fiction. We may think of it as the inverse of Virginia Woolf's *Orlando*: a novel written as a biography. *Writing in the Dark* finds company with Sarah Bakewell's *At the Existentialist Café: Freedom, Being, and Apricot Cocktails*, Stuart Jeffries's *Grand Hotel Abyss: The Lives of the Frankfurt School*, Francesca Wade's *Square Haunting: Five Writers in London Between the Wars* and D. J. Taylor's *The Lost Girls: Love and Literature in Wartime London*. As if to emphasise the fictionality and 'play' aspect of *Writing in the Dark*, Loxley takes a page out of Taylor's approach and refers to the historical figures in his book as a 'cast of characters' (p. ix).

Loxley's 'cast' is made up of well-known stars: Christopher Isherwood and W. H. Auden who receive top billing despite not being the book's central figures as well as Bloomsbury's most famous residents Virginia and Leonard Woolf. Yet *Writing in the Dark* focuses largely on modernism's up-and-coming and the second-billed – John Lehmann, Stephen Spender and Cyril Connolly – literary editors who steal scenes from those names the audience expects to see. This is not a fault with the book; instead, it is its strength. The reader feels as if they are uncovering new starlets of the World War Two literary scene who have only been kept in the background due to convention rather than talent or historical fact. And then there are the special guest appearances which round out the cast. In this group we find Dylan Thomas, Evelyn Waugh and, of course, George Orwell whom Connolly and Loxley crown *the* 'war-writer' of World War Two on the final page of the book.

BIRD'S EYE VIEW

Loxley's approach is called 'panoramic' by author John Sutherland on the book's cover blurb. But a more nuanced description of his perspective would be the bird's eye. Certainly, the scope of the work, detailing the lives of many London literary figures during the war, is expansive. It gives the reader the feeling that Loxley is looking at his subjects from above, like a plane scouting out its targets. This, of course, mirrors the era of aerial bombardment within which his cast of characters lived; indeed, we frequently see them looking to the skies in anticipation of the bombing to come. But while a panorama keeps its distance, Loxley does not. Like a bird he swoops down closer to his subjects, revealing aspects of their daily lives. He targets them individually, spending time with each before taking to the sky again to scan and search and see connections. It is an ambitious project in its mixing of breadth and intimacy.

BLACKOUT

Part of what makes Loxley's project a success is that he focuses on literary figures often hidden in the background of books about the literature of World War Two. Although Lehmann, Connolly and Spender are known for their editorial pursuits – Lehmann with Bloomsbury and *New Writing* and Connolly and Spender with *Horizon* – they are eclipsed by their own star authors. As Loxley writes: 'Old Bloomsbury cast a long shadow' (p. 86). And this shadow kept many newer authors, but specifically the poets of Spender and Lehmann, on the periphery and out of sight. But Lehmann, Connolly and Spender (and the women who worked beside them) are obscured – not only by the editorial desk – but also by an information blackout created by scholarly eyes trained to focus on shinier literary objects. *Writing in the Dark* does a tremendous amount of work in bringing the editorial, authorial and personal lives of these men out of the dark for a wider readership.

BOMBS

Loxley describes the terribly close quarters of Lehmann at the Hogarth Press and Connolly at the *Horizon* offices (they faced each other across Mecklenburgh Square in Bloomsbury, central London) as 'snipers' guns trained on one another' (p. 83). But the book is less about this antagonistic relationship and more about 'bombs': the literal ones falling from the sky and the metaphorical fear that writing and publishing during the war would be a failure. As Loxley shows, Woolf worried endlessly that her Roger Fry biography was doomed and turned her anxieties to her final novel *Between the Acts*, which she did not live to see in print. Lehmann and Leonard Woolf repeatedly battled over the future of the Hogarth Press; each worried that the other's ideas would lead to the downfall of the business. Connolly started *Horizon* in 1939, which he admits was an inauspicious time for anything to succeed (although *Horizon* will). Dylan Thomas's writer's block became so severe during the war that he failed to submit promised poems to Lehmann. And Orwell, who feared that he was not only failing his own political idealism, but also that world politics were failing him, was able to write numerous articles for *Horizon* and broadcasts for the BBC but did not publish a novel again until the war's end. In Loxley's portrayal of literary London, a fear of failure seems to be more crippling than physical bombs.

ALLIES

What makes *Writing in the Dark* such an engrossing read is Loxley's ability to unravel a complicated web of literary allies and envious enemies. Despite the numerous connections between the authors, Loxley makes it possible to follow because of the narrative he constructs. By default, there are always limitations as to whom and what a book can dedicate space to. But that doesn't mean as a reader that I didn't wish to see more – or perhaps different – allies. The book's sole female 'cast' member is Virginia Woolf. She loomed over Bloomsbury as she looms over modernism now. But I kept wishing for more. Elizabeth Bowen, for example, who is briefly mentioned but not a major focus in Loxley's book. Or perhaps the women at *Horizon* like Sonia Brownell and Lys Lubbock who, Loxley notes, ran the magazine while Connolly was in Europe in 1945. Or, perhaps, the inclusion of Mulk Raj Anand, who straddled between Bloomsbury and his friendship and work at the BBC with George Orwell. These gaps, of course, leave space for more work on this wartime literary network to be done.

Loxley's book makes a rather obscure topic accessible to a larger reading public, which is no small feat. It is a book in which academics and non-academics alike can find value. As I read this book, I couldn't help but think about how useful it would be for undergraduate and graduate students. Often, academic monographs and biographies are too narrow, making it seem as if an author wrote in a vacuum – an impenetrable ivory tower. Loxley's book shows that writing and editing are not solitary acts. War, although isolating at times, is not a solitary event. These are communal experiences. And it is ultimately community – friends, enemies, colleagues, partners, lovers, strangers – that helped these authors and their work find light in the darkest of times.

Melissa Dinsman,
York College,
City University of New York

Cold Warriors: Writers Who Waged the Literary Cold War
Duncan White
Little, Brown, London, 2019, pp 752
ISBN: 978 0 349 14199 2 (pbk); 978 1 408 70799 9 (hbk)

Before the Cold War, the West had been slow to recognise the propaganda value of literature and, indeed, culture in general. But once it took to it, it did so in style. In contrast, the Soviet Union, which in the 1930s had had all the best tunes, had almost none of them three decades on. Akhmatova, Pasternak, Solzhenitsyn – all in their turn fell out of official favour while foreign enthusiasts for communism like Arthur Koestler changed sides. Duncan White's *Cold Warriors* is the story of how this came to be, emphasising the part played by the CIA and its wartime predecessor, the Office of Strategic Services (OSS). Of particular importance was the Congress for Cultural Freedom (CCF) which acted as a conduit for the agency's funding, relaying it to seemingly conventional publications. The UK-based *Encounter* was probably the best-known of these but there was also *Preuves, Cuadernos, Tempo Presente* and *Der Monat*. According to White, the CIA 'were invested in the idea that literature that did not look like propaganda was much more effective at winning hearts and minds than polemical material' (p. 435). The role of the CCF was as a kind of front to keep the ultimate source of these periodicals' substantial backing secret. For a time, it worked. Stephen Spender edited *Encounter* for more than ten years apparently without knowing where the money came from.

While inevitably covering similar ground to Frances Stonor Saunders's *Who Paid the Piper?: The CIA and the Cultural Cold War* (London: Granta Books, 1999), *Cold Warriors* is, nonetheless, a captivating tale told with style and humour ('Socialist realism ... boy meets girl meets tractor') alive with facts that sometimes leave the fictions – Greene's Wormold in *Our Man in Havana* or James Bond in the pre-Daniel Craig era – standing (p. 508). For example, White traces the Americans' often farcical efforts to destabilise Cuba, which included plans to take out Castro with an exploding cigar, use chemicals to make his beard drop off, or – it would appear – down an airliner while making it look like the work of Cubans. Best of all was Edward Lansdale's scheme to play to the island's Catholicism by putting it about that Fidel was the Antichrist. The plan was to work the people up into a state of heightened religious anxiety, then fire flares from US submarines on All Souls' Day to signal the start of the Second Coming. 'This,' as White rightly says, 'was Wormold on acid' (p. 457). In comparison, an earlier agency frolic, the airlifting of copies of *Animal Farm* into Poland – a translation printed on special, lightweight paper so that copies could be sent over attached to balloons – seems almost sober.

Animal Farm and *Nineteen Eighty-Four*, along with Koestler's *Darkness at Noon*, were the essential Cold War readings. Though Orwell did not live to see much of the Cold War, he became, posthumously, by far the greatest of its literary assets. If Koestler's coy account of a repentant apparatchik has aged badly, Orwell's tales of soured revolution have outlived their context, working their way into the general culture like few other fictions. But both had to be tweaked when they were adapted into agency-backed propaganda films. This was done, not only to introduce a degree of optimism but also, in the case of *Animal Farm*, to ease out Orwell's message that the problem with the revolutionary pigs was not that they were revolutionary but that they had morphed into venal, capitalistic men.

BOOK REVIEW

'Cold Warrior' he may have been, Orwell nonetheless retained his faith in socialism to the end. In *Animal Farm* especially, he imagines a socialism productively and technologically superior to what went before it and more than capable of delivering a better life for all who contribute to it. It fails only because it is usurped by the corrupt and self-serving revolutionary elite, not on account of some inherent flaw. It is socialism gone wrong, not socialism as it must always be. The problem of Animal Farm, formerly Manor Farm, is not socialism, which Orwell supported, but Bolshevism. Not Stalinism — Orwell sees no discontinuity between Lenin and Stalin. Had Lenin lived, he wrote in 'Second Thoughts on James Burnham', 'there is no strong reason for thinking that the main lines of development would have been very different. Well before 1923, the seeds of a totalitarian society were quite plainly there. Lenin, indeed, is one of those politicians who win an undeserved reputation by dying prematurely' (Orwell 1998 [1946]: 274). In *Animal Farm*, the totalitarian side of the revolution is there more or less from the start. It begins with the pigs' expropriation of the first day's yield of apples and milk, and their subsequent propagandist rationale.

White sees Pasternak's *Dr Zhivago* as making a similar point, questioning the revolution right back to its Leninist beginnings and, thereby, exceeding the limited critical remit permitted by Khrushchev. Hence the author's 'unpersoning' at home and his official adoption in the West. According to White, the CIA enabled

Dr Zhivago to be published in Russian, copies being made tacitly available at the Vatican stand at the World Fair in Brussels in 1958. This proved a master stroke – a great Russian novel that Russians were prohibited from reading, its author out of official favour. *Cold Warriors* includes a moving account of how this affected Pasternak, and of the spontaneous and genuine way his many Russian admirers were able to honour him in death when all official recognition was prohibited.

White traces Orwell's antipathy towards the Soviet Union to his time in Civil War Spain. This was where he had witnessed the official communists turn against what he considered to be an authentic proletarian revolution: the 'wonderful things' he had seen in anarchist-run Barcelona (Orwell 1998 [1937]: 28). Orwell had served in the militia of the Partido Obrero de Unificación Marxista (POUM), the United Marxist Workers' Party that would soon be violently suppressed on the dubious claim that it was a Francoist Trojan Horse. The experience left Orwell wise to the power of the official lie, and with a concern that the very idea of objective truth might not be long for this world. Here, White includes a telling anecdote. Stephen Spender and communist author Sylvia Townsend Warner had been attending the International Congress of Writers for the Defence of Culture in Valencia in the summer of 1937, shortly after Orwell had left for home, a wanted man on account of his POUM connections. When the conference ended, Spender and Townsend Warner were driven over the border to France, their driver boasting of having killed six members of the POUM in the events in Barcelona the previous May. 'And what is so nice,' said Townsend Warner when they were safely across, 'is that we didn't see or hear of a single act of violence on the Republican side' (p. 80).

The POUM was a Marxist-Leninist grouping and, therefore, doctrinally close to the very people who were trying to suppress it. Though Orwell was never a member of the *Partido* itself – something he would regret – its influence on his assessment of the Spanish Civil War and of world affairs in general was considerable particularly in the immediate pre-war period. It led him to conclude that the Soviet system was insufficiently revolutionary, for example, and in its Spanish intervention, downright counter-revolutionary. And it formed his belief – which he maintained for a good two years – that liberal democracy and fascism were versions of the same malignant capitalism and, therefore, equally unworthy. Only with the advent of war in 1939 did Orwell move away from this latter position – far left still but now increasingly and fiercely respectful of democracy and other liberal freedoms, and of nationhood.

Orwell himself put the moment of awakening pre-war to his famous dream during the night before the Molotov-Ribbentrop

Pact in August 1939. Dream or not, he was certainly looking for war work early that September, several months before any serious bombing. But it was only in May 1940, when the battle for France was underway and going badly, that Orwell would come out in print (in *My Country Right or Left*) and declare himself supportive of Britain's war effort. Support for the war meant no lessening of his socialism. *The Lion and the Unicorn* sets out a programme the POUM could stand over. Capitalism will cost us the war, Orwell says, but socialism will win it. Orwell never cooled on this programme. His criticism of the Labour government elected in 1945 was that it was not radical enough. It was as a radical socialist that he made his infamous list for the Information Research Department (IRD), which was a creation of that same Labour government.

This was his most obvious non-literary contribution to the Cold War and White is inevitably perplexed by it. On the one hand, he says, it shows the lengths Orwell was prepared to go to damage Soviet communism. On the other hand, 'For the author of *Nineteen Eighty-Four*, this was a surprising act of complicity' (p. 245), a list that was shared with a branch of the state without knowing what would happen to the people who were named on it. As Peregrine Worsthorne noted: 'A dishonourable act does not become honourable just because it was committed by George Orwell' (see Saunders 1999: 300). In Orwell's defence, the ostensible purpose of the IRD list was to name the people he thought might be unreliable as Cold War propagandists. He may, therefore, have thought that, at worst, the people he had named would suffer no greater fate than to be barred from carrying out official propaganda work. Orwell had seen infiltration and had, especially in the aftermath of his Spanish experience, witnessed something of the power of the communists and their fellow travellers to sway the debate. It is conceivable he wanted to prevent the same from happening in this new and more tense Cold War situation. Then again, he must have known how these things work: that mud sticks.

It is not recorded what the IRD did with the names Orwell had provided. James Smith, in his 2013 *British Writers and MI5 Surveillance* (Cambridge: Cambridge University Press) states that the list was not used; indeed, that it was so naïve as to be unusable. It was certainly an amateur effort – 35 names culled from a longer list Orwell had drawn up as an odd kind of hobby. And it was eccentric both in terms of the people named (Charlie Chaplin, Hugh MacDiarmid) and what Orwell had to say of them (Naomi Mitchison, who had written to Orwell praising *Homage to Catalonia* when it was published in 1938, is a 'silly sympathiser') (Orwell 2008 [1949]). Then again, Peter Smollett was included. He is, these days, thought to have been an actual communist infiltrator in Whitehall

BOOK REVIEW

who may have nudged Jonathan Cape to turn down *Animal Farm*. 'Gives strong impression of being some kind of Russian agent,' Orwell comments adding, 'very slimy person' (Orwell 2008 [1949]). It might be that Orwell had the measure of him. Or was he just settling scores? The same may be said of Alex Comfort. Orwell had had frank and public disagreements with him when Comfort was an anarchist opponent of the war, but subsequently there had been something like reconciliation. And yet on the IRD list, Orwell, has him 'anti-British … temperamentally pro-totalitarian. Not morally courageous' (Orwell 2008 [1949]).

Was Stephen Spender also on the list? White comments: 'Amid the names of those he had publicly derided for their fellow travelling, there was one striking betrayal: Stephen Spender…' and 'His inclusion bespeaks either a callousness on Orwell's part, or perhaps more plausibly, a growing paranoia about the true reach of Stalinism' (p. 244). Spender, who may reasonably have considered himself Orwell's friend, was certainly on the author's *master* list of communists and fellow-travellers, which had some 135 names on it. 'Sentimental sympathiser, and very unreliable,' he is there described. 'Easily influenced. Tendency towards homosexuality' – Spender had been previously one of Orwell's Nancy/pansy poets – 'I am not one of your fashionable pansies like Auden and Spender,' he wrote to Nancy Cunard in August 1937. Discreditable, though, this is to Orwell, Spender is not, as far as I can make out, on the shorter list that went to the IRD. (I am going by the version that features in *The Lost Orwell*, the supplementary volume to the *Complete Works*, which came out in 2006).

What happened to the people on Orwell's list? Not a lot, I suspect. Or leastways not a lot on account of their having been listed. If Spender was, indeed, on the IRD list, it did not bar him from editing *Encounter*. And Michael Redgrave, who was definitely listed, ended up in the 1956 CIA-funded film version of *Nineteen Eighty-Four* in which he played 'O'Connor' (as O'Brien had, for complicated reasons, been renamed). Norman MacKenzie, the last of those on Orwell's list to die (in 2013) would go on to have a distinguished journalistic and academic career. His brief involvement with the far left was already well over at the time of Orwell's final months and, in the early 1980s, he would join the Social Democratic Party. Peadar O'Donnell was a far leftist in Dublin so his life was probably ruined anyway. And those who were in the long run damaged (Charlie Chaplin, for example) were damaged by others, not Orwell.

If those on Orwell's list survived being listed, the cultural opposition in the USSR was not so fortunate. White includes the bizarre, if unsettling, story of Koestler's friend Eva Striker Zeizel who served eighteen months in a Moscow prison having allegedly designed teacups with a subliminal swastika motif in the pattern. This was at the time of the Great Terror, he comments, when an estimated 1.5 million were arrested, just under half of whom died. Writers were not exempted. Some two thousand were detained of whom three quarters were either killed outright or died in the camps. Of the seven hundred who attended the first Soviet Writers' Congress in 1934, only fifty were in a position to make it to the second, when it was convened twenty years later. White's source for this arresting statistic is Robert Conquest's *The Great Terror: A Reassessment*, from 1990. Conquest, a self-declared Cold Warrior, in turn attributes it to the Soviet intellectual Ilya Ehrenburg writing in the literary journal *Novy Mir* in 1962. I have no figures as to the fate of the missing 650, but it is surely reasonable to assume that not all of them were killed or died in internal exile. Isaac Babel who, along with Gorky, had helped organise the inaugural conference, was not, as White notes, among the fifty who attended the later follow-up. He had confessed to working for the French, via Malraux, and to having been part of a Trotskyist conspiracy to kill Stalin. His fellow conspirators supposedly included the film director, Sergei Eisenstein, and Pasternak. Although he later withdrew this improbable story, he was found guilty and shot in 1940.

Mary McCarthy was another who found herself on the receiving end of hostile attention from the Communist Party, though fortunately, in this instance, only its American chapter. Her crime was to have inadvertently signed up for the Committee for the Defense of Leon Trotsky. As a result, she began to cool towards the party, having previously been sympathetic. Another McCarthy, the notorious senator, receives less coverage in this work than I would have expected. McCarthyism, the various blacklists and the House Committee on Un-American Activities (HCUA) – were important features of the Cold War in its cultural aspect and are, in my opinion, under-covered here. There was, for example, some crossover between Orwell's various lists and those who were affected by the Americans' sudden turn against the Soviets (which, in best Oceanic form, had been preceded by a period of mutual friendship epitomised by the Hollywood Stalinism of Michael Curtiz's *Mission to Moscow*, of 1943, made to garner support for the Soviet Union during the war). Orson Welles, Charlie Chaplin and Paul Robeson were listed by both Orwell *and* the HCUA, while Orwell's onetime friend, Dubliner Michael Sayers, would be on the Hollywood Blacklist until the 1960s.

White comments that the respective positions of the USSR and the West changed in the post-war era. Pre-war, the West and capitalism had seemed similarly enfeebled. Now both appeared resilient and superior, and the Soviet Bloc, in contrast, repressive and moribund. The Hungarian uprising of 1956, the suppression of the Prague Spring in 1968, and the Soviet interventions in Afghanistan and Poland in the 1980s all alienated considerable Western sympathy for Soviet communism. Each in its turn produced a fresh wave of disaffected communists. At the same time, the Vietnam War provoked significant Western opposition. White describes how Mary McCarthy went to Vietnam and joined in the general condemnation. She reported how Vietnamese villagers had been bombed from their homes by the American Air Force to stop them giving shelter to Viet Cong guerrillas – villages destroyed the better to save them, as the justification went. The displaced Vietnamese were then re-housed in camps. One of these, McCarthy said, had a banner that read: 'Refugees from communism.' That sign was intended, not for the 'refugees', few of whom knew English, but for the reassurance of the American soldiers and the Western media. Critical of South Vietnam, McCarthy had some admiration for the North, commending its efforts to build a school system and health service. But she failed, says White, 'to see beneath the officially mandated surface' – the unabashed Stalinism of the Viet Cong, say – and was, therefore, as credulous in her own way as Steinbeck who accepted the official American version of the war (p. 565). All in all, it was a 'dereliction of the narrator's duty ... a failure to read' (p. 566). Perhaps. But it was also, at least, a welcome challenge to the official version which had the propagandist power of the richest and most powerful country on earth behind it. The Viet Cong and their Hanoi backers had a constructive side; there was more to them than the propagandists allowed. If McCarthy was biased one way, she was so in the face of a massive bias in the opposite direction, voicing the subversive possibility that there might be popular support behind the Viet Cong's revolutionary war.

The anarchists in Spain were popular too. They established schools where there had been none and for children and adults alike who had previously had no prospect of education. And they modernised and streamlined factory production, including the introduction of safety measures. This was the socialism that roused in Orwell an enthusiasm so much so that, like Mary McCarthy in Vietnam, he would manage to overlook much of its darker side.

It would be wrong to say that Mary McCarthy, or Orwell, or any who were impressed by revolutionary movements were merely credulous. Writers who react critically to received opinion will be often drawn to alternatives. If Orwell was credulous, he was also inspired. Socialism, he would later write, was the idea that raised his writing above *belles lettres*. He understood socialism to mean goods and services being made as readily available as municipal tap water, approximate equality of income, classlessness and the making good of democratic deficits. As visions go, it seems benevolent enough. And though it was never feasible in this pristine form, working class people in much of the developed world would greatly enhance their political power, living standards and quality of life through the construction of democratic welfare states. This social democratic turn proved short-lived. Its time was approximately the period covered by this book, when the West, outside of the US, fearful of communism, prioritised equality as a policy goal. Both right and left adopted it. And both went off it around the time the Cold War ended, the Soviet experiment having run its course.

Towards the end of *Cold Warriors*, White describes John le Carré visiting post-Soviet Moscow and finding there a kind of internal siege with the houses of the rich heavily fortified – not a Cold War so much as the Hobbesian war of all against all. The cure in Russia – the sudden infusion of market forces – was looking a lot like an illness. Then Putin took the country in hand. And history, which had been laid to rest, was back in business.

It was useful for Cold War purposes, says White, that the West could field writers of the left against the Soviet Union: a reconditioned Trotskyist like Philip Rahv, for instance. It signalled that 'our' side was a broad church. You did not have to be on the right to be a part of it. The sensible left – the 'non-communist left', spoken of so often in CCF circles that it was acronymed to the NCL – was part of it too. In this respect, Orwell, had he lived, would have been the ideal recruit, convinced as he was that the Soviet myth had to be destroyed if socialism were to revive.

It is anyone's guess if he would have been biddable. True, he had worked for the BBC, but he had also come to believe he was being used by it. Nor was he, in general, any great joiner of movements. 'I'm afraid I cannot speak for the League of European Freedom,' he wrote to the Duchess of Atholl in November 1945. 'I am not in agreement with the League's ultimate objectives. ... I cannot associate myself with an essentially Conservative body which claims to defend democracy in Europe but has nothing to say about British imperialism. ... I belong to the Left and must work inside it, much as I hate Russian totalitarianism and its poisonous influence in this country' (Orwell 1998 [1945]: 384-385).

REFERENCES
Orwell, George (1998 [1937]) Letter to Cyril Connolly, *The* Complete *Works of George Orwell, Vol. XXI: Facing Unpleasant Facts*, Davison, Peter (ed.) London: Secker & Warburg

Orwell, George (1998 [1945]) Letter to the Duchess of Atholl, *The Complete Works of George Orwell, Vol. XVII: I Belong to the Left*, Davison, Peter (ed.) London: Secker & Warburg

Orwell, George (1998 [1946]) Second thoughts on James Burnham, *The Complete Works of George Orwell, Vol. XVIII: Smothered Under Journalism*, Davison, Peter (ed.) London: Secker & Warburg pp 268-284

Orwell, George (2008 [1949]) Names sent to Celia Kirwan (2 May 1949) *The Lost Orwell: Being a Supplement to the Complete Works of George Orwell*, Davison, Peter (ed.) London: Timewell Press

**Martin Tyrrell,
Queen's University, Belfast**

Re-Evaluation: Laurence Brander's *George Orwell* (1954)

How One of the (Now Forgotten) First Studies of Orwell Captured the Man and his Writings

Richard Lance Keeble.

Laurence Brander, the intelligence officer assigned to the BBC's Eastern Service while Orwell was working there between 1941 and 1943, generally has only a brief, walk-on part in the main biographies (see Bowker 2003: 295, 424; Crick 1980: 416, 418; Meyers 2000: 216; Shelden 1991: 377-378; Taylor 2003: 312).

Following a six-month trip to India, Brander reports to the Eastern Service director, L. F. Rushbrook Williams, on 22 September 1943 the results of a survey of listeners' preferences. Only 16 per cent vote for Orwell compared to 68 per cent for J. B. Priestley and 56 per cent for the philosopher C. E. M. Joad (*CWGO* XV: 247). In any case, very few people are tuning in to the broadcasts. As Taylor reports: 'Brander's conclusions were so depressing, Orwell confided to his diary that he could not bear to write them down' (Taylor 2003: 314). Soon afterwards, in November, perhaps not surprisingly, Orwell quits the BBC and joins the leftist journal, *Tribune*, as its literary editor. And thereafter, Brander disappears from the Orwell narrative.[1]

In fact, he writes one of the first full-length studies of Orwell (published in 1954).[2] And though now largely forgotten, it is fascinating, full of useful insights and, in some respects, pleasantly surprising.

Orwell has too often been associated with the doom and gloom of his dystopian masterpiece *Nineteen Eighty-Four*. Texts such as Alok Rai's *Orwell and the Politics of Despair* (1988) and Jeffrey Meyer's biography, *Orwell: Wintry Conscience of a Generation* (2000) (drawing on V. S. Pritchett's description) only served to reinforce this view. Rebecca Solnit, author of the recently published and highly acclaimed *Orwell's Roses* (2021), tells how, before embarking on her research, she saw Orwell (wrongly) as a 'grim, serious and pessimistic figure'.[3]

STRESS ON ORWELL'S HUMOUR

Intriguingly, in this early assessment, the stress throughout is on Orwell as a humorous writer and personality. So Brander points out the 'brilliant satire of the cheap private school' in *A Clergyman's Daughter* (p. 6); how his 'rich sense of humour which supported his thinking was at the mercy of his health' (p. 20); his description of the magistrate, U Po Kyin, at the start of *Burmese Days* 'is probably the richest piece of humorous writing in Anglo-Indian literature' (p. 79); *Homage to Catalonia* is his 'happiest and richest book' (p. 21); he displays 'the carefree, light, inevitable brightness of the essayist' in his *Tribune* 'As I Please' columns (p. 22); while his writings are 'not only stimulating; they form an introduction to a most likeable man' (p. 23).

Similarly Brander notes how his essay on Dickens is 'a good example of the quiet amusement Orwell enjoyed whether in reading or in life' (p. 41); no one had analysed boys' weeklies 'so amusingly' (p. 43); in his essay 'Lear, Tolstoy and the Fool', he finds in Shakespeare 'the joys he sought himself' (p. 55); the Paris part of *Down and Out* 'is the most cheerful writing he ever gave us. … He is content to describe for the sheer love of comic writing' (p. 58); in *The Road to Wigan Pier*, he points out the 'examples of Orwell's amused eye resting upon people and their surroundings' (p. 115). Winston Smith's belief in the common people expressed towards the end of *Nineteen Eighty-Four*: that the proles 'will inherit the earth because they are capable of happiness', Brander says, is 'nothing less than a gospel of joy' (p. 192).

ORWELL AS INTELLIGENT WRITER

Brander is also at pains, constantly, to represent Orwell as an *intelligent* writer. Chapter Two (pp 12-24) is titled 'An assessment' and Orwell is described as intelligent no fewer than 14 times. For instance, he says: 'In his books he deals with contemporary social and political problems with the detachment of fine intelligence' (p. 12). Orwell believed in decency, justice and liberty. 'He had the preacher's faculty for making these familiar words shine again with meaning. He reached them, not through academic training, but by the exercise of his native intelligence and much personal suffering in Burma and Europe' (p. 14).

Of *Burmese Days*, he says the novel is 'like any Orwell book, an intellectual achievement and it is satire and caricature which give the book its special quality' (p. 75). Later, he comments: 'Orwell's power of absorption was not imaginative but intellectual. His brain became red-hot when it was making a book like *Coming up for Air* or *Animal Farm*. Every incident and description is significant and one thing echoes another throughout the book' (p. 106).

FEAR IN NOVELS AND REPORTAGE

The role of fear in Orwell's novels and reportage is also interestingly highlighted by Brander. In *The Road to Wigan Pier*, Orwell tells how, after settling in a common lodging-house, he goes out expecting a fight. A hefty young stevedore lurches towards him with a 'dangerous gleam in his eye'. But the next minute the man has his arms around him inviting him to have a cup of tea. 'I had a cup of tea. It was a kind of baptism. Afterwards my fears vanished' (p. 67).

In *Keep the Aspidistra Flying*, Brander stresses how the central character, Gordon Comstock, wants to sink down through society to the irresponsibility of the down-and-out. But it's also a way to escape fear. As Orwell writes: 'He wanted to get away from all that, below all that. Down, down! Into the ghost kingdom, out of reach of hope, out of reach of fear! Under ground, under ground! That was where he wished to be' (p. 104).

George Bowling's fellow residents of Ellesmere Road, in *Coming Up For Air*, are all consumed by fear. The road was just 'a prison with cells all in a row. A line of semi-detached torture-chambers where the poor little five-to-ten-pound-a-weekers quake and shiver, every one of them with the boss twisting his tail and the wife riding him like a nightmare and the kids sucking his blood like leeches' (p. 154). Similarly, the customers of the Cheerful Credit live in constant fear: 'fear of not being able to pay the monthly dues on the house, fear of losing their jobs' (ibid). And then there's the fear of the grocer's assistant: 'The customer is always right. The thing you can see in his face is mortal dread that you might report him for impertinence and get him sacked. Besides, how's he to know you aren't one of the narks the company sends round? Fear! We swim in it. It is our element!' (pp 154-155). On growing up with his family in Lower Binfield and then on England during the years of the Depression, Bowling ponders: 'And what are the realities of modern life? Well, the chief one is an everlasting, frantic struggle to sell things. With most people it takes the form of selling themselves – that's to say getting a job and keeping it' (p. 160).

Orwell admires the novels of Henry Miller, because, in them, 'English is treated as a spoken language, but spoken without fear, i.e. without fear of rhetoric or the unusual or poetical word' (p. 46). And of the ghastly dystopia depicted in *Nineteen Eighty-Four*, Brander writes, 'he wanted to suggest that the steps from the present to that fearful future were not many or great' (p. 188).

OTHER FASCINATING OBSERVATIONS

Interestingly, Brander highlights what he describes as Orwell's 'four London novels', each having a specific topic which he wishes to examine (p. 92). Over-simplifying somewhat (and using capital letters erratically), he says: '*A Clergyman's Daughter* is about the Church, *Keep the Aspidistra Flying* is about Money, *Coming Up For Air* is about the Red Rash building between the wars, and *1984*, set in a London of future disaster almost beyond bearing, is about Propaganda in a husk of London's secular greatness. Labelled in this way, each novel becomes a Morality, and that is what they are.'

In another fascinating section, Brander examines 'The Theory and Practice of Oligarchical Collectivism', the manifesto of the dissident Brotherhood movement supposedly written by arch-enemy Emmanuel Goldstein. In it, the economic reasons for waging perpetual war are explained: 'War is a way of shattering to pieces, or pouring into the stratosphere, or sinking in the depths of the sea, materials which might otherwise be used to make the masses too comfortable, and hence, in the long run, too intelligent.' The manifesto stresses that a Party member must be 'a credulous and ignorant fanatic whose prevailing moods are fear, hatred, adulation and orgiastic triumph. In other words, it is necessary that he should have the mentality appropriate to a state of war' (p. 194).

Brander has some other useful observations about Orwell's life and works. He is rightly sceptical about his view on Eton: 'I did not work there and learned very little, and I don't feel that Eton has been much of a formative influence in my life' (p. 4). Brander adds: 'That sounds like the wishful thinking of the preacher of the classless society, and to anyone who knew him it was obvious where he had been to school' (ibid). On the Dickens essay, he writes: 'Future criticisms of Dickens will take Orwell's points for granted. He is original. As he clears away false appreciations, Dickens's work appears more fresh and strong, like a painting that has had its dull varnish removed. Orwell is so different from Dickens that he understands him well. Dickens fought his way up, while Orwell tried to go down in order to bring everyone up with him' (p. 43).

On *Burmese Days*, he suggests that nature 'along with U Po Kyin, is the most effective character in the story' (p. 87). In the novel, 'the problem is loneliness' compared to E. M. Forster's *A Passage to India* where 'the problem is the imperfect relationship between English people and Indians' (p. 89).

While Brander can be insightful, he is also at times somewhat pedestrian outlining – and at length – the central narrative of a novel. He wrongly states that *Nineteen Eighty-Four* is a deliberate warning about the 'incipient totalitarianism in English Socialism' (p. 184). As Michael Shelden says in his authorised biography (1991: 474): 'In a letter to Francis A. Henson, of the United Automobile Workers in America, Orwell made it clear that *Nineteen Eighty-Four* is a warning against totalitarian methods in general, regardless of time or place: "The scene of the book is laid in Britain in order to emphasise that the English-speaking races are not innately better than anyone else and that totalitarianism, *if not fought against*, could triumph anywhere." The italics are Orwell's.' A few factual errors creep in: for instance, he says Orwell was christened Eric Hugh (p. 2); ran a country pub for a while (p. 6 and 16), and at the end of his life, moved to a London nursing home (in fact, it was University College Hospital).

CONCLUSION: AN ENTERTAINING TRIP THROUGH ORWELLIAN LANDSCAPE

But overall Brander offers a wonderfully entertaining (and unjustly neglected) trip through the Orwellian landscape. In one instance he says, *en passant*: 'What a pity he never turned from men and animals to write a book about birds. It would have added something new to an immortal line. As it is, it would be possible to collect from his books one of the brightest aviaries in the whole of English literature' (p. 22). And in his analysis of *Nineteen Eighty-Four*, he mentions Winston watching the woman of the proles singing in her backyard – and then Winston looks up at the sky: 'It was curious to think that the sky was the same for everybody, in Eurasia or Eastasia as well as here' (p. 191). This leads Brander to reflect on other descriptions of skies in *Burmese Days* and *Homage to Catalonia*. Indeed, the place of birds and the sky in Orwell's novels and reportage: now there are a couple of interesting topics for possible future articles…

NOTES

[1] One exception is Les Hurst who writes to me (in an email, 31 January 2022): 'On Orwell's wider work, I have quoted a passage from the Introduction several times: "He was the inspiration of that rudimentary Third Programme which was sent out to the Indian student." Brander was writing in 1954 – I think that if he was writing in 1974 he would have seen the work that Orwell and he did as the forerunner of not only the Third Programme but the Open University. The connection was Jenny Lee, with whom Orwell worked at *Tribune*, who became the Minister introducing the OU. Conversations with Orwell about remote education must have stayed with her'

[2] I bought it for around £3 from an internet-based bookseller

[3] See https://www.csmonitor.com/Books/Author-Q-As/2022/0208/Q-A-with-Rebecca-Solnit-author-of-Orwell-s-Roses

REFERENCES

Bowker, Gordon (2003) *George Orwell*, London: Little, Brown

Brander, Laurence (1954) *George Orwell*, London: Longmans, Green and Co.

CWGO (1998) *The Complete Works of George Orwell, XX Vols*, Davison, Peter (ed.) London: Secker & Warburg

Crick, Bernard (1980) *George Orwell: A Life*, Harmondsworth, Middlesex: Penguin

Shelden, Michael (1991) *Orwell: The Authorised Biography*, London: William Heinemann

Meyers, Jeffrey (2000) *Orwell: Wintry Conscience of a Generation*, New York: W. W. Norton & Company

Taylor, D. J. (2003) *Orwell: The Life*, London: Chatto & Windus

NOTE ON THE CONTRIBUTOR
Richard Lance Keeble was the chair of The Orwell Society 2013-2020. His latest book, *Orwell's Moustache*, has just been published by Abramis, of Bury St Edmunds.

George Orwell Studies

Subscription information

Each volume contains two issues, published half-yearly.

Annual Subscription (including postage)

Personal Subscription

UK	£35
Europe	£38
RoW	£40

Institutional Subscription

UK	£100
Europe	£115
RoW	£120

Single Issue copies can be purchased (subject to availability)

Enquiries regarding subscriptions and orders should be sent to:

> Journals Fulfilment Department
> Abramis Academic
> ASK House
> Northgate Avenue
> Bury St Edmunds
> Suffolk, IP32 6BB
> UK

Tel: +44(0)1284 717884
Email: info@abramis.co.uk

www.ingramcontent.com/pod-product-compliance
Lightning Source LLC
Chambersburg PA
CBHW080401170426
43193CB00016B/2785